DEDICATED

to

*Bernard Herrmann and Hal Mohr, who did not
live to see this book in print; and to
James Card and Gerald Noxon, who taught
so many of us the cardinal rule
of film scholarship: never write about
a film you haven't seen.*

Preface
&
Acknowledgments

In October of 1973 a symposium was held at the International Museum of Photography, George Eastman House, in Rochester, New York. 300 delegates from the United States, Canada, England, and the continent of Europe gathered at the invitation of the University Film Study Center and the Graduate Film Program of Boston University, and with the support of the National Endowment for the Humanities, the New York State Council for the Arts, the Society of Motion Picture and Television Engineers, the American Society of Cinematographers, and the Academy of Motion Picture Arts and Sciences. They came to ponder the causes and effects of "The Coming of Sound to the American Film, 1925-1940".

This anthology consists (largely) of the edited proceedings of that symposium:

> in Part I, Raymond Fielding, Douglas Gomery, and
> James G. Stewart delineate the technological
> and economic context of the revolution;
>
> in Part II, Hal Mohr, Frank Capra, Rouben Mamoulian,
> Julius Epstein, Walter Reisch, and Bernard Herr-
> mann describe the transition and its aftermath as
> they lived and perceived it;
>
> in Part III, Gerald Noxon assesses the European
> contribution to the upheaval in America; and

> in Part IV, Lucy Fischer and the Editor give
> contrasting evaluations, from contrasting
> perspectives, of the implications of the
> period for film design, focusing on two films
> which bracket the era: Mamoulian's APPLAUSE
> (1929) and Welles's CITIZEN KANE (1941).

As coordinator of the symposium, I am indebted to Peter Feinstein, Barbara Humphreys, and the staff of the UFSC, and to Robert Doherty, James Card, George Pratt, and the staff of the Museum for their efforts on its behalf. I am indebted, also, to those participants whose contributions escaped encapsulation in this volume: especially Jean Arthur, George Bluestone, James Card, Leo Chaloukian, Debra Franko, Ted Gillings, George Korngold, Roger Manvell, Rosalind Rogoff, and Rayburn Wright.

As editor of this volume, I thank the participants whose contributions are herein included. Those which were submitted to me in writing, following oral delivery, are reprinted without emendation, for I respect the integrity of an author's text (the essays of Raymond Fielding, James G. Stewart, Gerald Noxon, and Lucy Fischer). Those culled from tapes of panel discussions or extemporaneous addresses have been resequenced to read as statements, but original word choice and phrasing have been retained wherever coherence would permit (the remarks of Hal Mohr, Frank Capra, Rouben Mamoulian, Julius Epstein, Walter Reisch, and Bernard Herrmann). Two of the essays were prepared for this volume: Douglas Gomery's replacing another essay presented to the symposium but already published (see Bibliography); and the Editor's final essay from an address to the Conference on Radio Literature at the University of Durham, England, in April of 1977, reprinted in their proceedings. The copyrights to the essays of Raymond Fielding, James G. Stewart, and the Editor remain with the authors.

Special thanks are owed two people without whose efforts this volume would not have appeared: William F. Wilbert, for emending and resequencing many of the articles prior to the final editing, and for preparing the Index; and my wife, Joan Evans-Cameron, for undertaking the arduous task of transcribing the tapes of the proceedings, and for assisting

(in Willard Quine's phrase) in the 'asymptotic labor' of spotting
errors in the typescript.

Lastly, I wish to thank Stanley Wolf, Linda Rogovin, and the staff
of the Redgrave Publishing Company for their encouragement, support,
and patience in the publication of this anthology. Few publishers have
the courage to issue volumes to limited markets, despite professed interests in truth and the elimination of cant. Stanley Wolf is an exception, and I wish him and this anthology a long and happy life.

E. W. C.
Pullman, Washington
March, 1979

Editor's Introduction

> "Every art has the right to stem
> from a previous art; it not only has the
> right to but must so stem . . . In art
> there is only slow or rapid progress,
> implying in essence evolution and not
> revolution."
>
> Bela Bartok[1]

The arts, as Bartok observed, are immune to revolution: innovations may percolate, but never subjugate. The history of artistic transformation is evolutionary without exception.

An immense question, then, confronts the historian of the cinema, and emasculates most theories of cinematic design, namely,

> Why did the advent of synchronous
> sound revolutionize the design
> and production of films?

By 1927 filmmakers were accustomed to changes wrought by technological innovation. Each advance in emulsion formulae, lens design, magazine size, lighting capacity, and projection technique had gradually reshaped the face of film production and distribution.

By 1927 filmmakers were accustomed, as well, to producing sounds to accompany movies. The cinema was never silent. When Lumiere first

projected movies to an audience in 1895, the flickering images were
seen as the sounds of a tinkling piano were heard. And for 30 years
thereafter filmmakers wedded to their works occasional music, spoken
words, and effects, hoping at best to deepen the emotional impact, and
at worst to mask the noise of gas lamps, projector gears, love making,
and upset stomachs.

Yet by 1930, scarcely three years after the 'first talking picture'
was released, not one asynchronous theatrical film remained in production (see Gomery below, p. 26). The prevailing traditions of film design, production, and exhibition, and the structure of the industry
which sustained them, had been shattered once and for all time. An art
had been exterminated at the zenith of its power, and something new –
something without precedent in human history – had taken its place.

If we are to understand the cinema – the sources of its power and
the roots of its dominant traditions – we must understand the causes
and effects of the revolution which occurred when synchronous sound
came to the American film. To do so, however, we must understand why
we hear as we do, and what part our ears play in that integrated perception of the world upon which our deepest emotional life rests. No
treatise on the physiology or phenomenology of perception is possible
here, but a sketch of the surface of what now seems to be true may
preclude misunderstanding of the depths. (See pp. 202–216 below for
further variations on the theme.)

II

> Were the choice forced upon you,
>   which would you prefer to lose?
> Your sight or your hearing?

Most persons to whom I have put the question, remembering perhaps
a blind man with a cane unable easily to cross a street or to avoid
objects he cannot see, answer unequivocally: hearing! Imagined blindness, but not deafness, strikes us with terror. Deafness seems, to

most of us, an inconvenience, whereas blindness is abhorrent beyond
comprehension.

But what happens when the choice is forced upon us, not in our
imaginations but in reality? Von Bekesy, winner of the Nobel Prize for
his probings into the physiology of hearing, gives us a hint in an atyp-
ically poignant passage of scientific literature:

> "We could do much to ameliorate the tragedy of deaf-
> ness if we changed some of our attitudes toward it. Blind
> ness evokes our instant sympathy, and we go out of our way
> to help the blind person. But deafness often goes unrecog-
> nized. If a deaf person misunderstands what we say, we are
> apt to attribute it to lack of intelligence instead of to
> faulty hearing. Very few people have the patience to help
> the deafened. To a deaf man the outside world appears un-
> friendly. He tries to hide his deafness, and this only
> brings on more problems." [2]

Statistics, unfortunately, confirm the observation: for the inci-
dence of acute mental disturbance among the deaf is many times greater
than among the blind.

Why the asymmetry? If our eyes and ears informed us about identical
aspects of the world, it would make no difference to our mental health
were we to be blind rather than deaf, or the converse. But such is not
the case. Deafness forces an inability to sense one's own identity
which has no parallel in blindness.

The question is inescapable:

> Why is hearing crucial to maintaining
> a stable personal identity, in a way
> in which seeing is not?

Our eyes convey to us information about visualizable events in the
world often supplemented by our ears. Often our ears warn us of the
presence of events to which we have not as yet attended with our eyes:
we hear the fire engine before we turn to see it, or we hear the door
opening behind us before turning to see who is about to enter the room.

Within the world, however, are <u>unvisualizable</u> events as well: happenings to which our eyes can have no access. Among them are musical
events: we see the tools which make music, and the making of it, but
not the music made, for a modulation from G major to E minor must be
heard, not seen. Among them, also, are mental events: we see our own
body and the bodies of others, but the thoughts and feelings which we
have, and which we infer others to have, cannot be seen.

We cannot see, in particular, either the self which constitutes our
own personal identity or those selves which constitute the identity of
others. We must infer both. How? We infer the identity of others
largely (indeed, almost exclusively) from what we <u>hear</u> them say, for
verbal expression is our most flexible tool for informing others of our
own mental and physical states, and we infer that the converse is true
as well. We infer our own identity by comparing ourselves to the in-
ferred identities of those about us. And we identify much of the remainder of the world by the values which we, as persons, project upon
it.

Our world, thus, divides into events to which our eyes are privy,
and events to which they are not. Our ears permit us to attend, by
inference, to those events to which our eyes remain unprivileged. They
grant us access to those unseen and unseeable events which define the
identity of ourselves, others, and the world beyond.

No wonder the deafened find identity elusive. Without sight the
nearby world of visualizable objects retains its identity, for we can
touch and often hear objects we cannot see. Without hearing, however,
the world of unvisualizable events remains largely beyond acquaintance.
Limited access may be had, by inference, to the grosser mental and emotional states of others, but the finer delineations which only spoken
language can express easily and well remain elusive, and with them the
identity of the world and everything of human value within.

III

Why, then, did the coming of synchronous sound revolutionize the

cinema? Through hearing we acquaint ourselves with those unvisualizable events, matched to the world of objects seen, from which we infer
the identity and value of ourselves, others, and the world about us.
Our deepest emotional engagement with the world, therefore, presupposes
the sustained, simultaneous, correlated, and integrated perception of
both seeable and unseeable events by our two distance senses, sight and
hearing.

Before 1927, the cinema, like all arts, was unnatural: neither
inartistic, nor ineffective, but qualitatively unlike nature. For
although filmmakers had learned to mimic the visual continuities of the
natural world without impediment (the absence of color and depth not-
withstanding!), they were unable to mimic its aural complement. Denied
the means of stimulating both distance senses naturally, the cinema,
like other arts, had no choice but to compensate – so it denaturalized
its visuals into art! Filmmakers, under constraint, learned to express
elegantly a few unsophisticated emotions through the visuals alone.
Stereotypical characters moved with grace through melodramatic situations, evoking emotions reminiscent of grand opera – for similar com-
pensations were being made.

When synchronous sound arrived, however, the need for compensation
disappeared. A natural art, unimpeded, sprang into being – an art to
which people could react with the same perceptual, conceptual, and emotional habits with which they reacted to faces, voices, gestures, and
the other patterns of seeable and unseeable events in their everyday
world. For the first time in human history persons could enter a room
in New York, face a darkened wall, and – without being psychopathologically maladjusted – see and hear a woman dying in an emergency ward
somewhere other than in New York. They would not see and hear a film
of a woman dying (barring elliptical descriptions), but rather would
see and hear a woman dying by means of a film – which is as different
as night from day.

No wonder a revolution occurred! Before 1927, created and natural
events were perceptually distinct. Unless one were psychopathologically
disturbed, one perceived painted flowers as 'painted', staged duels as

'staged', and narrated conversations as 'narrated'. Therein lay the
source of their genius, and the root of the conceptual compensation
which they demanded as the price of their transfiguration into art.

After 1927, however, the perceptual boundary between created and
natural events dissolved. The events upon which one could project
natural expectations and habits were no longer restricted to those
found in the everyday world, for the universe of happenings perceivable
as if real had been expanded. Created events could now induce reactions
physiologically indistinguishable from those caused by events in the
everyday world: cinematic happenings, unlike those of any other art,
could induce physical revulsion, epileptic seizures, hysteria, terror,
horror, and even psychotic trauma.

IV

It would take time, of course, for Hollywood, and thereafter the
world, to assimilate synchronous sound into the design of its films
with elegance and power. But not much time! By 1930 Hollywood was
ready to enter its 'golden age'. During the next 25 years Capra,
Cukor, Curtiz, Ford, Hawks, Hitchcock, Huston, Lang, Mamoulian, Milestone, Sternberg, Sturges, Vidor, Walsh, Wellman, Welles, Wyler, and
many, many others were to do their best work – work characterized by a
directness of human expression unsurpassed in any other art, and
equaled, I think, only by the splurge of musical creativity in and
around Vienna during the 135 years from Haydn's Op. 20 quartets to the
death of Mahler.

Frank Capra evaluated the revolution with respect to the cinema as
follows (see p. 80 below):

> "Films went all the way to what
> I think is real greatness when they
> got that third dimension of sound."

His assessment is apt, but understated. For unless history misleads us, the coming of synchronous sound to the American film was not only a cinematic revolution. It was also the sole cataclysmic event in the history of art, and hence a watershed in the history of mankind; for therewith a natural art for the first time found its métier. We live no longer within the perceptual boundaries of the natural world of our grandparents, for in 1927 those boundaries disappeared. Neither we, nor our world, will ever be the same again.

Evan William Cameron

Notes:

1. Bela Bartok, quoted by Erno Lendvai in "Duality and Synthesis in the Music of Bela Bartok", an article included in Module, Symmetry, Proportion, edited by Gyorgy Kepes (London: Studio Vista, 1966), pp. 181 and 187.

2. Georg von Bekesy, "The Ear", Scientific American, August, 1957, reprinted in Perception: Mechanisms and Models (San Francisco: W. H. Freeman & Company, 1972), p. 93.

CONTENTS

Part IV: COMPARISON AND CONTRAST

Part I:
The Technological Revolution

The Technological Antecedents of the Coming of Sound: An Introduction

by Raymond Fielding

Readers, it seems to me, should never be kept in the dark regarding a writer's assumptions and hypotheses. All of my work as an historian, at least in recent years, has proceeded from the premise that the history of the motion picture – as an art form, as a medium of communication, and as an industry – has been determined principally by technological innovations and considerations; that these, in turn, have had economic, legal, and operational consequences which have determined the artistic evolution of the medium, the choice of subject matter and themes, and the impact which it has had, in competition with other arts and media, upon the general public.

There is a temptation for film historians to interpret the development of the motion picture teleologically, as if each generation of workers had sketched out the future of the art far in advance of the technology required for its realization. In fact, however, the artistic evolution of the film and its selection of images, sounds, subject matter, and themes has always been associated intimately with technological change, just as it has, in less noticeable fashion, in the other arts. The contribution of a Porter, Ince, and Griffith followed as much from the availability of portable cameras, larger magazines, interchangeable lenses, and improved emulsions as it did from their individual artistic vision and talent. Similarly, the <u>cinema verite</u> movement of today could not possibly have appeared and prospered twenty years ago, prior to the miniaturization of camera and sound equipment, and without dramatic improvement in film stocks.[1]

The influence of technology upon film style, content, and theme is
subtle but profound. The technology involved is more intricate and costly than that used in any other art. More important still, it is a technology which renders film a corporate art, for with a few exotic exceptions, motion pictures cannot be made by individuals. They require the
collaboration and orchestration of tens or scores of highly-paid artists
and technicians both in front and in back of the camera. The operational problems and economic waste involved in the production of successful
films is further aggravated by the fact that the technology which is
employed obsoletes rapidly and continuously.

Finally, and perhaps most importantly, unlike most other artistic
products, the motion picture cannot be viewed directly. A painting,
when completed, can be hung upon a wall and admired at once. A book,
once printed, can be carried in the hand of the reader and examined at
will, the ideas and language of the writer being presented immediately
to the intellect as the pages are turned. But the motion picture film
is worthless in itself. The images which it carries must be further
reproduced, technologically, before we can perceive them, projected in
succession onto a screen within a darkened room, where, for economic
reasons, they must be viewed in concert by a relatively large number of
people - or, in a variation, viewed individually by relatively large
numbers of people geographically separated, on television. It is this
play of light and shadow, formed upon a screen or on the phosphors of an
electronic tube, which is the artistic and informational end result.
From beginning to end, it is an art born in the laboratory, continuously
sophisticated by engineers, and both sustained and constrained by a mas-
sive economic investment.

All of which brings us to the particular subject of this paper, for
in the history of the motion picture no technological innovation brought
so much impact and change to its form and structure, to its directorial
and acting styles, and to its content and themes, as did the successful,
commercial, widespread introduction of sound in the late 1920's.

Having said as much, let me reveal still another premise upon I
proceed, which is that there never was any such thing as a silent film -

at least insofar as audiences were concerned. From the earliest days
of motion picture exhibition, theaters featured a variety of sounds in
more or less synchronous accompaniment to the images which appeared on
their screens. These included music, sound effects, and speech, and
they were produced at each individual theater on a custom basis. The
music was provided by pianos, organs, vocalists, musical ensembles, and
orchestras. Sometimes, as was common in the case of piano and organ
accompaniment, the music was extemporized on the spot from well-known
melodies or phrases, as the musician followed the action on the screen.
With the introduction of more elaborate theaters devoted exclusively to
the exhibition of the motion picture, and the financial growth of the
industry, special scores were oftentimes produced by composers and ar-
rangers for particular films, the various movements, phrases, and melodies being scored in appropriate order and tempo so as to insure a reasonable synchronism between the live music and the projected images.
The use of such custom-made scores, beginning at least as early as 1908,
represented the first widespread system for pre-determining and guaran-
teeing a particular sound and image relationship from performance to performance and from theater to theater.

    Sound effects of a variety of sorts also were introduced regularly
into early motion picture exhibition. Some of these were generated by
elaborate organs or special effects machines such as the Noiseograph,
the Dramagraph, the Kinematophone, the Soundograph, and the Excelsior
Sound Effect Cabinet, and from whose keyboards and associated equipment
came galloping horses, railroad whistles and bells, rooster crows, hen
cackles, cow bawls, canary chirps, mockingbird calls, tugboat whistles,
auto horns, cowbells, anvil strikes, marching feet, gun shots, tom-toms,
thunder, temple bells, castanets, frog croaks, slide whistles, tambour-
ines, telephone bells, glass crashes, auto chugs, water splashes, and
the blowing of noses.

    And finally, speech was frequently added to the motion picture pre-
sentation. Most commonly this took the form of a master of ceremonies
who spoke from the front of the theater while the films were projected.
His role was somewhat analogous to that of the 'benshi' in Japanese

Kabuki drama, and he served at least three functions. First, as a conventional master of ceremonies, he provided a link between the new and
somewhat disreputable motion picture and the more respectable music hall
and vaudeville traditions with which audiences were familiar. Second,
he read the sub-titles, which were then, as they are today, crucial in
introducing abstract ideas of any intellectual complexity into the silent motion picture experience. This was an especially important service for those members of the audience who either could not read English
or could not read at all. Finally, he interpreted the motion picture
experience artistically for the members of the audience - a crucial contribution at a time when the form and structure of the film, particularly insofar as it involved changes of camera position or editing, was
likely to confuse audiences. Unsophisticated as their contribution may
seem today, these masters of ceremonies fulfilled one of the most important roles of a critic in any one of our arts - they interpreted and
explained innovations in style and form to the uninitiated and inexper-
ienced patron.

Another kind of speech was also introduced into the early motion
picture from time to time when exhibitors hired actors and actresses to
stand behind motion picture screens and to read or extemporize dialogue
in synchronism with the performers on the screen. The systematic use of
such live performers during motion picture presentations began at least
as early as 1897 with the work of entrepreneur Lyman H. Howe, and during
the first decade of the century a number of professional actor's companies were founded to provide such services to theatres on a regular
basis. These included the Humonova, Actologue, and Dramatone companies.

In fact, then, the 'silent film' is a myth. It never existed. Furthermore, the term was rarely used prior to 1926 - only afterwards.
What an irony! Today, pre-1926 films are widely shown in university film
courses and film society programs in a manner which was never intended by
their makers and which never prevailed during the period of their original release - in silence!

What was introduced in 1926 was an entirely different kind of sound,
permanently recorded by technological means in a single, particular ver-

sion for each particular film, and reproduced so that exactly the same
sound performance accompanied that film from day to day, theater to
theater, and screening to screening. Furthermore, it was intended that
these sounds would be precisely synchronized with particular actions
which occurred on the screen. Most noticeably, this applied to dialogue,
but in just as significant a manner it applied to music and sound effects
as well.

If the technology involved in the introduction and sophistication
of the so-called silent motion picture had been complicated, that which
was necessary for commercially satisfactory talking pictures was even
more so. It required that solutions to four broad classes of technical
problems be reached, and that the technology which resulted was sufficiently sophisticated, reliable, and high in quality as to insure its
commercial success.

These four sets of problems included, first, a method for the permanent recording of sound; second, a method for the reproduction and
amplification of the sound; third, a method for positively and reliably
synchronizing the sound with the accompanying images on the screen; and
fourth, the international standardization of technique, hardware, software, and operations involved in such an enterprise.

As for the first of these problems, a more or less satisfactory
method of recording sound had appeared as early as 1877, when Thomas
Edison introduced his fabulous phonograph. A remarkable breakthrough,
the phonograph was virtually unanticipated by other inventors, and was
granted a so-called 'basic' or 'master' patent.

Fourteen years later, in 1891, Edison applied for a patent for the
kinetograph, which he and W.K.L. Dickson had developed – the world's
first practical motion picture camera which incorporated all of the essential features which were to survive in such instruments for the next
three-quarters of a century; to wit: a ribbon of perforated photographic
film, a single-lens optical system, an intermittent movement, a satisfactorily high frame rate, and a synchronized shutter of proper design
which allowed for exposure of the film during its brief stationary periods.

If we are to believe Edison's statement, published in the June, 1894 issue of <u>Century Magazine</u>, three years following application for a patent on the Kinetograph, it was his intention, from the beginning, to link the phonograph and the motion picture camera so as to produce sound motion pictures.

Edison never licked the problem of motion picture projection, but he did introduce the world's first practical motion picture viewing system in 1894 – a peep show which he called the Kinetoscope. And a few of these – probably no more than 50 in number – were modified a year later so as to present sound motion pictures. They were called Kinetophones and combined in one machine a motion picture peep show and an Edison cylinder phonograph. Only one of these machines is known to survive, and on the basis of an examination of it, it is known that the sound and picture were not, in any strict sense, operated in synchronism. When a coin was inserted into the Kinetophone, the separate sound and picture reproducing machines were set in motion at approximately the same time, and sound which was appropriate to the picture was heard by the viewer by means of a stethoscope attachment.

Edison continued to experiment with sound motion pictures and introduced a quite elaborate synchronous motion picture sound system in 1913 which he also called the Kinetophone. This system employed a 35mm projector in its booth at the back of the theater and an acoustic phonograph at the front of the theater near the screen. The two were synchronized by a belt which, in a continuous loop, ran the entire length of the theater, between the projector and the phonograph. The projector was hand-cranked, and, according to a 1913 account in <u>Motion Picture News</u>,

> "A synchronizing device, like the one attached
> to the camera, is also attached to the projection
> machine. This device is so constructed that it con-
> trols the operator, preventing him from turning the
> crank at any speed than that demanded by the phono-
> graph. After the start he can turn his back to the
> picture and maintain synchronism to the exactness of
> a fraction of a second."[2]

This version of the Edison Kinetophone ran for about sixteen weeks at Keith's Colonial Theatre in New York city with some success, as well as

in other American cities and foreign countries; but in the end it was
closed out and disappeared from the technological scene.

Other systems, based upon similar principles, were introduced to
the public prior to 1910 by Leon Gaumont in France and Oskar Messter in
Germany. As was the case with the Edison system, however, they had a
short commercial life.

The phonograph systems which were used during these early years
reproduced sound acoustically, the needle in the record's grooves transmitting its movements to a diaphragm, the vibrations of which were perceived by the human ear as recognizable sounds, whether music or speech.
These faint sounds were made louder by linking the diaphragm to a horn
which amplified the sounds acoustically. The larger the horn, the greater the amplification, within limits, these limits being both theoretical
and practical. Further acoustic amplification could be achieved by using a mechanical power amplifier on the pickup, or by using the vibrations of the diaphragm to modulate a stream of compressed air.

The machine used by Edison for his 1913 Kinetophone employed a horn
several feet long and a mechanical power amplifier between the stylus
and the diaphragm. Despite its size, however, it was not really very
effective, and the quality of sound was quite poor. Today we are charm-
ed by the anachronistic sounds which are produced by turn-of-the-century
antique Edison cylinder phonographs, but by any contemporary entertainment standards, either then or now, the quality of sound was metallic,
crude, and unnatural. Like Dr. Johnson's walking dog, it astonished by
its very existence rather than by its performance.

As for the system employed by Edison to achieve synchronism between
the projector and the phonograph, it was simply absurd from an engineering point of view, and according to engineer-historian Edward Kellogg,
no further attempts of any consequence were made, at least in the United
States, to utilize mechanical sound-on-disc recording for motion picture
purposes following this 1913 presentation of Edison's, until the development and introduction of Warner's Vitaphone system in 1926.

As for the problems involved in achieving reasonable high fidelity

in reproduction, and in amplifying the resulting signal for large numbers of people, this was gradually solved during the next couple of
decades, following the patenting in 1907 of the Audion tube by Lee de
Forest. This epochal invention, the patents to which were acquired by
the Western Electric Company, a subsidiary of American Telephone and
Telegraph Company, and its gradual sophistication by other inventors and
engineers during the next couple of decades, together with the subsequent development of electrical loudspeakers ultimately provided solutions to the problems involved in recording, detecting, amplifying, and
reproducing recorded sound. From both engineering and commercial points
of view, however, this gradual sophistication of hardware and technique
was a very slow process, involving the founding, development, growth,
financial support, and utilization of an entire new field of electronic technology. Without taking the time here to describe that evolution,
we will note, however, that by the early 1920's, the electrical recording of phonograph records had been achieved. It meant the end of the
acoustic reproducer and the beginning of the kind of electrical/electron-
ic phonograph reproduction system with which we are familiar today.
Much work remained to be done in the years that followed, of course, especially following the Second World War, in reducing surface and system
noise, in expanding the frequency response, in eliminating or reducing
various kinds of electronic and mechanical distortion, and in extending
the length of play of the recording media. Nonetheless, by the middle
1920's, electrical recording systems, employing discs, had been sufficiently perfected so as to provide commercially satisfactory sound quality, as well as for the amplification of the resulting signal to large
audiences. And it was with such a system, employing electrically recorded phonograph discs, that the so-called sound motion picture was successfully introduced into the American commercial film industry in 1926 under
the trade name of Vitaphone.

    The Vitaphone system originated in the Bell Telephone Laboratories
in one of two separate research groups which had been set to work to
develop a practical sound motion picture system, the one group developing sound-on-disc, the other sound-on-film. Both groups worked under

the general supervision of Bell's Executive Vice-President, Edward B.
Craft, while the disc group worked directly under the supervision of
Dr. J. P. Maxfield.

Discs in what became known as the Vitaphone system were cut on a
turntable which was driven in synchronism with a motion picture camera
by means of separate selsyn motors. The discs which were used were 13-
16 inches in diameter and about two inches thick, composed of metallic
soap, commonly called 'wax', upon the surface of which the recording
stylus moved from the center outwards at 33-1/3 RPM. From this original
wax recording a negative master, and then a stamper, were produced from
which final pressings were made.

Within motion picture theaters Vitaphone installations required
considerable modification of and addition to the motion picture equipment. The conventional drive motors of the projectors were removed and
replaced with electrically regulated motors which provided what was for
those days a remarkable measure of precision and constancy in operation
so as to reduce wow and rumble in the sound system to an acceptable minimum. Next to each projector a phonograph turntable and pickup arm were
mounted, the turntable and the projector being positively synchronized
in their movements by mechanically geared drives which connected the
two pieces of equipment. Power supplies and controls for the projectors,
turntables, sound pickups, amplifiers, changeover, and volume level were
located close at hand.

A standard projection reel of 35mm film in those days held 1000
feet, for a maximum running time of 11 minutes, assuming that the film
ran at 90 feet per minute. A separate phonograph disc was provided for
each reel of film. At the conclusion of each reel's projection, a changeover was made not only from projector to projector but from turntable to
turntable.

From an engineering point of view, the system was a monstrosity.
The use of discs made it very difficult to achieve any artistic or
story-telling modification or refinement of the sound track once it had
been recorded in the studio (although there were, in fact, some attempts
to dub sound from disc to disc during post-production stages). As a

consequence, the sound track dominated the picture absolutely. Cuts
could be made in the picture to conform to the track, but not vice
versa.

The discs which were played in theaters were quite fragile and
were supplied in multiple copies for each program so that replacements
were at hand when the inevitable breakage occurred. More seriously and
expensively, multiple copies of each of the picture reels also had to be
supplied since, if the film broke, it could not be spliced together in
normal fashion - to do so would have destroyed its synchronization with
the recording. Nor was it possible to 'slug' the projection print with
blank leader since that would produce a momentary loss of picture on the
screen. And so, if breakage occurred, the entire reel of film had to be
replaced.

Nonetheless, the quality of sound reproduction was reasonably good
and demonstrations of the system were made by Edward Craft of Bell Laboratories as early as 1922. Craft moved slowly, cautious not to push the
system before its quality had been established, and it was not until
1925 that a much improved system was shown to producer Samuel L. Warner.
On the basis of Sam Warner's enthusiasm, Warner Brothers Studios committed itself to sound film production and on April 20, 1926, the Vitaphone Corporation was founded, and entered into a contract with Western
Electric which provided exclusive rights to the Bell Telephone Laboratories system of disc recording and reproduction.

On August 6, 1926, Warners presented to the public its first major
Vitaphone feature production, DON JUAN, starring John Barrymore, at
Warner's Theater in New York city. This was fundamentally a silent film
which was musically scored and recorded using the Vitaphone system. It
carried sub-titles and had no spoken dialogue. It was accompanied on
the program, however, by several synchronized shorts, including a talk
by Will Hays and songs by Martinelli, Marian Talley, and others.

By the end of 1926, Western Electric had equipped about twelve
theaters with Vitaphone sound installations. In April of 1927, Warners
acquired 100% of the Vitaphone Corporation by buying out financier W. J.
Rich's interests in the company, and on October 6, 1927, Warners pre-

miered THE JAZZ SINGER, starring Al Jolson, in New York city. This,
too, was fundamentally a silent film with conventional subtitles, accompanied by musical scoring throughout and occasional spoken dialogue. It
was an enormous success, both financially and artistically, and provided
a turning point in film history by infusing reluctant producers and investors with an enthusiasm for the economic potential of the sound motion picture.

Nonetheless, as we have said, the sound-on-disc system was a monstrosity from any engineering point of view. Paralleling the development and sophistication of the sound-on-disc system, a variety of sound-
on-film systems had been evolving over many decades and in the minds and
laboratories of many different workers throughout the world. As Edward
Kellogg has written:

> ". . . photographic recording [of sound] represented
> a new medium, which seemed to offer promise of much super-
> ior results. A mechanical system seems inherently crude
> where such delicacy is needed as in reproducing sound; in
> contrast to which recording by a beam of light would seem
> ideal. The experimenters have all been conscious of the
> handicap imposed by the necessity of making ponderable
> mechanical parts vibrate at high frequency."[3]

Indeed, attempts to record sound on photographic film began long
before motion pictures were invented.

As early as 1878 Professor E. W. Blake of Brown University published a paper entitled "A Method of Recording Articulate Sounds by Means of
Photography", while two years later, in 1880, Alexander Graham Bell patented a method for using selenium cells for detecting sound signals
transmitted over a modulated light beam.

By 1886, both variable-area and variable-density methods of recording sound-modulated light beams through small slits onto photographic
film had been patented variously by Alexander Graham Bell, C. A. Bell,
and S. Tainter.

All sorts of attempts were made by different individuals to modulate the intensity of various kinds of light sources with sound modula-
tions. These included open gas flames, arc lamps, gas discharge tubes,

and oxy-acetylene flames, reproduction of the sounds usually being accomplished in those early days with selenium cells. Other inventors
attempted to vibrate, oscillate, or pivot mirrors with modulated sound
signals and to reflect a steady-state light source from these moving
mirrors onto photographic film.

Some of the more important inventors working during this early
period included the German Ernst Ruhmer, who began publication of his
work on sound recording in 1901, and who invented a photographic sound
camera called the photographophone. Another was Eugene Lauste, who
worked first in the United States for Thomas Edison, under the immediate
supervision of W. K. L. Dickson, beginning in 1887. Mr. Lauste's interest in photographic sound recording began as early as 1888, while still
with the Edison organization. Later in England, after the turn of the
century, he made good progress in photographic sound recording employing a sound camera system which used rocking mirrors and a grate-type
light valve. Lauste was one of the first to conceive of the idea of
combining picture and sound on the same piece of film, securing a British patent which incorporated this notion in 1907. He is believed to
have first successfully recorded sound and picture on the same piece of
film at his Brixton, London studio as early as 1910. Between then and
1914, he photographed thousands of feet of composite sound motion pictures; however, he lacked a means of amplification with which to properly
reproduce these recordings. In 1911 Lauste returned briefly to the United States where he photographed and subsequently demonstrated what may
have been the first composite sound-on-film motion pictures made in the
United States. Shortly thereafter, he returned to England where his
financial resources became exhausted, and where the First World War interrupted his work. A pity, it seems, for according to his biographer,
Merritt Crawford, writing in the Journal of the Society of Motion Picture
Engineers in 1931,

> "But for the fact that his capital was limited
> and the later interruption of the war, it is quite
> possible that the sound picture might have made its
> public appearance at least a decade before its com-
> mercial possibilities were demonstrated by [others]
> . . ." 4

Back in the United States, important contributions to the state of
the art were made by Professor Joseph T. Tykociner of the University of
Illinois whose earliest interest in photographic sound recording had
begun before the turn of the century. In those days he employed a man-
ometric gas flame as a light source for his sound recording, modulated
by means of sound waves striking a diaphragm, the resulting photographic
record being of a variable density sort, and being reproduced by means
of a selenium cell. Like Lauste, however, he lacked electronic amplifying devices for reproduction, as well as having to rely upon the relatively insensitive and sluggish selenium cell for such reproduction as
he was able to achieve.

Having set aside this work, and after an interval of many years,
he renewed his experiments in photographic sound recording in 1920, by
which time he now had available to him the photoelectric cell which had
been invented in 1913 by Professor Jakob Kunz of the University of Illinois, mercury vapor lamps which could be modulated by sound signals, and
the then recently announced and refined vacuum tube amplifiers and os-
cillators.

By June of 1922 he was able to demonstrate to a professional audience a relatively advanced example of a composite, sound-on-film motion
picture, a product of what he called the Phonoactinion system.

Professor Tykociner never bothered to patent his inventions, nor
did he or his university ever benefit financially from his work. The
quality of his sound pictures was quite crude by today's standards, but
many of the principles and much of the engineering which was involved in
it were substantial, and he proved that photographic sound recording coul
be successfully undertaken.

In the end, however, it was the work of Theodore Case, originally
in association with Lee De Forest, and with the assistance of Earl Sponable, which rendered sound-on-film a successful, commercial reality.

De Forest, the inventor of the Audion tube and the father of 20th-
century electronics, began experimenting with sound-on-film motion pictures sometime around 1918, and filing patents as early as 1919.

Theodore Case had begun experimenting with sound recording as early as 1911 while a student at Yale.

The two men began dealing with each other by 1920, by which time De Forest was using a so-called 'Thalofide Cell' which Theodore Case had developed for reproduction of recorded sound tracks. Sometimes working together, sometimes separately, Case and De Forest and their respective staffs worked throughout the early 1920's to innovate and perfect a practical sound-on-film system. Progress was slow. Suitable light sources, methods of modulating the recording light, suitable photosensitive cells for reproducing recorded sound, and loudspeakers for transducing the reproduced signal into audible sound waves, all had to be invented and refined. By 1922, according to De Forest,

> "I well remember the grim satisfaction I felt when for the first time in reproducing a photographic record of my voice, I was able clearly to determine whether or not it was being run backwards." [5]

By 1922, Case had developed as a recording light source the so-called 'helio' or 'aeo-light' - a helium-filled vacuum tube which operated on relatively low direct currents of 200 to 400 volts and which gave off an intense, highly actinic radiation. This proved to be a practical light system, capable of being modulated by sound signals for recording purposes.

By 1923, a sound camera designed for Case Laboratories by Earl Sponable was in operation and giving promising results. At the De Forest organization, by March of that year, eight composite, sound-on-film motion pictures had been completed using a Case aeo-light for recording, a Western Electric amplifier, and a Case thalofide cell to reproduce the sound tracks. The quality of the De Forest demonstrations to the press during this period was oftentimes quite poor, however, both with respect to sound quality and mechanical motion irregularities. De Forest persisted, however, He called his evolving system the 'Phonofilm' and presented the first public exhibition of it at the Rivoli Theater in New York city on April 15, 1923.

By August of 1923, a contract had been concluded between De Forest
and the Case Research Laboratories granting De Forest a commercial license to use the Aeo-light and the Thalofide cells in the making and reproducing of sound pictures.

Commercial exposure of the De Forest Phonofilm system moved ahead.
By the spring of 1924, he had about twenty exhibition outfits giving
roadshows in theaters throughout the United States. Among the films
made during this period was one which appears to be the first sound
talking news film of any consequence - spoken remarks by President Coolidge and Senator LaFollette in Washington, D. C., photographed on August 11, 1924.

Despite De Forest's hard work, however, he did not succeed in
interesting film producers or financiers in the potential of his system.
Perhaps, as some have suggested, the industry was doing too well financially at that time to be very much concerned, while the quality of
sound recording and De Forest's selection of subject matter was not
terribly good.

In September of 1925, the business relationship between Case Laboratories and De Forest was terminated, and Case and his associates proceeded on their own. From this period onward, De Forest's influence on
and contribution to the development of sound motion picture technology
declined rapidly. Interestingly, De Forest was quoted during this period as believing that the silent dramatic picture could never be improved by the addition of sound, and that sound pictures would never
replace silent ones. About the same time, in 1926, Thomas Edison was
quoted as saying substantially the same thing.

Meanwhile, back at Bell Telephone Laboratories, where development
of the sound-on-disc system had been proceeding hard-a-pace, a separate
group of researchers were at work on a sound-on-film system.

The patent position at this time was very complicated, some of De
Forest's original patents having expired, and both Western Electric and
General Electric claiming rights to public address amplifier systems.
The General Electric and Westinghouse Corporations were at work on their

own sound-on-film systems, and with the growth of the electronics industry and wireless communication, many electronics patents had already
been turned over to a holding company, the Radio Corporation of America.
Just to complicate things further, RCA now claimed for itself the exclusive right to use amplifier patents in connection with talking pictures.

Gradually, at least two things became clear. Case Laboratories had
the aeo recording light and the photoelectric reproduction cells which
Western Electric needed, and Bell Telephone Laboratories, the Western
Electric research branch, had the high-quality amplifiers and loudspeakers which Case Laboratories needed.

By March of 1926, Case had begun negotiations with Courtland Smith
of the Fox Film Corporation, and in May of that year the Case Laboratories system was demonstrated to the satisfaction of producer William
Fox. Following extensive tests of the Case system at Fox Studios, an
agreement was entered into in July of 1926 between the Case and Fox
companies whereby Case turned over all patents and rights to a new organization, the Fox-Case Corporation.

Lee de Forest brought suit against both Fox and Case at this point,
charging infringement of a variety of patents, but this legal action was
never carried forward to a conclusion.

At the new Fox-Case Corporation, Courtland Smith became general
manager, joined by Earl Sponable and D. B. Elred of Case Laboratories,
and the trade name 'Movietone' was selected as the name for the system.

At this time, negotiations were undertaken between Fox-Case and
General Electric to secure rights to General Electric's vacuum-tube
amplifier patents, but these negotiations were unsuccessful. As Sponable
has noted,

>   ". . . if this arrangement had gone through,
> the whole setup of the future sound business would
> have been changed. The Western Electric Company
> would probably have concentrated more and more on
> disk, and the Fox General Electric group would have
> led in the development of sound-on-film." 6

In the end, Fox-Case secured a sub-license from Vitaphone Corporation to

use the Western Electric amplifier patents, on which Fox agreed to pay
an 8% royalty of his gross business in the sound film field. Still
later, by April of 1927, Fox was able to by-pass the Vitaphone Corporation and arranged a new licensing agreement with ERPI, Electrical Research Products Incorporated, a newly-founded subsidiary of American
Telephone and Telegraph Company, for non-exclusive licensing of the
Western Electric amplifier patents. The terms of this arrangement were
subsequently modified to provide for a flat $500.00 per negative royalty
to Western Electric for domestic release and another $500.00 for foreign
release.

The first demonstration of the Fox-Case sound-on-film system to the
public occurred at the Sam Harris Theater in New York city on January
21, 1927 - a screening of Movietone short subjects at the premier of the
film WHAT PRICE GLORY. However, it was the newsreel or news film which
was selected by Fox-Case to introduce its new system commercially to the
general public. Fox sent sound camera crews all over the world under
the supervision of Jack Connolly to record images and voices of celebri-
ties and political leaders - Mussolini, George Bernard Shaw, King Alfon-
so of Spain, King George V of England, the Prince of Wales, President
Paul von Hindenburg of Germany, Marshal Ferdinand Foch of France, David
Lloyd George and Ramsay MacDonald of England, Queen Marie of Romania,
President Calvin Coolidge, General John J. Pershing, Alfred E. Smith,
Thomas Edison, John D. Rockefeller, and many others - all spoke for the
Fox Movietone cameras and microphones.

Of all these news-film short subjects, the most successful was that
of Charles Lindberg's take-off on his trans-Atlantic flight from Long
Island on May 20, 1927, and his subsequent welcome home by President
Coolidge at ceremonies in Washington D. C. on June 12, 1927. The screening of this and other sound-film subjects was sensationally successful
with audiences, and Fox Movietone moved directly to produce a regular
sound newsreel series, The Movietone News, the first issue of which was
shown at the Roxy Theater in New York city on October 28, 1927. Movietone News was a success from the beginning. Introduced as a once-a-week
release, its frequency was gradually increased until four issues each

week were presented in theaters across the country, doing a one hundred thousand dollar a week business for William Fox.

In Los Angeles, the design and construction of sound stages were undertaken by the Fox Corporation, and in September of 1928 a new sound-film production complex in Beverly Hills, called Fox Movietone City, was dedicated. This subsequently became Twentieth-Century-Fox Studios.

During the same period, Fox began production of sound-on-film features, some of the first of which were IN OLD ARIZONA, the first sound film known to be recorded principally out-of-doors, and the all-talking productions THROUGH DIFFERENT EYES and HEARTS IN DIXIE.

At the same time, out in Schenectady, New York, beginning in 1925, a group of General Electric engineers, headed by C. A. Hoxie, had developed a sound-on-film system of their own, originally called the 'Pallo-photophone', and then, at the time of its demonstration to the press in February of 1927, the 'Kinegraphophone'. It was this group which prepared a quite complicated music and sound effects track for the release of Paramount's production of WINGS towards the end of 1927. Finally, in 1928, the work of this General Electric group and that of engineers at Westinghouse Company was combined into a sound-on-film system which turned over to a subsidiary of the Radio Corporation of America for commercial exploitation. This system employed a variable area track, in contrast to Western Electric's variable density, and was marketed by RCA under the name 'Photophone'. Subsequent to this, in October of 1928, RCA entered the film production business with acquisition of the B. F. Keith and Orpheum circuit of theaters and the FBO Producing Company, the resulting production organization being named 'RKO' for Radio-Keith-Orpheum. Their first production was THE PERFECT CRIME, the variable area sound track of which carried musical accompaniment and some dialogue.

By 1928, then, more-or-less satisfactory prototype systems for permanently recording sound on film existed, as did systems for amplifying the recorded sound and for providing positive, reliable, convenient synchronism between picture and sound. The standardization of technique, hardware, software, and operations, on both national and

international levels, took several more years, however, No other art
form is so dependent upon such a vastly complicated set of technological
understandings and agreements as between creators and exhibitors of the
product as is the motion picture. Because of the conflicting technological, legal, and commercial interests involved, these understandings
were hard to come by. Until they had been reached, films made in one
part of the country, or by one company, might not be capable of being
screened elsewhere by a differently equipped organization; this was especially the case as between film makers in the United States and exhibitors overseas. In Germany, for example, three inventors, Engl,
Massole, and Vogt developed a sound-on-film system called Tri-Ergon.
Similar to, although apparently inferior in design to that of the Fox-
Case system, the patents which they secured for it in Germany kept all
ERPI-licensed films, such as those of William Fox, from being shown in
that country until an international agreement was worked out by a committee headed by Will Hays in June of 1930.

We have not the time in this brief survey to review the process
whereby the technological confusion of the late 1920's was finally resolved. Suffice to say that, according to Earl Sponable, by the end of
1929

> ". . . there were 234 different types of theatre
> sound equipment in use; most of these, produced by the
> independents, were for sound-on-disk. The total number
> of theaters equipped for sound of all makes in the Uni-
> ted States was 8,741. Of these installations, ERPI and
> RCA had provided 4,393."[7]

The effects of this new sound-film technology upon the motion picture industry were profound. It led to the penetration by broadcasting
interests into the motion picture industry, and the intimate, permanent
association, through shared technicians, artists, patents, and inter-
locking directorates, which prevails to the present day. It also led to
the widespread purchase of radio stations by motion picture interests.
The need for new capital, together with the financial reorganization of
the industry which was necessary following the great crash of 1929, led
to an uneasy but enduring liaison between Wall Street financial houses
and the motion picture business. New corporations rose and prospered,

while others fell and disappeared. The inevitable tendency towards
monopoly within the motion picture industry began to operate at once.
William Fox nearly took over the entire film business, acquiring control of Loew's and MGM in February of 1929, then acquiring Theodore
Case's stock in the company, and then negotiating a merger of interests
with the Hearst organization. During this same period, Fox also introduced a wide-screen, sound-on-film process called Grandeur Films, which
premiered in September of 1929. Extending himself at an historically
inappropriate time, Fox went under with the crash of 1929 and was
obliged to sell out of the film business entirely.

Technologically, then, the period from 1926 to the middle of the
1930's was chaotic. New kinds of studios had to be built, insulated
from the sounds of the outside world and acoustically appropriate for
the recording instruments employed within. Because of the difficulty
experienced in shooting in natural, exterior locations, a new repertoire of special effects techniques, such as the Dunning multi-film process and background projection, had to be developed in order to artificially transport the outside world into the sound stage. Happily, the
first of a new generation of duplicating film stocks began to appear
about this time which facilitated the development of such special effects
techniques.

Noisy arc lights which sputtered, whistled, hummed, and whined either had to be redesigned and silenced, or replaced with incandescent
lights, the latter of which were much less effective when used with the
black-and-white film stocks then available.

Cameras were at first imprisoned within sealed containers built
like giant ice boxes so as to silence the noisy camera movements then
employed. This in turn resulted in the elimination or severe reduction
of camera movement for some time to come. Later, cameras were operated
from within portable sound-insulated containers, and still later, self-
blimped cameras appeared which again offered a reasonable amount of mobility to directors and cameramen. Some camera manufacturers, such as
Bell & Howell, which were reluctant to re-design and re-engineer their
cameras for sound-film production gradually saw their equipment replaced

on sound stages by entirely new designs such as those of the Mitchell
Corporation.

The introduction of the microphone boom onto sound stage sets in
the late 1920's, and the difficulties involved in lighting around it,
increased on-stage production time and costs immensely. In doing so,
it rendered the director of photography an even more important sound
stage figure than he had been from an operational and economic point of
view.

The state of the sound recording art being as limited as it was in
1927, it was required that the speed with which film passed through the
camera and projector be increased from 60 feet per minute to 90 feet per
minute, so as to minimize wow and rumble on the sound track. This 50%
increase in running footage printing costs didn't seem so bad in 1927,
but with the introduction of expensive color print stocks in later years,
the industry was to discover by the late 1950's and early 60's that it
could save tens of millions of dollars in laboratory print costs if the
frame rate were dropped from 24 per second back down to 16 per second,
and serious proposals along that line were made by both commercial and
military film producers. By that time, however, wide screen formats had
become a permanent part of the production/exhibition scene, and it was
found that a reduction in the frame rate, although satisfactory from a
sound reproduction point of view, would also produce a flicker in wide
screen formats. And so the proposal had to be dropped.

The demand, from 1926 onward, for directors capable of supervising
actors and actresses in speaking roles brought many theatrically talented
people from Broadway to Los Angeles. Many of these were completely ig-
norant of motion picture technique, however, and for some time thereafter
a good many films ended up being directed by cameramen and editors. Some
silent directors never could get the hang of sound motion pictures, and
dropped out of the big parade for good. Others not only adapted successfully but began to experiment and to innovate artistically with their
very first sound films.

The introduction of sound to motion pictures was a great adventure.

Like many such adventures, it left a lot of casualties. It bankrupted
some investors and severely disillusioned many others. It broke the
hearts of some inventors. And it destroyed the careers of many creative
artists. By 1930, the pantomime party was over, and those who couldn't
learn to talk were not invited when the new party got underway next door.

But for every person the sound film injured, it benefited another.
Out of this change, disruption, pain, and readjustment, a new art form
emerged, with its own rules, aesthetics, pioneers, and leaders. However
much some of us still love the so-called silent film, it is a necrophilic
love for a dead art. The era of the talking picture is now nearly half
a century old, complete with its own myths, legends, heroes, villains,
failures, and achievements.

But that, of course, is another story!

Notes:

1. This paragraph is an amended version of one to be found in Raymond
Fielding, A Technological History of Motion Pictures and Television.
Berkeley: University of California Press, 1967. p. (vi).

2. Motion Picture News, January 18, 1913, p. 9.

3. Edward Kellogg, "History of Sound Motion Pictures", Journal of the
SMPTE, June, 1955, p. 292.

4. Merritt Crawford, "Some Accomplishments of Eugene Augustin Lauste -
Pioneer Sound-Film Inventor", Journal of the SMPE, January, 1931, p. 108.

5. Lee De Forest, quoted in E. I. Sponable, "Historical Development of
Sound Films", Journal of the SMPE, April, 1947, p. 286.

6. Sponable, op. cit., May, 1947, p. 408.

7. Ibid, p. 422.

Hollywood Converts to Sound: Chaos or Order?

by Douglas Gomery

Most film historians argue that once THE JAZZ SINGER proved how popular sound movies could be, the American film industry 'panicked' and 'rushed headlong' into the production of talkies. This description is of an industry 'confused' – in a 'chaotic state'. On the other hand we learn that during the transition to sound, Hollywood monopolists grew more powerful. Profits for giants such as Paramount and Loew's (MGM) rose steadily higher. The unresolved question is: Why would such powerful and profitable firms permit such disorder? I argue that previous historians have misled us; the transition to sound films was not only rapid, but also smooth, orderly, and extremely profitable. Speed of diffusion must not be mistaken for chaos or confusion. Only the small independent companies experienced significant difficulties, little profits, and no growth. In this article I will describe and analyze how the Hollywood monopolists cooperated to eliminate all important problems and insure maximum profits and growth for themselves. Consolidation and merger, not panic or anarchy, should be the labels we use to characterize the switch to sound by the U. S. motion picture industry.

I

Paramount, Loew's (MGM), and United Artists signed for sound with Western Electric's newly formed subsidiary, Electrical Research Products Incorporated (ERPI), on 11 May 1928. The other majors soon followed and the diffusion of sound motion pictures began. Hollywood moved to create sound features first; soon after came newsreels and shorts. Warners and Fox led - at least temporarily - in the conversion. Yet Paramount, Loew's, and RKO caught up within one year. Paramount's conversion was typical: it released its first feature with a musical score in August, 1928, its first with talking sequences in September, 1928, and its first all-sound film in January, 1929. The majors distributed silent and sound versions of all films during the 1929-30 season, and moved completely to full sound features for the 1930-31 season. MGM trailed Paramount by one month; Universal and United Artists followed three months later at each stage. The only significant exception to this quick one-step transition was Radio-Keith-Orpheum (RKO). Since the merger which created RKO occurred in October, 1928, time was needed to establish basic operations. By September, 1929, RKO had caught up with Paramount and the other majors. Independent producers lagged six months to a year behind even the slowest major company. The first all-talkie independent feature was not released until July, 1929, a year after Warner Brothers and seven months after Paramount. The independents continued to produce and release silent films well into 1930. The differences in speed and ease of conversion can best be seen in Figure I. The transition for the majors was rapid (about one year) and smooth. The independents trailed the majors at every point, and were seemingly undecided as to corporate strategy well into 1930. [1]

For shorts and newsreels, the changeover was not as smooth or rapid; less profit was at stake. Only Warners and MGM initially moved into shorts. Consequently there were opportunities for independent producers. Disney advanced significantly at this time. Fox led the way for sound newsreels. By the fall of 1929, Fox was releasing four different newsreels each week, and had seventy production units in the field. Pathe, MGM, Paramount, and Universal followed and all-sound newsreels were commonplace by the spring of 1930. Small newsreel firms, such as Educational's Kinograms, did not survive the conversion to sound. [2]

FIGURE 1

Silent Film Releases as a Portion of Total Releases:
the Majors and the Independents (computed as a
three-month moving average)

Percentage of releases
which were silent

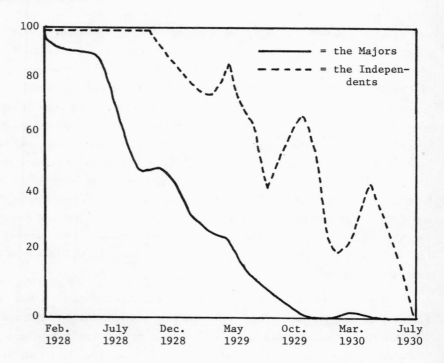

Source: Gomery, Ph.D. Dissertation (see Note 1), pp. 480-481

The Hollywood monopoly capitalists pooled information during the diffusion of sound, and minimized all potential problems. The Academy of Motion Picture Arts and Sciences (hereafter referred to as the Academy) coordinated the collection and transmission of all knowledge to the major Hollywood studios. On 2 May 1928, when it became known that the majors would sign the recording license agreements, the Academy held its first educational seminar. As early as 5 June 1928 twenty committees were established to gather and distribute information, and to consult with physicists and speech experts from the University of Southern California and University of California at Los Angeles. During 1929 the Academy formalized its activities and set up a school in which to train studio personnel concerning the fundamentals and newest advances in sound technology. Nearly six hundred employees enrolled in sessions supervised by Irving Thalberg of MGM. Elsewhere the Academy set up a special committee to solve the technical problems an individual studio could not solve on its own: silencing lights and cameras, finding the best materials for sets and props, and improving release print quality. This committee, also supervised by Thalberg, worked for twelve months. It published the most significant findings and solutions in the Academy Technical Digest. In 1930 all reports were collected and published as a book. [3]

Individually, the majors took less than one year to plan and construct their new sound stages. The only setback came on 16 January 1929 when one of Paramount's nearly completed sound stages burned to the ground. Paramount immediately initiated rebuilding operations, not even pausing for one day. The cost of the new Hollywood construction was enormous. Conservative estimates placed the investment at $23,000,000; others saw the total running closer to $50,000,000. All this came when the original studios, built over a 15 year period, were valued at only $65,000,000. Hollywood was not the only area which prospered. In order to minimize expenses for using Broadway, radio, and vaudeville talent, Paramount reopened its Long Island studio in July, 1928. During the summer of 1928, MGM, First National, Warner Brothers, Universal, RKO, and Fox all activated studios in the New York city area. New York

studios boomed throughout 1929 and into 1930. During a typical week ten
features, and as many shorts, were in production. Paramount always led
in activity; for example, in 1929 it produced over 30 percent of its
output in New York.[4]

The distribution branch of the motion picture industry was the
least affected by the coming of sound. The majors continued their dominance over national and international distribution. States'rights distributors decreased in number as their operations became less profitable.
The exchanges themselves became more careful in handling prints as any
dirt, oil, or grease could severely distort the sound. There was one
important change. Prior to the coming of sound, most films rented for
a flat fee. Since revenues from silent films could not be used as a
guide, distributors began to demand a percentage of box-office revenues
supported by a minimum guarantee. The major producer-distributors would
share in the excess profits if a film did well and be protected if it
did not. Independent exhibitors vigorously protested for they did not
wish to expose their accounts to constant surveilance by the majors.
Still these independent exhibitors gave in quickly; they did not want to
lose access to the highly profitable 'talkies'. Producer-distributors
then hired checkers to monitor audience size to guarantee accurate
accounting. [5]

Immediate access to sound films increased the importance and profits of the theatres affiliated with the Hollywood major corporations,
and accelerated the rate of disappearance of the independent house.
Chains easily absorbed the additional costs of wiring, quickly substituted vaudeville acts recorded-on-film for live presentations, and in
sum lowered operating costs. In response, during the fall of 1929,
smaller independents began to add vaudeville presentations to their silent film shows as a counter-programming strategy. This only helped for
a short time. Moreover, the automobile caused great difficulty for
independent theatres in small towns. Roads had improved during the
1920s and thus significant numbers of patrons could easily drive to nearby cities to large chain theatres. Independent exhibitors began to complain to their representatives in Congress: the majors were now even

more of a trust than before. To head off adverse governmental action,
the Motion Picture Producers and Distributors Association, the film
industry's trade association, appointed a committee to monitor com-
plaints, arbitrate disputes, and even compensate certain theatre owners.
In sum the committee did little except generate reams of public relations releases arguing how fair the current system really was. [6]

II

The most difficult problems for Hollywood came from outside forces.
As soon as the majors signed with ERPI, an adversary relationship developed. ERPI continually pushed to strengthen its terms of trade.
Interchangeability became the supreme question: Could ERPI demand that
all licensees only rent films to exhibitors using ERPI equipment? ERPI's
management pushed vigorously to eliminate all competition - especially
RCA - and thus produce a complete monopoly. In May, 1928, ERPI's
licensees added riders to their exhibition contracts requiring all films
to be run only on ERPI equipment. During May and June, 1928, this re-
striction presented no problems; the few theatres wired for sound (all
chain-owned) used ERPI equipment. By July, however, RCA - ERPI's principal competitor - had completed several installations and rendered its
Photophone system completely compatible. RCA pressured ERPI to initiate
a new decision rule regarding interchange. ERPI retaliated and warned
exhibitors: interchange, and face a long legal battle! One potential
solution could have been a merger of ERPI and RCA. There were preliminary discussions but no concrete action; each thought it alone would
become the dominant monopolist. [7]

In October, 1928, the Hollywood majors faced a no-win situation.
Irate exhibitors from all parts of the U. S. protested as their rental
contracts were terminated because of interchangeability restrictions.
ERPI seemed totally recalcitrant. Finally Elik Ludwik, general counsel
for Paramount, formed a committee to press for a solution. This committee met weekly with ERPI's top management starting 26 October 1928.
Early on, ERPI's negotiators declared that they would not press for a

strict interpretation of the interchangeability clause, alienate the
licensees, and drive them to RCA. Simultaneously sales managers for
the majors began to furnish films to theatres wired with non-ERPI equipment. A member of the sales staff would inspect a newly installed system, approve it, and then the producer-distributor would treat the theatre as if it had installed ERPI equipment. The committee pressed for
complete elimination of the clause, and on 14 December 1928 ERPI sent a
letter to all its licensees officially dropping the interchangeability
clause. ERPI would raise several smaller issues during the early 1930s,
but always the committee played ERPI off RCA, and resisted all changes.
The significant battle with ERPI was over in December, 1928, and had
taken only six months to be resolved in favor of the Hollywood monopolists. [8]

Labor unions also threatened the Hollywood monopolists' smooth and
profitable transition to sound. Most motion picture unions were quite
passive. Only the projectionists, members of the International Alliance
of Theatrical Stage Employees (IATSE), had a strong union. Consequently
when a theatre wired for sound, IATSE demanded and received new contracts
raising wages and doubling the required minimum number of projectionists
to be employed. Nationally by 1929 the number of employed projectionists doubled, and earnings rose nearly fifteen percent. The musicians
who accompanied silent films did not have as much power. Exhibitors had
installed sound movies in order to substitute technology for labor and
effect a large cost reduction in the long run. The American Federation
of Musicians recognized the threat immediately and in June, 1928, organized a defense fund of $1,500,000 and began an educational campaign to
convince the public of the benefits of live music. During the summer
of 1928 the union lost contracts in St. Louis and Milwaukee. [9]

The musicians union made its strongest stand in Chicago. In July,
1928, Chicago's dominant exhibitor, Balaban & Katz, removed its orchestra from a Loop theatre, the McVickers. Local union president, James
C. Petrillo, demanded immediate reinstatement; Sam Katz, president of
Balaban & Katz, refused. Petrillo threatened a strike. Contracts for
fifty important neighborhood houses expired on Labor Day, 3 September

1928. On 28 August Petrillo announced the union's demands: six musicians per theatre for a guaranteed forty-four weeks. Jack S. Miller,
representing the theatre owners, declared such requirements meant bank-
ruptcy. The six musicians would cost as much as rental for a Movietone
system, and would not provide for the showing of the new popular talkies.
The contracts expired and on 4 September more than 700 musicians left
their jobs. [10]

Quickly Petrillo and Miller began serious negotiations. Although
Petrillo threatened to request that projectionists honor the picket
lines, both sides knew that the exhibitors, supported by the Hollywood
majors, were much stronger. Petrillo wanted jobs, not a prolonged
strike. He dropped the demand from six to four musicians, and by 8
September a new agreement was reached. Both sides claimed victory, but
the number of required musicians per house, the length of their contract, and their wages had fallen. Only the threat of a sympathy strike
by the projectionists averted total disaster. By the end of 1929 even
assistance from other unions could not prevent mass layoffs in all U. S.
cities. During the 1928-29 season over 2,600 musicians lost their jobs.
Many moved into radio, or relocated to Hollywood to work in studio orchestras. By December, 1930, the situation had reached an equilibrium.
Only the deluxe first-run theatres in the largest cities retained musicians. For most local unions it meant a 50% unemployment rate. Even
in New York city, with its vast opportunities in radio, the rate reached
53%. [11]

In Hollywood the Academy mediated in all labor disputes and kept
all difficulties to a minimum. Most workers quietly prospered with the
increase in business. The only disruption came from outside. As is
well known, Hollywood raided Broadway for speaking talent; over four
hundred stage actors and actresses moved to the West Coast in 1929.
Most stage personnel were members of Actors Equity (hereafter referred
to as Equity). Equity had attempted to organize silent film actors and
actresses in 1924 and 1927, but failed. The producers, through the
Association of Motion Picture Producers, continued to recognize the
Academy as the sole bargaining unit. In January, 1929, however, as

more and more stage performers emigrated to Hollywood, Equity's new
president, Frank Gillmore, sent a questionnaire to all members; an overwhelming majority desired a new effort to unionize Hollywood's actors
and actresses. On 4 June 1929 the assault began. Gillmore proclaimed
that from then on Equity members would sign only Equity-approved contracts. No member would work on a film unless all other actors and
actresses belonged to Equity. Most employment contracts expired in the
summer months. Thus Gillmore knew that if this action was successful,
Hollywood would become a closed shop during the summer of 1929. [12]

Twenty-four hours after the announcement, Fred W. Beetson, secretary of both the MPPDA and the Association of Motion Picture Producers,
called a meeting of the production heads of all the major studios in
Hollywood. After a four-hour session, Cecil B. DeMille, representing
the producers, issued a statement defying Equity:

> "We will continue to engage artists for our
> productions only under the fair and just form of
> contracts which was approved by representatives
> of both producers and motion picture actors. We
> decline to be restricted as to the sources of our
> talent." [13]

The producers knew that only one-tenth of all of Hollywood's currently
employed actors and actresses belonged to Equity. Quickly the producers rallied important stars to their side: Lionel Barrymore, John
Gilbert, Norma Talmadge, and Marie Dressler publicly declared that they
knew of no labor abuses in Hollywood. Moreover, the major studios continued to operate normally, trading personnel when needed, and post-
poning no films. In July Ethel Barrymore, Equity's vice-president, per-
suaded Gillmore to meet with the producers. Gillmore demanded a partially closed shop. The producers offered only an open shop. On 11
August 1928 Barrymore released a statement to the press accusing Gillmore of misleading the membership. Barrymore felt that the producers
offered a reasonable settlement. This split Equity's leadership, and
quickly Equity's membership broke ranks. Large numbers of players began to sign standard Academy contracts. The labor unrest was over.
Equity retreated to Broadway. Substantial changes in Hollywood's labor
relations would begin three years later, when there was a real economic

upheaval - the Great Depression. The coming of sound only proved, in
this area too, how powerful the major companies had become. [14]

III

The switch to sound happened so rapidly because of the high profits
the major companies earned on their new investments. Costs increased
but revenues rose much faster. Accurate data for specific grosses are
unavailable, but all reports indicate that Warners' THE SINGING FOOL,
released during September, 1928, grossed a record $5,000,000. Other
new sound films did nearly as well and thus the majors' profits reached
new peaks. In 1929 Warners made over fourteen million dollars, Paramount fifteen million, Loew's eleven million, and Fox nine million.
Moreover, growth in profits was phenomenal. From 1928 to 1929 Warners'
profits grew an incredible 609%, Paramount 78%, and Fox 59%. All the
majors sought expansion and takeover. Here the actions of the Radio
Corporation of America (RCA) and its subsidiary, Radio-Keith-Orpheum
(RKO) are best known. By 1930 RCA controlled two major radio networks,
a small movie studio, the old Keith-Albee-Orpheum vaudeville chain, and
the Victor Phonograph Company. Still RCA never achieved great success
in its thrust into movies; other operations provided most of its profits. [15]

Of the other majors, Warners moved first. During the fall of 1928
it took over the Philadelphia-based Stanley theatre chain. Warners
needed theatres, Stanley a source of sound films. Stanley owned 250 key
theatres in southeastern Pennsylvania, Maryland, Washington, D. C., and
New Jersey. Ownership of such a chain guaranteed Warners parity with
Paramount, Loew's, and Fox. Stanley also owned one-third of First National, and thus Warners began its acquisition of that studio. By the
fall of 1929 Warners had complete control of First National studio.
Goldman, Sachs issued new Warners stock and raised the necessary
$10,500,000. Thus by the fall of 1929 Warner Brothers included two
production units, and one of the most powerful theatre chains in the
United States. [16]

Fox provided the next spectacular merger in the spring of 1929.
Fox had grown phenomenally in 1928. It had acquired the Poli chain of
theatres in New England, and gained majority control of West Coast Theatres, and with it one-third of First National. (Fox later sold this
share of First National to Warners.) Still Fox sought more power. The
opportunity came in September, 1927, when Marcus Loew died and his widow
and sons inherited almost one-third of Loew's stock. Nicholas Schenck,
Marcus Loew's long time assistant, assumed control. William Fox approached Schenck, and convinced Schenck to organize a pool of executives
and the Loew family to sell their stock - a majority. On 3 March 1929
Fox announced the purchase. The Fox-Loew's combination was now the
largest in the motion picture industry, surpassing even Paramount. The
new corporation held assets over $200,000,000 and possessed an annual
earnings potential of $20,000,000. It controlled over 750 theatres in
the best locations. Fox-Loew's purchased 115 additional theatres in
May, 1929, to bring the total to nearly 900.[17]

Not to be left behind, Paramount also sought takeover. On 1 September 1929 Paramount announced it would merge with Warner Brothers to form
'Paramount-Vitaphone'. This new company would be the industry's largest entertainment combine, exceeding the asset base and earning of
either Fox-Loew's or RCA-RKO. Paramount-Vitaphone would own over 1,400
theatres, six studios, a system of vaudeville presentation units, the
Columbia Broadcasting System, and the Columbia Phonograph Company. Now
three giants - RCA-RKO, Fox-Loew's, and Paramount-Vitaphone - would control four industries: motion pictures, vaudeville, radio, and phonograph. [18]

The Paramount-Warner Brothers merger never took place. As President Herbert Hoover installed his administration during the summer of
1929, the new Justice Department began to investigate the proposed merger as well as the Fox-Loew's and the Warner Brothers-First National
combinations. In October, 1929, the Justice Department threatened to
sue Warners and Paramount. Both backed down. The motion picture industry's structure was set. Four firms dominated this and the three
allied entertainment industries: Fox-Loew's, RCA-RKO, Paramount, and

Warner Brothers. Three smaller motion picture companies still existed:
Universal, Columbia, and United Artists. As for the independent motion
picture producers and states-rights distributors, most had gone out of
business. Those remaining represented only a tiny fraction of the market. The powerful independent exhibitor chains were also gone, verti-
cally integrated into the four majors. Only marginally profitable,
small independent theatres remained. [19]

IV

The transition to sound by the American film industry monopolists
was fast, orderly, and profitable. All adjustments were made in fifteen
months. The Academy, the Association of Motion Picture Producers, and
the Motion Picture Producers and Distributors Association coordinated
the flow of information, and arbitrated nearly all disputes in quick
fashion. Profits skyrocketed, and the motion picture monopoly capitalists expanded, absorbed other firms, and concentrated and centralized
power into four large units. Rather than confusion, these monopolists
created more order by gaining control of the inputs to and outputs from
their enterprise. The coming of sound facilitated this greater monopoly
power, and shaped the structure of the U. S. film industry - a structure
which survived both a depression and a world war well into the 1950s.

Notes:

1. J. Douglas Gomery, "The Coming of Sound to the American Cinema: A
History of the Transformation of an Industry", (Ph.D. Dissertation,
University of Wisconsin-Madison, 1975), Appendix C, pp. 467-481.

2. Maurice D. Kann (ed.), The Film Daily Yearbook - 1929 (New York:
Film Daily, 1930), p. 889; Variety, 25 July 1928, p. 34; Variety, 3
October 1928, p. 12; Variety, 28 November 1928, p. 22; Variety, 5 December 1928, p. 7; Variety, 6 February 1929, p. 39; Variety, 20 March 1929,
p. 7; Variety, 15 May 1929, p. 28; Variety, 16 April 1930, pp. 35 & 51.

3. Academy of Motion Picture Arts and Sciences, Annual Report for 1929
(Hollywood, 1929), p. 13; Lester Cowan (ed.), Recording for Sound Motion
Pictures (New York: McGraw-Hill, 1931); Irving Thalberg, "Technical

Activities of the Academy of Motion Picture Arts and Sciences", Journal
of the Society of Motion Picture Engineers, #15 (July, 1930), pp. 3-16;
Variety, 16 May 1928, pp. 9, 16, & 42; Variety, 26 June 1929, p. 5;
Variety, 30 October 1929, p. 26; Variety, 19 February 1930, p. 10.

4. Variety, 30 May 1928, p. 10; Variety, 6 June 1928, p. 7; Variety,
27 June 1928, p. 3; Variety, 11 July 1928, p. 10; Variety, 8 August 1928,
p. 10; Variety, 28 November 1928, p. 5; Variety, 23 January 1929, p. 50;
Variety, 16 March 1929, pp. 1, 60; Variety, 3 April 1929, p. 6; "Talkies
Require Concrete Construction", Concrete, #35 (August, 1929), p. 56;
Howard T. Lewis, (ed.), Cases on the Motion Picture Industry (New York:
McGraw-Hill, 1930), p. 19.

5. Variety, 24 April 1929, p. 17; Lewis, Cases, pp. 590-594; Trevor
Faulkner, "The Maintenance of Sound Film in Exchange Operation and the
Degree that Sound Reproduction is Affected by the Continued Use of the
Sound Track," Journal of the Society of Motion Picture Engineers, 14
(October, 1930), pp. 501-508.

6. Variety, 18 July 1928, pp. 20, 23; Variety, 29 May 1929, p. 30;
Variety, 17 July 1929, p. 5; Variety, 8 May 1929, p. 29; Variety, 7
August 1929, p. 185; "Economic Relief for Small Town Exhibitors," The
Motion Picture, September, 1929, p. 3.

7. U.S. Federal Communications Commission. Staff Report on Electrical
Research Products, Inc., Volume II, Report B (Pursuant to Public Resolution No. 8, 74th Congress), pp. 258-272; Kann, Yearbook - 1929, p. 495;
Variety, 23 May 1928, p. 9; Variety, 11 July 1928, p. 7; Variety, 18 July
1928, p. 5.

8. United Artists Collection. O'Brien File. Manuscript Collection.
(Wisconsin Center for Theatre Research, Madison, Wisconsin), Box 84-4,
letters, Dennis O'Brien to George Pratt, 31 October 1928, Dennis O'Brien
to Al Lichtman, 1 November 1928, and 10 November 1928, Al Lichtman to
Dennis O'Brien, 29 October 1928, George Pratt to Dennis O'Brien, 9
November 1928; FCC, Staff Report, volume II, pp. 76, 278-284; General
Talking Pictures, 18 F. Supp. 650, Record, pp. 2937-2945; Variety, 20
February 1929.

9. Francis E. Ziesse, "America's Highest Paid Labor," American Federa-
tionist, 37 (May, 1930), pp. 570-575; Variety, 16 May 1928, p. 16;
Variety, 23 May 1928, p. 5; Variety, 30 May 1928, p. 21; Variety, 25 July
1928, pp. 4, 37; "Effects of Technological Changes Upon Employment in
Motion Picture Theatres of Washington, D.C.," Monthly Labor Review, 33
(November, 1931), p. 1007; "Effects of Technological Changes Upon Employment in the Amusement Industry," Monthly Labor Review, 33 (August, 1931),
p. 263.

10. Variety, 13 June 1928, p. 20; Variety, 11 July 1928, p. 17; Variety,
18 July 1928, p. 19; Variety, 1 August 1928, p. 14; Variety, 22 August
1928, pp. 24, 37; Variety, 29 August 1928, p. 16; New York Times, 2
September 1928, II, p. 9; New York Times, 3 September 1928, p. 14; New

York Times, 3 September 1928, p. 14; New York Times, 4 September 1928, p. 25; New York Times, 5 September 1928, p. 25.

11. New York Times, 6 September 1928, p. 23; New York Times, 7 September 1928, p. 16; New York Times, 8 September 1928, p. 19; Variety, 12 September 1928, p. 11; "Effects," Monthly Labor Review, November, 1931, pp. 8-9; "Effects," Monthly Labor Review, August, 1931, pp. 2-3.

12. Variety, 13 June 1928, p. 5; Variety, 18 July 1928, p. 49; Variety, 25 July 1928, p. 49; Variety, 8 August 1928, p. 44; Variety, 19 September 1928, p. 5; Variety, 10 October 1928, p. 1; New York Times, 5 June 1929, p. 1; Equity, July, 1928, pp. 7-8; Equity, June, 1929, pp. 7-14; Alfred Harding, Revolt of the Actors (New York: William Morrow and Company, 1929), pp. 532-542.

13. New York Times, 6 June 1929, p. 19.

14. New York Times, 7 June 1929, p. 28; Variety, 12 June 1929, p. 5; New York Times, 10 June 1929, p. 3; Variety, 26 June 1929, pp. 6-7; New York Times, 28 June 1929, p. 5; Equity, July, 1929, p. 8; Variety, 3 July 1929, p. 6; Variety, 24 July 1929, pp. 7, 42; New York Times, 21 July 1929, VIII, p. 4; Variety, 7 August 1929, p. 191; Variety, 14 August 1929, pp. 1, 6, 7, 14; Equity, October, 1929, p. 51.

15. Variety, 2 January 1929, p. 17; Martin Quigley (ed.), Motion Picture Almanac, 1934 (New York: Quigley Publications, 1935), p. 15; New York Times, 22 August 1928, p. 15. For the history of RCA and RKO see Gleason L. Archer, Big Business and Radio (New York: American Historical Company, 1939), pp. 322-351 and Carl Dreher, Sarnoff (New York: Quadrangle, 1977), pp. 103-133.

16. Koplar (Scharaf et al., Interveners) v. Warner Bros. Pictures, Inc. et al., 19 F. Supp. 173, 1937, Record, pp. 578-608; Variety, 29 August 1928, pp. 5, 11; Variety, 19 September, 1928, p. 5; Variety, 17 October 1928, p. 19; Variety, 24 October 1928, pp. 11, 16; Variety, 26 December 1928, p. 17.

17. Barrons, 30 August 1928, pp. 20, 28; Variety, 10 October 1928, p. 5; Variety, 27 June 1928, p. 51; Barrons, 25 September 1928, p. 8; FCC, Staff Report, Volume II, pp. 474-78; Variety, 6 March 1929, pp. 5, 10; Variety, 8 May 1929, p. 29; Barrons, 11 March 1929, p. 11; Variety, 7 August 1929, pp. 185-234.

18. Barrons, 26 August 1929, p. 29; Variety, 11 September 1929, p. 5; New York Times, 22 September 1929, II, p. 14; Variety, 2 October 1929, pp. 1, 4; Variety, 16 October 1929, p. 35; Barrons, 21 October 1929, p. 15.

19. Barrons, 7 October 1929, p. 20; Barrons, 28 October 1929, p. 15; Variety, 9 October 1929, p. 6; Variety, 30 October 1929, p. 9; Variety, 6 November 1929, p. 7.

The Evolution of Cinematic Sound: A Personal Report

by James G. Stewart

Since what I have to say will be in the form of reminiscence, let me preface my remarks with a bit of personal background.

My interest in sound goes back to the early days of radio broadcasting. Frank Conrad, whose experimental station 8XK at Wilkinsburg, Pennsylvania, was the forerunner of station KDKA (Westinghouse) at East Pittsburgh, was a friend of my father's, and through this connection I had a small share in the operation of the station. At the age of fourteen I took the streetcar on Friday nights to Wilkinsburg where Mr. Conrad allowed me to announce the records being played to a few hundred crystal receivers in the vicinity of Pittsburgh. My interest in radio continued and I was employed part-time while going to school by various dealers who were selling the early receivers. Servicemen were at a premium and any person who knew anything at all about the functioning of a radio set could get part or full-time employment.

This activity led to my employment a few years later by an RCA distributor in Pittsburgh as service manager, and ultimately I had contacts with RCA in New York. On a trip there in 1928 I learned of the establishment of RCA Photophone at 411 Fifth Avenue for the distribution of recording and reproducing equipment for sound pictures. I applied for a job and became employee No. 4 of the theatre installation and maintenance department.

This was in May of 1928. Two years earlier Warner Brothers had produced and exhibited DON JUAN which, while not a talking motion picture, did have synchronized sound and music. This was followed by other similar efforts and culminated in the release on 8 October 1927 of THE JAZZ SINGER. While still not a full talkie, it was the first film to attract the wide attention of audiences to sound pictures. This was followed by THE LIGHTS OF NEW YORK which was the first all-talking motion picture. All of these pictures were recorded and exhibited with Vitaphone sound-on-disc. The Western Electric Company, through its subsidiary Electrical Research Products, had done the experimental work and produced the early equipment.

In 1928 RCA was just beginning to market equipment produced at Westinghouse and the General Electric Company for both sound recording and theatre reproduction. This had been preceded by several years of experimentation, principally at the General Electric plant in Schenectady.

For several years Lee De Forest and others had been experimenting with sound-on-film, and in 1927 Fox-Case had begun producing and exhibiting the Movietone News.

In the summer of 1928 Mr. George Eastman came to New York to purchase sound equipment for the Eastman Theatre in Rochester. When he came to Photophone I was assigned to show him around the plant. On that same day he ordered complete equipment and asked that I be assigned to supervise the installation. This early equipment was quite elaborate. It consisted of two complete systems, each powered by a motor generator, installed in an attic-like deck above the projection booth. Mr. Eastman was much interested in the equipment and visited the theatre throughout its installation; and I remember that after the work was completed he insisted on climbing the ladder with me to inspect the generator installation.

Theatre Sound

The introduction of sound had a tremendous effect on the motion
picture theatre. Prior to sound, theatres had had no acoustical or
noise problems. Reverberation if anything enhanced rather than detracted from the organ music which usually accompanied films in the
better houses. Synchronous sound changed all this. The vaudeville
houses suffered least since they, while not acoustically perfect, nevertheless had upholstered seats and heavy drapes which tended to cut down
reverberation and made speech reasonably intelligible. But in the average house intelligibility was very low, and with the poor quality of
early recording this became a real problem.

Western Electric in their pioneering of theatre equipment had used
a horn-type reproducer which was quite directional, resulting in a concentration of sound energy on the audience - where it was needed - with
a minimum reaching the reflecting walls and ceiling. Since the audience
formed the major portion of the sound absorption within the theatre,
the results with the use of this equipment were reasonably satisfactory
even in reverberant houses.

When RCA entered the field in 1928 they decided to use 12-inch cone
speakers mounted on large baffles at either side of the screen. These
were essentially non-directional. Not only did they provide a wide beam
of sound to the audience, but the backs of the speakers were open and
equal energy was delivered to the backstage area, which in the houses
that were presenting stage shows was quite large and very reverberant.
The result was that the RCA equipment was on the borderline of acceptance for speech reproduction.

RCA had so many problems with these non-directional loudspeakers
that early in 1929 it became apparent that something would have to be
done to improve the directional characteristics of the system. Since
I had more field experience than most of the other installation engineers, and was more aware of the nature of the problem, I was assigned
to head a group of Westinghouse, General Electric, and RCA engineers and
make a theatre study. We experimented with various types of reproducers

in a number of theatres, using intelligibility tests in empty theatres
to determine the relative merits of the systems tried. Nothing was
particularly successful until J. D. Seabert of Westinghouse went to the
plant at East Pittsburgh and returned with what came to be known as a
directional baffle. It was simply an exponential horn of square cross
sections five feet long, mounted on a fully encased cone-type speaker.
The first installation was in a small theatre in Pennsylvania where the
reverberation was extremely severe. It was installed so that it was
possible to shift from the old system of cones to the new system. The
results were satisfactory and left no doubt that this was the answer to
our immediate problem. We gave a demonstration for some of the 'high
brass' of RCA Photophone, and the speaker was put into production. RCA
replaced the older type installations with the new baffle.

Another problem that plagued RCA was the introduction of the P-2
projector. The first projectors of this type in commercial use were
installed at the Eastman Theatre. Prior to 1928 projectors were designed exclusively for high quality picture projection. Sound introduced
new problems, due to the differing types of motion required for picture
and sound. The picture movement is intermittent, since the film must
remain stationary during the time that the picture is visible. Then it
must move very rapidly to the next frame while the screen is dark. This
is accomplished by the use of sprocket holes driven by a device known as
an 'intermittent'. Sound, on the contrary, must move with constant linear velocity past the photocell. Since these two systems are only 20
frames apart (in 35 mm) something must be done to remove the residue of
intermittent motion between the picture head and the sound head. If
this is not done, the sound reproduction is greatly impaired by bad
motion.

The old nitrate-based film was unstable and the number of sprocket
holes in a thousand feet of film could vary by as much as 1% due to
shrinkage. As a result, the sound and picture drive systems could not
be locked together. The P-2 projector surmounted these difficulties by
having the sound driven at constant velocity by a drum, while between
the sound and picture heads a device known as the 'compensator' was

incorporated which made it possible via slight variations in the picture
speed to compensate for the variable shrinkage of the motion picture
film being projected. Sound quality from the P-2 was excellent, probably the best available from commercially produced equipment.

Unfortunately, this projector had been tested under laboratory
conditions on a small screen. When these projectors were installed in
the Eastman Theatre, it proved impossible to keep the picture on the
front wall of the theatre, let alone on the screen! The chief projectionist at the Eastman Theatre, Mr. Townsend, was very helpful in over-
coming, at least in part, the picture projection difficulties of the
P-2; and he along with myself and engineers from General Electric were
able finally to produce a satisfactory result for the opening of the
Theatre in December of 1928. Due to similar experiences in other theatres, as well as high maintenance costs, the P-2 was eventually abandoned.

Other solutions of the motion problem were being studied, such as
filtering devices between the picture head and the sound head. This
work culminated in a highly satisfactory filter which, in some derivative
form, is used in all recording and reproducing equipment today.

Production Sound

In September of 1929 I was sent to the West Coast to head a group
installing the new directional baffle speakers in theatres. We also
made such alterations in the equipment as had been found desirable in
the experimental period. This brought me into close contact with motion
picture studios, and in 1931 I left RCA Photophone to work for RKO Studios. I was first employed as an engineer to develop new equipment, but
with the onset of the Depression the studio abandoned independent development and experimentation, relying on RCA to accomplish this. I transferred to the production department and began work as a boom man .- the
man who pursues the actor with a microphone during production.

Much has been said regarding the many changes in motion picture
production which sound necessitated, but very little about the transi-

tion that was necessary in radio sound to adapt it to motion pictures. Radio had been perfected over a period of ten years with fixed microphones and movable performers. The shows that were on the air during the early days of motion picture sound were excellent in both quality and presentation of oral material. Those of us coming from radio into the motion picture field were faced with the problems of translating our techniques into methods which could be used in motion picture production. We had been accustomed to stationary microphones, and had never regarded the performer as a moving target.

At first the emphasis was on sound quality. The cameras were installed in soundproof booths six feet on a side, depriving the cameraman of the freedom of panning, tilting, etc. By mid-1929, however, blimps came into use (smaller soundproofed enclosures for cameras), and with these the camera regained much of its mobility. The cameraman was also faced with a number of other problems which had not existed in the silent days. In the early sound pictures he was forced to light for two or three cameras at once, which made it difficult for him to get the desired quality in all camera angles.

The director in silent pictures had been able to talk to his actors and give them instructions during a take. Now sound muted him. Before and after the take he was a director. During the take he was a critic. He was now forced to instruct his actors, watch a take, and then reinstruct them. Movement on the screen was extremely limited. Microphones were non-directional and were suspended from above or hidden behind flower vases, underneath tables, or in back of curtains. The actor was unable to speak while in motion from one pick-up point to another. Looking at some of the early talking pictures you get the impression that it's '1-2-3-4-speak', '1-2-3-4-speak'!

The actors suffered severely. In many cases the introduction of sound terminated careers. The industry turned at first to stage plays, and we had a series of parlor-bedroom farces and serious dramas imitating stage plays. These prospered primarily because of the novelty of sound. Performers who had been very adept in the silent days were now forced to speak, and in many cases they had had little training. Often their voices were inadequate, or their accents were unacceptable.

During all of this the sound man had his day! The technicians who
arrived in Hollywood came mostly from radio broadcasting and from the
engineering firms which were producing the equipment. Few of us had
any training in dramatic art. We were inclined to limit visual freedom in order to favor sound quality. Later, however, we were instrumental through our technical training in creating advances which made it
possible for the business to return in large degree to the satisfactory
production techniques that had existed in the silent days.

The first method devised for moving the sound pick-up with the
actor was a heavy microphone which was hand-carried along the parallels
above the set with an amplifier in a suitcase. This obviously was unsatisfactory. During 1930 microphone booms came into use. Due to the
weight of the mikes, the first booms were ponderous, difficult to move,
and occupied a great deal of stage space. Later smaller microphones and
lighter booms were developed. Then it became possible to use a fishpole for shots which could not be reached with a boom (a fishpole being
a long light-weight aluminum, bamboo, or wood shaft with a mike mounted
on the end and maneuvered either from the floor of the stage or from
the parallels above). With time, improved equipment and techniques were
developed, and most of the restrictions introduced by sound were eliminated.

Types of Sound Tracks

Originally there were two types of optical recording: variable
density and variable area. In variable density recording the density of
the track varies longitudinally along its length. In variable area recording only two densities are present, opaque and transparent, and the
modulation is accomplished by varying the ratio of the width of the
track occupied by each of the two densities.

Commercially variable density made its appearance first. It was
being used in 1927 for the early Movietone News. When area track began

to be used a year later, it showed superiority in the reproduction of
music due to its higher output and greater range, but it suffered by
comparison with the density track in dialogue reproduction. The area
track seemed to have serious volumetric distortion - individual words
and portions of words exceeded tolerable volume limits and were offen-
sive to the ear. At first it was believed that non-linearity existed
in the area recording. This conclusion was based on the assumption that
density recording was a linear system. Investigation failed to reveal
non-linearity in the variable area system. From 1928 until 1935 this
problem was a serious drawback to the use of area track.

In 1935 Rouben Mamoulian's BECKY SHARP, the first of the big Technicolor dramas, was produced at RKO Studio. At previews the track proved
unsatisfactory because of obvious dialogue distortion; and nothing that
we were able to do in the rerecording process produced a satisfactory
track. The area track was finally transferred to variable density, and
this was used in the release.

A comparison of the variable area and variable density tracks on
this picture gave us our first clue to the nature of the problem. There
was no doubt of the superior smoothness of the transferred density track,
and assuming that the density system was linear, there was no explana-
tion of why our distorted area track should be improved by being transferred to variable density. We began a new set of experiments based on
the assumption that the area track was linear and the density track non-
linear. These tests indicated that the density system, as used, had
considerable peak suppression. The distortion resulting from this was
not disagreeable to the ear.

Experiments with electronic devices resulted in the design and use
of a compressor for variable area recording. The first of these was
developed at RKO Studio and began to be used on the dubbing stage in
1936. We realized at the time that for the best results to be obtained
from such a device it would have to be installed on the original recording channels. During the transition period, however, considerable improvement was found to be possible by utilizing the compressor on all
dialogue rerecording, even though the original had distortion. In 1937

RCA delivered to RKO the first of the RCA compressors to be used on
original recording. Some compressors of this design are still in use
today.

Finally a paper which we had written in 1937 for the Society of
Motion Picture Engineers (later the Society of Motion Picture and Television Engineers) was published in April of 1938, and a demonstration of
the effect of compression was conducted. Soon compressors were used in
all variable area recording. The superior volume-range of area track
made itself felt, and, beginning about 1945 and continuing through 1955,
density track was gradually phased-out. After the introduction of magnetic recording in 1958-59, variable area track became the only optical
track in use for motion picture or television release.

Picture Editorial

Let's consider how editorial techniques were changed by the introduction of sound. In the silent era the editor had great freedom of
expression. He was unrestricted in time or content. The dialogue written for scenes was seldom spoken word-for-word by the performers. Dialogue titles made it possible to alter in many ways the structure of a
story to suit the editing.

With sound all this changed. In the first sound-on-disc films,
scenes were required to run from 8 to 10 minutes in order to be recorded
completely on a 16-inch disc. Scenes were shot with multiple cameras
and the picture was then edited to fit the sound. This meant that the
original pace of the scene could be in no way altered. Since this pace
had already been restricted by sound, many dramatic effects long established in silent pictures were lost. In sound-on-disc this problem was
eventually solved by shooting shorter scenes and rerecording them onto
a single disc for release.

With sound-on-film, difficulties of a different sort beset the editor. Since the lens and the sound head of a projector cannot be located
at the same point, there must be a displacement in the position of the
picture and the sound on a composite release print for theatrical dis-

tribution: the sound recording must lead the picture by 20 frames (in 35mm filming). At first the editor worked with this composite print. He was interested, rightly, in cutting the picture. In doing so he was forced to cut sound at improper points. Short sections of sound unrelated to the picture would result. (This remained true only during the editorial process. When the picture was completely edited, the sound track negative was properly cut, and then a new composite was printed from the picture and sound track negatives.)

This cutting difficulty was eventually eliminated by printing the picture and sound on separate pieces of film so that they could be cut independently. With the introduction of the 'movieola', which runs picture and track locked together, the editor was able to cut the picture as desired and match the track to it. The picture and the sound track were kept in sync by machine-coding both with identical numbers. The movieola, with minor improvements, is still in use in the studios for all editorial purposes.

Until about 1933 if you made and distributed a picture, you usually had to release it simultaneously on both sound-on-disc and sound-on-film, for about 200 theatres were owned by the companies that were manufacturing sound-on-disc equipment. The problem of maintaining sync between disc and projector, however, was insurmountably grievous, and thereafter only sound-on-film remained in use.

Post-production Sound

From 1928 to 1931 the major emphasis had been on production sound, with little thought given to the possibilities of improving the sound after the original recording had been completed. The rationale that sound as originally produced was necessarily the final product was a holdover from the days of radio, when transmissions were broadcast directly over the airwaves.

As the quality of photographic recording and reproduction improved, however, it became obvious that many alterations could be made in the level and quality of original dialogue. There was also a great advantage in putting sound effects and music into the product after it had been completed on the stage and edited in the cutting room. The result was a gradual shift in importance from production recording to rerecording, with increased emphasis being given to the latter. Objections on the part of the production mixer during exterior shooting were answered by the statement: 'We'll fix it in the rerecording!' This covered a large number of defects, such as extraneous noise, which was an increasing problem with more low-level airplanes and heavy traffic, or poor pick-up of voices due to the physical position of the microphone. Thus rerecording, which started out involving only those portions of the picture requiring music and effects, finally became the process which produced the entire release track. As a result, there was a growing interest on the part of directors and producers in this area.

The importance of music, not only in production numbers but as background for scenes, resulted in more and more attention being given to the dubbing process. This interest created several new professions: the music editor (a job requiring a knowledge of both picture techniques and music), the sound editor, and the dubbing mixer. The dubbing mixers became the heroes of the rerecording process, which detracted considerably from the importance of good sound and music editing. No highly satisfactory job of release sound has ever been done without great contributions from sound and music editorial work. It was not, however, until the economics of television entered the picture that this work received full recognition for its contribution.

The sophistication of dubbing and sound cutting grew together during the 1930s and 1940s. In the beginning the original dialogue track plus possibly one or two effects tracks (usually only one) and one or two music tracks represented the maximum number of tracks required on the dubbing stage. The devices employed by the dubbing mixer for alteration of the level and frequency characteristics of the original were simple and easy to operate. Shortly, however, elaborate equalizers were added to the equipment on the stage, and then dialogue equalization became a prime factor in a satisfactory release product. Additions of compression and noise suppression further complicated the work of the dubbing mixer.

By 1934-35 the supervising dubbing mixer on a production attained about equal rank with the editor of the picture, and was included in all preview trips and all discussions about the release picture. At RKO, where I was in charge of dubbing and sound editing, I would see all important productions in first cut. From then on I would be in contact with the producer and director on editorial changes. Thus, by the time of first dubbing, I would have seen the picture three or four times.

Just prior to dubbing there would be a reel-by-reel running with the people involved in decisions. These would include the producer or producer-director, the editor, the composer assigned to the picture, and whatever sound cutter was going to prepare the picture for dubbing. These runnings produced a typed analysis of everything that was to be done to the picture in rerecording. This was intended not only as a guide for the sound cutter, but also as a means of clarifying issues in the event of later misunderstanding. Upon completion of the sound cutting, the picture would be scheduled for the dubbing stage.

Depending on the complexity and importance of the picture, from one to two reels a day could be dubbed satisfactorily. Where there were differences of opinion, several takes might be made to be run the following day and intercut to produce a temporary review track. This intercutting was all done on the positive track.

On an important picture there would be several previews, the number depending upon audience reaction. Editorial changes would be made after each preview and, where necessary, additional rerecording would be done. After the last preview final changes were made, the rerecorded negative was assembled to match the positive track which had been cut during the preview sessions. This was then printed in connection with the edited picture to produce the release composite picture and track.

This is not the technique in use at present. The magnetic process which was introduced in 1950 has drastically altered all of the rerecording and editing techniques. I shall speak of this later.

Post-production Dialogue Recording

From 1935 to the present the use of 'looping' (post-production dialogue recording) has been continually growing. In view of the high
noise conditions existing in areas close to Hollywood, less and less
attention is given to original sound quality and more and more dependence placed on the introduction of lines recorded after the actual
shooting is completed. Today it is not unusual to find a picture in
which 60 to 90% of the dialogue in the release negative is made after
the completion of production.

Whenever the action is photographed in very long shots, it is possible to use 'wild' lines; that is, lines recorded with no particular attention to synchronization. With closer shots, however, it is essential
that the dialogue be in exact sync with the lips. There are several
ways in which this is accomplished during post-production recording.

In all systems, the actor hears the original dialogue over headphones. In the older method the picture and track are broken down into
'loops'; that, short sections of film spliced together end-to-end to
form continuous loops which can be repeated time after time. For rapid
work this is sometimes done without picture, the performer working only
to the sound track. Here again there are two methods: one is for the
actor to hear a short section of original dialogue and then, during a
silent period, to repeat the same words. The other method is for the
actor to repeat what he hears in exact synchronization with it. This is
the more desirable method, since it results in better synchronization
with the lips.

All of these systems are inferior to a method introduced in the late
1960s-early 1970s called ADR - Automated Dialogue Replacement. In this
system the picture and track are not broken down but the entire reel is
put onto a special projector and reproducer which are controlled by a
computer. The editor prepares a work sheet with the dialogue, and indicates the beginning and ending of each line to be replaced. When the
reel advances to this point, the computer is programmed to play the
track and picture between the two indicated footages repeatedly through

the headphones to the actor. This process continues until the actor is
fully rehearsed. Then the record button is pushed, and the new dialogue
recorded. If no other controls are activated the computer will play
back the newly recorded dialogue to the picture. If the take is unsatisfactory, the record button is pushed again and on the next round
another take will be automatically made. By the use of multiple channels three takes can be made and saved for later selection. As each
line is judged satisfactory, the computer is re-set for the following
line and the process continues until the sequence is completed. The
track can then be played back to the picture for final judgment and possible corrections. The editor receives from the ADR stage a complete
track on which he has to do no cutting either of the sequence or the
entire reel! The system on the stage is somewhat slower than the use
of loops alone, but since it necessitates no breakdown of the original
track or picture, and delivers to the cutter a completed reel of track,
it is in wide use today.

If dialogue replacement is done under careful supervision with due
attention to recording quality and satisfactory performances on the part
of the actors, the results are good. Unfortunately speed and economy
necessitate that post-production recording for television be a rapid,
routine operation.

Stereo Sound

It is impossible to cover in a short essay the many aspects of
stereophonic sound, particularly in relation to wide-screen processes.
A brief history, however, seems pertinent to our discussion.

In 1933 the Bell Telephone Laboratories staged the first stereophonic, or directional, sound demonstration in Washington, D. C., reproducing sounds originating on a stage in Philadelphia, 200 miles away.
It was an attempt to simulate the presence of an orchestra. It was
accomplished with multiple-channel transmission over telephone lines.
They followed this in 1940 with a demonstration of a recording system
employing more or less the same technique as was used in the 1933 live

demonstration. The cost of producing the necessary track for this type
of distribution and exhibition was at that time regarded as too great
to warrant its extensive use.

In November of 1940 Disney's FANTASIA was projected stereophoni-
cally on special equipment on a roadshow basis. In 1955 Spectra Sound,
developed by Loren Ryder at Paramount Studio, was introduced, and this
was followed by many other systems, both photographic and magnetic.
These systems developed simultaneously, and their growth was accelerated
by the introduction of the various wide-screen processes. The wider
screens offered greater possibilities for the use of multi-channel sound.

Of these systems, Cinerama and CinemaScope have survived the longest. The original Cinerama system required three separate projectors.
Later it was adapted to single-projector operation. It is used today
only on the hard-ticket, roadshow type of presentation, and is extremely
effective visually and aurally.

In theatres, however, CinemaScope has much wider possible distribution, since probably as many as 2000 theatres in this country are equipped to project it. But the costs of producing multi-track magnetic
sound, which requires a magnetic transfer process to produce each individual print, mitigates against its use except on very high-budget pictures. On such pictures a multiple sound release is made, and for ordinary distribution an additional standard single-track optical system is
provided. A recent widely-distributed CinemaScope picture was JESUS
CHRIST SUPERSTAR, and I know that the equipment in theatres throughout
the country had fallen into such disrepair that it was necessary to send
out a field crew from Universal Studio to implement the rejuvenation of
the system in order that it might be used for this picture.

I might talk for a moment about the aspect ratio, that is, the
ratio of the height of the picture which you see to its width. Edison
established the original ratio of 1 to 1.33, which simply means that the
picture was one-third wider than it was high. The human field of vision
has no such aspect ratio, being something much more like 1 to 2, with
peripheral vision spreading out well beyond this. Almost all pictures

today are shown with an aspect ratio of 1 to 1.66 or 1.85 or greater, and consideration must be given to this in the original photography.

The development of all of these systems has been covered in numerous SMPE and SMPTE papers, and I cannot go into further detail here.

Directors and Sound

Most of the early directors and producers were essentially visually trained, and came to regard sound as an adjunct to the picture. There were some, however, who realized that sound could be used creatively. Among the directors who come to mind quickly in my personal experience are George Stevens, Frank Capra, Rouben Mamoulian, John Huston, and Val Lewton. I worked on many pictures with them during the 1930s and 1940s.

Another director of this type was Orson Welles, who came to RKO in 1939. Mr. Welles had extensive and successful experience in radio, and was noted for his creative use of sound. After exploring other story ideas, he produced and directed CITIZEN KANE on which I did the rerecording. Orson's knowledge of sound and his appreciation of the subtleties of its use were responsible for the innovative use of sound in CITIZEN KANE and his later pictures. His prestige was initially great, and there was very little restraint placed on him in relation to time or money spent on sound. This made it possible for me and my department to develop his ideas, even though this might entail numerous failures and repeated recordings to accomplish the final result.

Orson's method, at least with me, was to run a sequence, give me an idea of the effect he wished to achieve and several suggestions as to how it might be done, and then allow me full play in producing it. We would then run the completed track with the picture. He would make comments and suggestions. I would then re-work the track until he was satisfied with the result. At times I was carried away by this freedom, and in one particular sequence - the Madison Square Garden scene in CITIZEN KANE - elaborate reverberation was used to give the feeling of space and size. After running my first attempt at this, Orson turned to me and said, 'You know, you're a bigger ham than I am. Nobody's going to listen

to me with all that going on!' He was right, and we redid the sequence
with somewhat less emphasis on sound. (This is a point to remember:
sound should enhance the performance, not detract from it.)

In one sequence in THE MAGNIFICENT AMBERSONS, where the cast is
riding in the park in an early horseless carriage, a problem of real
magnitude was presented due to the manner in which Welles had photographed the sequence. I was busy on other pictures and knew nothing of
how the scenes were being shot until I received a call from Mr. Welles's
secretary saying that he wished to see me downtown on the refrigerated
stage where he was shooting. At this time the Union Ice Company maintained a stage at their plant in downtown Los Angeles which could be
iced over to represent an exterior, snow-covered scene. Orson had a
park set constructed on this stage. With the techniques available at
that time, it would have been extremely difficult to record dialogue in
the horseless carriage; and even if hidden microphones had been used,
the stage itself was so reverberant that no sense of being outdoors
would have been achieved.

Orson's approach to this problem was to make a temporary recording
of the all the dialogue of the scene in his office on a disc recorder,
then play this back to the actors on the stage. Unfortunately it was
difficult for the actors to hear the dialogue clearly and to mouth it,
and the original track was of no particular use since the quality of the
recording was typical of home acetate recorders at that time.

When I showed up downtown and observed how this was being down, I
was considerably taken aback. Orson's only comment was 'Jimmy, you're
going to have quite a bit of trouble with this sequence'. And I did.
There were six principals involved in the dialogue, and I recorded each
one separately to the picture. This was done without Orson being on the
stage. I then combined these tracks and rerecorded them with the necessary motor-noise of the old type automobile.

On running the result with Orson, he said 'It's all right technically, but it's no good from the standpoint of realism. I don't feel
that the people are in the automobile. There's no sense of movement in

their voices; they're not responding to the movements of the car. The
voices are much too static.'

So I went back to the recording stage and redid all of the lines.
This time they were done with the actor or actress and myself seated on
a 12-inch plank suspended between saw-horses. As we watched the picture I simulated the movement of the car by bouncing the performer and
myself up and down on the plank. After a week of bumping, I had a track
which I then rerecorded and ran for Welles. His only comment was 'That's
very good'. Orson was not given to exaggerated praise of anyone's efforts.

Of late there has been considerable discussion as to how much Mr.
Welles contributed to the production of CITIZEN KANE. I can only comment on my own area, that of sound. He was the only person on the production with whom I had any contact, or from whom I received any motivation for what was done in the way of sound in CITIZEN KANE. I've always
felt that I owe to him much of my knowledge of the imaginative use of
sound and the motivation for my continued interest in this sphere.

1945-1950

In 1945 I left RKO to go with David Selznick's organization and
head-up a newly formed sound department. I eventually ended up in
charge of all technical departments in both production and post-production.

The Selznick organization was virtually self-contained. The post-
production unit consisted of 30 people engaged in picture, music, and
sound editing, sound recording and rerecording, and special effects.
This department also handled distribution of prints and censorship problems.

During the next five years Selznick produced three pictures under
the Vanguard Films label: DUEL IN THE SUN, THE PARADINE CASE, and POR-
TRAIT OF JENNIE. All of these pictures were released through SRO, the
Selznick Releasing Organization. On DUEL IN THE SUN censorship resulted

in our having some 30 different versions of the picture playing simultaneously in the United States.

Working for Mr. Selznick was a 24-hour-day, 7-day-a-week job. At
one point we had a crew in New York shooting PORTRAIT OF JENNIE, an editorial crew doing the censorship cutting on DUEL IN THE SUN, and a crew
in Hollywood editing THE PARADINE CASE. This resulted in my spending a
great deal of time in airplanes between Hollywood and New York.

Mr. Selznick always insisted that PORTRAIT OF JENNIE pre-dated both
CinemaScope and other wide-screen processes, not only in the use of a
larger screen but also in the use of multi-track sound. This was of
course not the case. Warner's had used the big screen fifteen years
before, and multiple tracks had been used on FANTASIA and other pictures.

In the last reel of PORTRAIT OF JENNIE there is a storm sequence
which culminates in the final disappearance of Jennie. Mr. Selznick
decided that the spectacular scenes, with the waves breaking over the
lighthouse and sweeping Jennifer Jones and Joe Cotten off their feet,
could best be shown on a large screen. I fell heir to the job of im-
plementing this process.

I decided that in addition to the big screen I would try to do something special with the sound. I did this without informing Mr. Selznick
of what I was doing. The wind and the waves crashing on the beach and
against the lighthouse and rocks were recorded on a separate track. We
built an attachment for the projector to play this track. The output of
this special soundhead was fed to a separate amplifier and then to 20
speakers that were placed on the sidewalls of the theatre and in back of
the audience, both in the balcony and in the auditorium proper. We had
a 250-watt amplifier to feed these speakers.

After we had completed the picture it became necessary to find a
preview theatre where a large screen was available. The use of this
type of screen had been discontinued some years before, but we scouted
around and found the Fox Theatre in Oakland, California. The screen was
not in usable condition. The mechanical device for pulling back the
side curtains to disclose the large screen had not been used for years,

and, if I remember correctly, it cost something like a thousand dollars
to get the screen ready for the first preview.

At the preview I had a separate gain control on the secondary
sound system. As the curtains opened on the lighthouse at the beginning
of the storm, I gradually raised the volume on the side speakers. Mr.
Selznick was sitting alongside me, and the entire 250 pounds of him
practically left the chair! The effect was dramatic and greatly improved the impact of the big screen. Typical of Mr. Selznick, after the
preview he asked me nothing about how I had produced the effect. As we
came out of the theatre he said 'Jimmy, we want 100 of those'. He had
no idea what it would have cost to distribute the picture with that kind
of projection and sound. Even if the funds had been available, there
were very few houses capable of using that kind of screen. That approach
was used in only about 5 or 6 houses in this country and a few in Europe.

In 1950 when Vanguard shut down its operations, the motion picture
business was entering a slump period. Fortunately I had continued to
function in my primary capacity of rerecording supervisor and mixer on
the three Selznick pictures. The Selznick experience gave me a broader
view of motion picture production and for this I am grateful. What I
had learned in my varied other activities was useful in the television
field, which was just beginning to come alive. I became a part of it
when I went to work for the Glen Glenn Sound Company.

Production Magnetic Recording

During the period from 1945 to 1950 the development in sound was
evolutionary, with increasing complexity in both equipment and techniques. But it was not until 1950 - with the introduction of magnetic
sound recording which had been long anticipated - that really great
changes in both areas took place.

At most studios the first form of magnetic recording to be used was
sprocket-driven film with magnetic coating. This was the product most
readily adapted to the existing recorders and reproducers. The industry

had been completely dependent upon sprocket holes and sprocket-driven
equipment to keep picture and sound track in sync. Quarter-inch magnetic tape had long been used for high quality recording, but it had never
been used in synchronous motion picture work due to the impossibility
of keeping it in exact synchronization with the picture.

At Glen Glenn the interest in the use of quarter-inch synchronous
equipment for motion pictures was primarily economic. The rapid growth
in the demand for recording equipment by independent television producers
made it difficult for us to expand our sprocket-driven equipment rapidly
enough to take care of the increased number of pictures. Mr. Glenn had
been in touch with Colonel Ranger of Rangertone in New York, and we had
done experimental work with a synchronous device on quarter-inch tape
recorders which he had originated. It employed a low-level, low-fre-
quency tone which, when picked-up on reproduction, maintained strict
sync between the original camera, the recorder, and the projection machine. This equipment was much more portable than our existing optical
recording equipment, and we put it into service in early 1950.

The synchronizing devices on this early equipment were cumbersome
and required considerable maintenance, but they made it possible for us
to expand our recording facilities without a large expenditure. After
the original recording had been made on quarter-inch tape, we transferred the dailies to optical track to be delivered to the editor.

Editors were reluctant to use magnetic tracks since they felt that
being unable to see the modulation would make cutting difficult. This
objection gradually disappeared, and soon transfers were made to 35mm
magnetic recording stock. (This is a 35mm film base coated with magnetic recording material on one edge inside the sprocket holes.)

The major studios were averse to accepting quarter-inch recording
as an original medium since they believed that the electronic methods
of maintaining sync were insufficiently reliable. It was not until we
had done five or six hundred television shows with no synchronous failure that quarter-inch tape came to be accepted and adopted at the major
studios. Today it is virtually the only method used for original recording on filmed shows.

Magnetic recording not only changed original recording methods, but
resulted in a virtual revolution in post-production sound. After editors had become accustomed to cutting both music and sound effects
tracks on which they could see no modulation, magnetic recording became
universal.

New rerecording equipment was installed with separate channels for
dialogue, music, and sound effects. These three channels were fed separately to a multi-track recorder. This recorder uses a different stock
than the magnetic stripe which is used on production or other single-
channel recording. This stock is fully coated between the sprocket holes
with magnetic material, and up to six or eight tracks can be placed in
this area. At present only three tracks are used: one each for dialogue,
music, and sound effects.

We now had a recording medium with which we could make repeated
copies without any significant loss in quality. We were able to record
a reel completely, and then go back to the head of the reel and start
again, making corrections in any one of the existing tracks by making a
dupe copy (or, as it is now called, an 'X' copy) of the original. This
eliminated the necessity of redoing an entire reel in order to make min-
or alterations in the relation of sound effects, music, dialogue, or
other corrections which we felt desirable.

Up-date Rerecording

Next came reversal rerecording on the dubbing stage, which we also
pioneered at Glen Glenn. This process, which is now standard practice
in all major Hollywood studios and independent sound companies, enables
the mixer to stop in the middle of a rehearsal or take, reverse for ten
or fifteen feet, and then start rerecording again. We can stop whenever
there is a difference of opinion about how a sequence should be handled,
or if there is a mechanical error on the part of the cutter or mixer.
We can then reverse to a suitable point, and then go forward, rerecording to make the necessary change.

Some people objected at first to this process, asserting that you could not get the feel of the individual scenes in relation to the whole reel. I felt from the start that this was a lot of nonsense. As one producer said after using this process for the first time: 'This is the only time I have ever seen a reel dubbed exactly the way the mixer and myself wanted it to be dubbed.' Where refinement is desirable, we can go back and make corrections in the recorded track. We don't have to make a copy, but can record on one or more of the three channels; that is, we record dialogue, music, and sound effects, and make the corrections on that individual track without the necessity of rerecording the other channels.

The reduction in rerecording time by this process has been phenomenal. For most TV shows the time on a reel can be reduced to an hour, resulting in a single dubbing stage being able to do two half-hour shows in a single 9-hour day. This can be accomplished without any loss of quality or compromise on dramatic effect. Rerecording of pictures for theatre release requires more time. Depending on the nature of the show, dubbing can take from two days to two months.

Until recently a method of up-date recording for videotape was unavailable, but we now have a system that is comparable in every respect to that used in film. The only difference between film and videotape rerecording, as far as the dubbing mixer is concerned, is that with videotape he's looking at a 25-inch monitor rather than a screen. Otherwise the situations are identical. The controls are the same. With tape, as with film, you can reverse, stop, go forward, start rerecording, do anything you want at any time during the reel. But with tape this is accomplished without sprocket holes since the sync is maintained electronically through the use of a time-code - a coding system which is read-out electronically by the machines and which can also be reproduced visually on the monitor. The videotape (that which would correspond to the workprint in film) is a one-inch slant-track video recording. Superimposed on the image on the monitor is a small block that has in it the hours, minutes, seconds, and frames identical to the code numbers recorded electronically on the sound track. This synchronization system

interlocks and maintains sync between the videorecorder and any other
machines we wish: half-inch, quarter-inch, 8-track, 16-track machines,
etc.

As a result of the introduction of the time-code and the impact of
videotape upon the economic structure of the television industry, more
and more television shows are being done from start to finish on videotape. I shall speak more of this later.

General Observations on Sound

If I were called upon to put a label on the function of motion
pictures, the obvious word to use would be 'entertainment'. What is
sometimes forgotten is that to entertain you must first communicate.
This takes place at various levels. Factual communication is primarily
accomplished by recorded speech. But in addition to transmitting fact,
a good actor is also transmitting content deeper than the purely factual.
The better the actor, the more involved the communication. This psychological communication is both aural and visual.

Ours is a visual culture. Despite years of radio and hi-fi, we are
still much more easily reached through the eye than through the ear.
First of all, vision is much more discriminating than hearing. The eye
is many times more perceptive than the ear. From birth our eyes receive
more involved training than our ears. Only in the trained musician or
sound engineer or students of speech do you find anything like acute
aural perception. This point is important in any consideration of the
contribution that sound makes to an entertainment picture. Sound is
secondary to picture. This does not mean that audience enjoyment and
understanding cannot be enhanced by an imaginative sound track.

There are three basic elements in a sound track: speech, music, and
sound effects. The proper relation of these elements is vital if the
track is to be effective. First of all, let's consider speech. At one
time I was a proponent of 100% intelligibility. I've written papers
saying that you should be able to understand not only every word but
every syllable. I have come to realize that this is wrong. In looking

at older pictures, I am struck by the lack of reality in some scenes.
In particular I remember one scene in a railroad train where two people
were talking. The train noises were easy to hear, and with the car
shaking you knew you were on a train. But the voices did not sound like
conversation. The scene was being defeated by the fact that I <u>was</u>
understanding every single word, which under the visual circumstances
would not be the case.

On the other hand, I do not go along with the present trend to see
how difficult you can make it for an audience to understand the dialogue.
There is a definite limit past which you must not go, or you lose the
attention of your audience. Once you have lost that you have ceased to
communicate. There is a basic principle: before you can communicate you
must have the attention of the listener or the viewer. In poor intelligibility there is an element of irritation which causes the audience to
reject what you are telling them.

The proper shading of speech, both in frequency characteristic and
in range, is not a science. It is really an art. All theories about
this grow out of practice. Results come first and from these results
theories are evolved. No broad theory, however, gives the answer. Only
extensive experience in dealing with speech, then listening to that same
speech reproduced in theatres or on television, can give you the knowledge that enables you to do this job expertly. Unfortunately I find
that too few of the directors and producers with whom I work are aware
of the possibilities of what can be done to speech on a dubbing stage.

The other two elements in a sound track - music and sound effects -
have separate and distinct functions which are sometimes confused. Both
are capable of transmitting factual information in creating an acoustical
environment to give the viewer a sense of reality that is in keeping with
the visual image. But there is the much more subtle and difficult field
of emotional and pyschological transmission. In this area music is the
leading factor. Sound effects, however, cannot be ruled out in this
dramatic area, since they can be used to produce sudden shock, tension,
horror, or excitement.

Many producers work on the assumption that 'loud is good', and they
apply this to both music and sound effects, or combinations of both.
Psychologically, nothing could be further from the truth. Effective use
of sound does not depend on sheer volume. It depends on the change in
volume of the sound, or in technical terms, the loudness range. The ear
has a protective device. After listening to loud sound for a long period, you develop short-term partial deafness and it ceases to be loud.
Continuous loudness defeats itself as far as emotional effect is concerned. This is true of both sound effects and music.

Another grave mistake is to use sound effects and music simultaneously to convey the same idea. This does not mean that music and sound
effects cannot be combined in a single background, but if they are simultaneously attempting to say the same thing they defeat one another.
It's as if you were listening to someone tell you something in one language while another person is trying to tell you the same thing in another language. I have often had composers tell me on the dubbing stage
'I had no idea that there was going to be that kind of sound effect in
the chase'. If it were possible, in an action sequence, to first produce a sound effects track and then allow the composer to hear it, he
would have a much better chance to further improve the track by the proper introduction of music. But this requires pre-planning, and is very
difficult to achieve, not only from a monetary but from a time standpoint as well.

In television the acceptable volume range of sound is extremely
limited. In your home the range from the lowest sound to the highest
sound that you can hear and tolerate comfortably is much less than what
is acceptable in a motion picture theatre. Many early TV shows violated
this rule in their recording, and hence when they went on the air the
electronic devices employed in television stations to limit the range
destroyed the dramatic effect created by this excessive loudness. The
result was less satisfactory than it would have been if the loudness
range had been limited in the original recording. In the years since,
this fact has been accepted and the devices employed in the stations to
limit the range have been improved. If you do exceed reasonable limits,

the product will no longer be ruined by electronic compression.

The virtual elimination of sheer loudness as a means of producing dramatic effect in television has had one good result: more and more attempts are being made in the TV and theatre product to produce subtle differences in sound rather than sheer bombast. In theatre motion pictures, unfortunately, there is still considerable dependence upon plain loudness to produce dramatic effect. It's understandable. The easy way to achieve an effect is to make something loud. It doesn't require much thought to turn up the volume control on sound effects or music and believe that you are producing a dramatic effect, even though nothing could be further from the truth.

The relation between the three elements in a sound track - speech, music, and sound effects - is an important factor in communicating with the audience. This ratio depends entirely upon what the scene is trying to say. If plot lines are being spoken, and if the primary consideration is to convey information, then speech is the paramount factor. When you depart from fact and come to emotion, the relation of these elements becomes very complicated, and it requires perception and skill to know how far you can go in losing intelligibility in favor of artistic effect. It's good to make an audience work a little to understand what your actors are saying, but if you go too far their attention wanders and you lose them. The producer or director who is on the dubbing stage knows every word of the script. Even if the dialogue were not present he would know what the actors were saying. This sometimes makes it difficult to convince him that the speech he is listening to is only about 25 to 30% intelligible to the average person. He doesn't take into account that perhaps we're dealing with accents, poor enunciation, poor sound pick-up, or high ambient noise in the original recording.

There is also the factor of personal taste. If the producer's taste dictates a certain approach, that's his prerogative, and what you must do as a recording engineer is to adhere as closely as possible to his taste and at the same time try to produce a reasonably commercial product. I sometimes think that a really good dubbing or rerecording supervisor is only part technician (sometimes only a small part), and that his chief function is psychological.

I quarrel with cinema education, based on what I feel is a lack of
appreciation of the possibilities of sound. Our cinema schools seem to
be turning out people visually trained but not aurally trained. If more
attention to sound were present in the college curricula, I believe that
students would enter our business and over a period of time improve the
level of appreciation of sound.

Videotape Recording

At this point I should like to mention briefly videotape recording;
that is, recording of a visual image magnetically on tape. This began
to be used in television broadcasting in 1956. There have been tremendous advances in the quality of images produced by this system since that
time. With the present electronic editing techniques available, videotape is becoming a serious rival to the film process in production, particularly in television. Work is being done on a satisfactory technique
for transferring the tape image to 35mm film for theatre use, and there
is every indication that within a few years this will be readily acces-
sible and produce picture quality comparable to or better than what we
now have on a straight film process.

The motion picture industry, I believe, is at the beginning of a new
technical revolution. The substitution of video cameras for the present
film cameras on a motion picture stage will not produce any vast change
in the methods employed there. The entire structure of post-production
operations in both sound and picture, however, will be dramatically
changed. As to pictures, the techniques and equipment are now available
in which the editorial process will be accomplished without the editor
ever laying his hands on a piece of film. All the work will be done
with an electronic image and remote control of the tape reproducers and
recorders. This is taking place now in the television field. Sound
editorial work will also be completely altered, since it will be a process involving recording from master sound effects and music tracks onto a multi-track recorder.

The post-production videotape field is in such a state of flux and
rapid advancement that it cannot be adequately covered in this essay.
(See, however, my earlier comments on up-date rerecording.) The one
point I would like to make is the tremendous importance that I place on
the development taking place in this field, and the vast changes that I
see taking place in the very near future.

Economics have always been a tremendous spur to technical development, and there is no doubt that there is great economic advantage to
the extension of the use of videotape in both television and motion pictures. The transition will be rough, entailing changes almost as great
as those that resulted from the introduction of sound in 1927. New
professions will again be created, and once the tumult has died we shall
have a healthier industry.

Sound of the Future

We have just begun to realize the possibilities of sound, not only
in entertainment but in other fields. Multiple-track magnetic recording offers potentials far beyond our present accomplishments. Quadri-
phonic sound is a first attempt to achieve some of what I see in the
future.

With 16 or 24 magnetic tracks available to us on present recorders,
I envision looking at a 3-dimensional picture and listening to sound
originating not only at the screen but all around me, so that if the
scene is in a railroad station, I am in the railroad station by virtue
of the sound surrounding me. It is now possible to have a changing
acoustical environment in keeping with the scene being presented. This
is being done in a limited sense in theatres today.

In real life we hear sound on all sides of us. If a car passes you
you not only hear it approach and go by, but you know where it went by —
in front of you or in back of you. All of this can be simulated for an
audience. It will require knowledge and artistry in both the original
recording and in the rerecording to produce this authentic ambience.
The obvious objection to such an endeavor is economic. Whether a suf-

ficient audience will be available to make this kind of entertainment
commercially feasible I do not know. But in connection with this it is
interesting to note the tremendous growth of appreciation for motion
picture subtlety among young people. I believe our cinema schools and
colleges are developing a new crop of creative people. Those who do not
make a profession of motion pictures will certainly be a more perceptive
future audience, capable of enjoying sophisticated forms of visual and
auditory entertainment.

With the increased interest in home entertainment and the prospect
of more leisure time, the extension of sophisticated recording and reproducing equipment into the home seems likely. At present there is a
percentage of our population sufficiently affluent to indulge themselves
in stereo equipment in the two thousand dollar class, and videotape recorders for home use are now on the market and beginning to enjoy popu-
larity. With 8 and 16-track recorders available and in use today in the
music and television field, we could soon have a truly audio-visual room
in the home complete with an artificially created acoustical environment.
This could involve a 3-dimensional video screen or a mood inducer to
supply whatever you needed in the way of audio relaxation without picture.

Another new profession would then result for cinema students - a
combination of talent and training. This work would become a part of
our environmental program, and we would have new college courses in
audio ambience engineering. I hope to be around long enough to see some
of this take place.

Part II:
Reminiscence
and Reflection

Hal Mohr, Cinematographer

I saw my first motion picture shortly after the San Francisco earthquake and fire, which goes back long before many of your parents were around. The picture I saw was of a train passing before the camera. That's when I went into the motion picture business and first started as a cameraman - and that ruined my educational career. I'd been playing with magic lanterns and that sort of thing up to that time, but from then on it was a case of 'How was that picture made to move?', and 'I'm gonna do it too!' I've been doing it ever since!

There was nobody to teach us then, of course, or to tell us how it was done. No way of learning about this except to learn it the hard way. So I proceeded to learn it the hard way. I quit school and got a job in the Miles Brothers Film Exchange in San Francisco. The Miles Brothers were the people who photographed the earthquake (you may have seen some of their footage). When the films would come back to the Exchange after being run in a theatre, we'd have to inspect them to repair the damage that the projection machines had wreaked on the film - sprocket holes being torn, and so on.

Amongst the junk in the basement of the place I found a little projection machine that was almost a toy. This was the forerunner of the Motiograph. It was called an 'optigraph', and those of you who know your history of motion pictures will recall that the optigraph was a tiny thing with a barrel shutter and two little sprockets, one at the

bottom and one in the top, to create the loop. This loop was the thing
on which the Motion Picture Patents Corporation claimed to have its
patents, and which they used as justification for confiscating cameras
of their competitors which used it. (Oddly enough it was the sewing
machine which broke the monopoly of the Patents company. The inter-
mittancy of the thread being pulled down by the shuttle on the sewing
machine was the legal precedent that was later invoked to negate the
company's patent claim on the projector loop.)

I used this projection machine to make a camera of my own which
used a loop. I put it inside a black box, got hold of some short ends
of film, and photographed little news events in San Francisco with it.
The lens that I had (I know you're going to disbelieve this) was the
projection lens that was on the machine! It was a little 2-inch projection lens with a fixed stop, and I photographed news events with it,
such as the breaking of ground for the Panama Pacific International
Exposition in San Francisco by William Howard Taft, who was then President of the United States. I was getting pretty active. Sidney Grau-
man's father, who ran the Empress Theatre in San Francisco, was my best
customer. He'd buy these short news items and run them in his theatre.

One day two gentlemen appeared at my home, a man by the name of
Smith and another by the name of Kelly. They said that they were oil
well operators in the Bakersfield area, and wanted me to make some moving pictures of their oil well operations. Well, I knew about the Patents company, and I knew that if anybody got to see how my camera operated I was out of business. But I was very young and quite gullible,
and I believed these two wretched people, who turned out to be two detec-
tives from the Motion Picture Patents company! I showed them my camera
and they served papers on me and immediately seized it.

We took the camera down to a building on Marcus Street in San Francisco and turned it over to their attorneys. The attorneys had a marble
floor in their old offices. When I brought the camera in, I said (or
words to this effect) 'Gentlemen, here's what you claim I'm infringing
on, and you can have it'. I then threw it on the floor, because I was
not going to let anybody else use my camera! When the thing shattered

and the box broke into pieces, I realized that it was just a projection
machine again. So I said, 'But unfortunately it is not a camera, so
therefore your patents don't apply'. I then picked the thing up and
walked out of the office! I subsequently built it into another camera,
which I still own. That was my involvement with the Patents company.

I later was under contract to Warner Brothers. We were very happily making silent pictures - with all the permissiveness with respect
to our activities on the set that was then allowed - when Sam Warner
brought about the introduction of Vitaphone to our studios. It created
a whole new elephant for those of us who had been making silent films.

In the early days of making sound pictures, the experts on sound
came from the telephone laboratories, and we were terrifically awed by
the eggheads who came onto our stages to tell us how we were going to
put sound on our silent films. They'd walk authoritatively onto the
stage and say, 'We have to put baffles here'; or 'You can't have lights
there, because that's sound reflecting'; and so on and so forth. Unsurprisingly, after we made the first sound pictures (including THE JAZZ
SINGER) it looked as if sound pictures were going to be very short-lived,
because, by the prevailing standards of making motion pictures, they
were so bad! We did suffer tremendously from the inadequacies of being
unable to meet the problems that sound put to us.

Those of us who had any voice at all in the making of motion pictures finally convinced our mentors - the producers with the purse
strings - that they were short-changing themselves by making such an inferior amusement product, and that we'd better start making movies again.
The sound man at that time had been the supreme god on the set. If he
said 'You can't have that light there', then that light disappeared; or
if he said 'I want that microphone down here', that's where the microphone was placed, despite the fact that an actor had to deliver the
lines and we had to photograph him. So finally we reached the point
where we said 'Now fellows, we're going to start making movies again.
You just get the best sound that you can get, and if it ain't good
enough, that's too bad!' We then found a happy compromise: they worked

with us and we worked with them, and the result is that we're still
making bad movies!

In the early days sound was put directly onto discs, and hence
each scene was recorded in its entirety from beginning to end. It was
impossible to cut the scenes. It was impossible to extract a bit of
the film here and a bit of the film there. We had to do an entire section of a film - the entire scene - in one operation. I imagine that
the reels were then a thousand feet long, which was about 11 minutes of
film; so the duration of the accompanying phonograph record (or disc)
could be up to 11 minutes of sound. If the film was short, then the
reel was short; and then the disc was also short because the disc had
to be exactly the same length as the reel of film. At the very beginning some of these reels of film, and their accompanying discs, were as
short as a minute-and-a-half or two minutes, which made it necessary for
the operators in the projection booths to move pretty darn fast to be
ready for the next changeover by the time the end of that reel would
come about. If a scene was terribly short, therefore, we'd often try
some way of stretching it out so that we could make it last long enough
to get enough film onto the projector to permit the projectionist to have
enough time to thread the other projection machine.

The discs were rather short-lived as components in the process of
producing motion pictures because of the impracticality of holding sync.
The operators in the projection rooms would watch through the porthole -
if they were good operators - and would see the sound getting out of
sync. If the sound was ahead of the picture, they'd put a thumb on the
disc and slow it down a little bit, or if it was behind they'd juice it
ahead a little bit to try and catch up with the picture.

It stayed that way until dubbing was invented. The man who first
made it possible to take portions off of records, and in fact to 'cut'
sound, was named Hermann Heller. He initiated the practice of having
multiple turntables operating from which he could extract different sections of the sound, and thereby cut scenes.

In the silent days we had been accustomed to having our noisy cameras standing on a little piece of 3-legged apparatus someplace on the

set. We had the whole stage and the whole surrounding area in which to
place our lights, gobos, or the chairs for visitors or members of the
cast or whomever was watching on the sidelines, without getting in each
other's way. All of a sudden came these trememdous soundproofed camera
blimps we called 'iceboxes'. Each camera had to be encased in a completely silenced booth. If you had more than one angle of a scene to
photograph at a time, it was necessary to have one camera doing the master long-shot of the scene, another camera doing a two-shot with two of
the principal players, and perhaps two or three other cameras doing individual close-ups. If you had four or five cameras operating at once,
you had four or five of these huge 'iceboxes' surrounding a small stage,
which left no room for lights; and often the director had to sit atop
one of the iceboxes in order to see what was going on. Your cameras,
in addition, all had to be operating simultaneously, so that whenever a
particular actor spoke up, or played a portion of the scene that was
supposed to have dialogue in it, they would be at the proper moment in
relation to the disc that was being recorded in the little booth on the
side. These cameras were supposed to all start together, but in many
cases useless film was ground through. Often a 1000 foot roll of film
would go through a magazine for an extraction of a 10 foot piece of film
to be used in the scene. And if the cameras didn't start together, you'd
never be in sync! At the beginning it was all at once or not at all!

We had a little playback room on each stage, and immediately following the conclusion of photographing a scene, everybody would rush
back to the little room to play back the dialogue and see how the actors
were doing. Well, that didn't last very long, because Mr. Warner and a
few of the others who were holding the purse strings found that about
half of our time, instead of shooting film, was being spent listening to
the mistakes that we had made so we could make them over again!

This illustrates only one of the tremendous number of problems the
cinematographer - in particular - faced when sound came in. Because of
the iceboxes he had no place to put his lights; and, after all, you can't
photograph without lights. In those days lights in great numbers were
necessary, because the exposure ratings of the films were very slow.

Our films were rated at a very low ASA (although we didn't call it
'ASA' at that time), and we had to use considerable light to register an
image.

When sound came we went to an entirely different kind of film and
light. Having been a silent cameraman, but not having been in on the
preliminary Vitaphone shorts, I used what was generously entitled
'orthochromatic' film. 'Plain' film would have been the proper name for
it, I think (and I believe that the people from Eastman will possibly
agree with what I'm saying). It was sensitive to blue light only. If
an actor had blue eyes, or an actress had light blue eyes, we had to use
a little spotlight covered with a filter to reflect in their eyes in
order to make their eyes photograph dark so they wouldn't be bald-eyed.
As you may recall, many of the actors of that period seemed to be bald-
eyed!

When we went to sound films, we could no longer use arc lights,
because they were too noisy, and we hadn't as yet found a way of master-
ing that noise on the arc circuit. So we had to go to a light that was
completely impossible with respect to the orthochromatic film that we
were using. We had to go to the red end of the spectrum on a panchromatic emulsion, which was sensitive to the red light and not to the blue
light. So here we were working with a new medium as far as we, the
silent cameramen, were concerned: a different emulsion sensitive to a
completely different end of the spectrum, and lights of a wave length
completely different from the wave length to which we were accustomed.
It opened up a whole new set of problems.

The problems were tremendously hard to overcome, and I'm so happy
that I was fortunate enough to be around at that time to participate in
helping to solve some of those problems. It was a great challenge.

Even today we haven't gone as far as we can go. I hope the day
never arrives when we do, because if it does, that's when we'll start
reversing ourselves and going backwards.

I think that the age of camera mobility has been a wonderful improvement on the static conditions that we were forced into in the

early days of sound. In the silent films, of course, we had mobility
to a degree, though not to the extent that you do now. But I do believe
that camera mobility is one of the most valuable tools that has been
developed insofar as new methods of photography are concerned.

But let me caution you! Don't let that be an encouragement to
overplay your hand! When the zoom lens came in, for example, I can recall many pictures that were shot with zoom lenses as if the cameraman
were playing a trombone! Many a novice of today uses the zoom lens in
the same way, and I think that's a great mistake. I think that any
tool, be it a zoom lens or a method of mobility that might be something
new, is only as useful, as progressive, and as great as its application
to the particular problem that you are relating it to. To try to make
a universal tool of it would be a terrible mistake.

Whenever new technical innovations are introduced to any industry,
they bring with them new innovations in methods. But I do think that
we who are presently in the industry (and I say this guardedly) recognize the fact that these transitions are bound to happen, and that you
must welcome them. I agree with a great deal that has been claimed
about video tape being the 'coming thing'. I don't think there's any
question but that the usage of tape is a very desirable thing. I think
there are things that must be done first, however. I believe that in
order to get sufficient resolution to make it possible to use tape for
theatrical distribution - to get an enlarged image so it will look in
focus and at least the equal of film in resolution - they'll have to
increase their scanning by about twice what they're doing now. On a
25-inch television screen a slightly blurred image is acceptable; but
you can't put that up on a theatre screen (assuming, that is, that you
are going to have theatres in the future, about which there is a certain
amount of debate).

But I welcome the transition to tape, if it is a transition. I
think it's going to be used more and more. I think that eventually
there'll be a new medium to take the place of tape, maybe a thermal
development process. God knows what's going to come next! But in the

final analysis those of you who are interested in learning about motion pictures - about the technicalities as well as the creative factors of making them - have nothing to fear. The knowledge that you are gaining now will be just as usable and just as acceptable in these new media as the ways of the old media are acceptable to us old fogies who are still hanging on!

Frank Capra, Director

I'd like to give you an idea of how the transition from silent to sound films appeared from a director's viewpoint. When Al Jolson sang 'Mammy' in New York in October, 1927, I think it was, it caused an earthquake in Hollywood. Hollywood just shook! Sound had been talked about before, of course, and little sound pictures had been made. But this was something new. THE JAZZ SINGER was such an enormous success that no one could now deny that sound had arrived - and then the inmates took over the asylum! Everything had to be redone.

I worked for Harry Cohn at Columbia Pictures. Cohn was afraid of nothing, absolutely nothing. He was crude, heavy-handed, fearless, and a gambler. He was passionately in love with film, and hence one of the finest studio executives there ever was. But sound panicked him! He got orders from New York, and said to me, 'We've got to make talking pictures from now on - but what the hell is a talking picture? What's a sound picture? You tell me - you went to Cal Tech!' I said, 'Sound's a great new tool, Harry. We're going to be able to use it to hear people talk. It's a third dimension added to movement and sight - a wonderful dimension - and it can only help.' 'Sure', he said, 'but they want me to spend hundreds of thousands of dollars. 'microphones', 'decibels' - I don't know what the hell these terms mean! I'm scared of them.' So I'd try to calm him, and say 'Well, don't be afraid; it's just photographing sound as well as faces'.

The thing that frightened him the most, of course, was that he was
told that he had to use all stage actors, and he wasn't from the stage.
He was afraid of the stage, as I was. Anybody who was from the stage
panicked me, too. I didn't know anything about the stage. But I did
know sound. I had had a technical education, and when you know about
something it doesn't scare you as much. So I got Harry to make a half-
talking picture! We had to rent a barn, put some blankets all around it,
get the use of some equipment, and get ourselves a rental studio. The
picture was called THE YOUNGER GENERATION, and the last part of it was
a talking picture!

The actors, of course, were the greatest sufferers in all this.
Technicians and directors suffered too, but not like the actors. We
were accustomed to shooting and projecting the film at 16 frames per
second. For some reason, however, the sound track had to pass through
the recorder at 24 frames per second, which is roughly 50% more speed
than we were used to using. That meant that we had to use twice as
much light, and hence generate about three times as much heat! The
actors melted in the enormous heat from the lamps we had to use in order
to photograph at 24 frames per second. They were already scared to
death of sound, having to learn lines for the first time; and now they
had this extra heat. About every hour they'd have to change their
clothes!

Actors also had to work now in silence, complete silence, for the
first time. The making of a silent picture was anything but silent!
People yelled all the time. The director had his megaphone, and he'd
yell directions while the scene was being shot. The cameraman might
yell at his grip at the top of his voice, or someone might be building
on the set next door, hammering and sawing. If there was something
funny going on in the scene, everybody would laugh.

When sound came, however, all of a sudden you had to work in the
stillness of a tomb. If you belched, or if you coughed, you'd wreck a
scene. We actually had to be careful what we ate and drank!

The sound man at that time was one of the biggest prima donnas you
have ever seen. We had one sound man who was unflappable until a scene

started and he had to flip the little dials. He always wore enormous
headphones on his ears, and insisted that he had to have his ears washed
out by a doctor every day at 4 o'clock. He actually had us believing
it! He'd leave the set, and we would all wait while this man went to a
doctor to have his ears washed out so he could hear better! Finally we
said, 'We'll bring the doctor here'. He said, 'No, I've got to go to
his office'. 'No, no', we insisted, 'you bring the doctor here'. So
the doctor came and did it in the dressing room. We saved a little
time that way.

Right in the middle of scenes the sound man would suddenly say
'Cut, cut, cut, cut', and he'd go onto the set and bawl the actors out.
'Mr. Herschel, you cannot talk between movements. When you're talking
into the microphone here in this drawer, you've got to talk into it! You
can't look at the other man. Talk in there, then walk over here to this
flower pot - but don't talk in between!' The sound man got away with it
for awhile, but finally we said, 'Hey, just stay the hell off of this
set, will you? And don't you dare come in and talk to these actors
again!' He complained: 'But you don't want bad sound, do you?' I said,
'Never mind what I want, just leave all the mikes open!'

Then, of course, we had to contend with these great big camera
booths to muffle the camera noise. The first cameraman that I had was
Ben Reynolds. He weighed about 350 pounds and was about 5 feet tall.
He looked like a whiskey barrel on two fireplugs, and it wasn't surprising that you couldn't see his neck. Ben would go to sleep anywhere; he'd
just sit down and go to sleep. He wouldn't fall over because he was too
big. He'd sleep 10 seconds, wake up, say 'What did you say?', and then
go back to sleep again. Well, he was the cameraman on my first sound
picture. We pushed him into this booth with the camera. There was no
air in those booths, no ventilation at all. There was more air in a
man's lungs than there was in the booth. So Ben immediately went to
sleep. It didn't matter because the camera couldn't move anyway.

It wasn't easy to get rid of those booths, to get faster film so
that the actors wouldn't die of heat, and to get microphones out of
flowerpots and onto a boom so we could follow the actors. Yet the prod-

ucers immediately saw that silent pictures were dead, so the transition
was made very quickly. I don't think it took over a year, or 18 months,
for every studio to be equipped to make sound pictures. They worked
night and day, and didn't lose any time. It was a remarkable transition. But we didn't stop making movies in the meantime! Movies kept
being made: silent, half-silent, all talkies. And then, of course, the
theatres had to be renovated. They had to tear the guts out of the
theatres and put in mare's nests of cables and boxes and other things
for sound. Again, it was an amazing time. But within two years it was
all done. Within two years everybody was making talking or sound pictures for distribution.

I don't think any of the studio heads, or the executives, or the
directors, or even the writers said sound wasn't going to work, or
hated it, because I think they just had to go with it. If they didn't
go with it, they didn't go! The transition was fast and necessary, for
we had found a voice! Films went all the way to what I think is real
greatness when they got that third dimension of sound.

Let me return for a moment to the problems of acting, and the relationship between actors and directors. Film is a director's medium. The
actor has to rely on the judgment of the director to tell him where he
is. Actors and actresses, especially those who have big names and big
careers, are staking their careers on the judgment of one person - the
director. They haven't got a big audience. They never play their part
completely from beginning to end. We shoot scenes out of continuity in
order to conform with schedules for monetary purposes. If your picture
begins in Hong Kong and ends in Hong Kong, you don't go to Hong Kong
twice; you go there once and shoot the beginning and the ending. Yet
these shots, these scenes, are supposed to show a gradual growth of the
relationship between the characters. Only the director has the knowledge of where the characters are supposed to be in space and time in
these scenes. Nobody else in the hierarchy of motion pictures can carry
this in his head: no executive, producer, cameraman, soundman, or actor.

This is why film is a director's medium. The mechanics of it make
it so. Only the director knows what scene 50 is in that story, what will
come before, and what will come after.

Hence the relationship between the actor and the director must be one of great trust and actually great love. Because the actor or the actress depends entirely on an audience of one. Only the director knows where everything is, and how it should be played, what the pitch and tempo should be, and what the scene is all about in relation to the rest of the story. If the actor or the actress hasn't got confidence in the director, you're going to have problems. You're going to have an actor questioning the judgment of the director. And when that happens you get uneven performances. This is one of the great problems in filmmaking: the actors and the director not seeing eye to eye. It's unfortunate when that happens. But if the actors have confidence in the director, then there is a unity that is wonderful to see on the screen. Part of the whole task of directing is to insure that the actors have confidence in your judgment. When you think a scene is right, they will accept it. When you think there's something wrong with the scene and you want to change it, they will accept that.

I must, therefore, have control over everything: the actors, the cutting, the music - everything. I don't think film is a great collaborative effort between many people. Many artists work on films, of course: writers, technicians, artisans of various kinds. But they all must work for the director if they are to have a common aim! If they all work at cross purposes, and all contribute their little bit, you get a mess. That's how the camel was built, not the horse!

Few people have succeeded in being both the lead actor and the director of a picture. The problem is that you're being called upon to be objective and subjective at the same time. It's a pretty difficult thing to do, and not many people have done it well. Chaplin did it, because he invented his character and therefore knew his character better than anybody else. He's the most successful example that I can think of. But most actors who try it give it up. I talked to Clint Eastwood the other day. He directed a couple of his own films, and I said 'How are you, Mr. Director?' He said, 'Yes, Mr. Director is right. When I direct I can't act.' So he directs now, but doesn't feel he acts as much. He's found that doing both is too difficult. This is one of

those things I don't think one can do well unless you're some sort of a
genius. Normally it's an unworkable idea.

Directing, after all, is difficult enough. No two directors are
alike, and they shouldn't be, because they're different human beings
and they achieve their results differently. I like to speed up the
pace of my films. The pace of my films is much faster than normal, because I think things slow down on a large screen. I don't know if stimuli affect people more quickly because a thousand pairs of eyes and ears
are perceiving something simultaneously, or if those thousand pairs of
eyes and ears simply accept stimuli faster than we think. But I do know
that persons in a crowd react faster to images than a single person
would. I know that you have to speed film up to make it look natural to
a thousand people.

I really believe this, but not everybody agrees with me. George
Stevens does it just the other way around. He slows the pace down until
it is almost so slow that you can't bear it. But he gets wonderful effects at that slow pace with those long slow walks, because it gives you
a chance to think about what that young woman may be thinking as she is
walking - what's in her mind. He gets his effects that way; I don't.

There are no rules in directing. It's just how the individual
director feels he can get the best effects. If anybody tells you there
are rules, they're wrong. There are no rules. There are no two directors who work alike.

This goes for working with actors, too. Lubitsch, for instance,
acted out all the parts, and the actors imitated him. If they imitated
him correctly, they were doing fine, because he was a fine actor. He
blue-printed his scripts and shot them without changing anything. Somebody else might do it differently.

I constantly change things. I change my conception of the characters when the cast comes in. When Gary Cooper steps into a part, that
part has to be tailored to Gary Cooper. Each actor brings in his own
particular clout. I don't care where the clout comes from. All I want
is a good tale so that the audience is interested in it.

I rehearse quite a bit, but I always think the first take is the best unless there's something mechanically wrong, because there's a rough feeling to that first take. There's a feeling of extemporaneous quality about it that is what I'm after - something that is not quite perfect.

I used to have arguments with Jean Arthur about this, because she came from the stage and thought this was complete heresy. I'll tell you what she would do! She would come onto the set having studied and worked hard, knowing her part perfectly. She'd have the part perfected, and I would say 'Wait a minute', and then I'd take sentences right out of the middle of her speech! That way she'd have to think the things through anew. I wanted her to think of that scene right at that moment. I wanted her to think those words - words that weren't rehearsed - just as they came out. I wanted her to react for the first time. I usually screw the actors up a bit, and try to do things with them that'll keep them from being as set as they get emerging from one rehearsal after another.

One of the tricks that I used was to keep the camera running after a scene had been shot, call the actors back, and do retakes of it. I originally developed this technique to defeat Harry Cohn, who, to save money, would only let us print one take of a scene. If I never stopped the camera, then I could get to see three or four takes on one scene! But this technique worked well for the actors,too. They'd come back in, find their places and their marks, and start again without a stop. Then I'd do it again and again. By the third or fourth time they'd be sweating, their hair would be mussed, they'd have forgotten to look for their marks, and suddenly they'd be playing that scene as if there were some urgency about it - playing it with real feeling. I wasn't after a style, you see - I was after reality. (And Harry Cohn didn't catch on for quite a while!)

Reality is not visuals and sound balanced, but integrated - one indivisible unity. I don't think that you should weigh the visual against the audial aspects of film. You're telling a tale, you're not making balances between the sound and the visuals. You don't measure

these properties in terms of inches or yards. You're telling a tale;
you're communicating. This whole business is communicating from people
to people. Not from camera to people, but from actors to audience. If
the machinery gets in the way - if you notice too much sound or too much
visual - you lose your audience, because you lose the communication and
the involvement. You can't involve people in machinery. It's very difficult to hold their attention for long with machinery, but it's not
difficult to hold their attention with actual living human characters
that seem to live and breathe up there on the screen. They're really
shadows - the whole thing is one grand illusion - but you must keep the
audience involved with the people on the screen. I always think in terms
of involving the audience in the lives of those people. Theatrical films
are people-to-people communication. Neither visuals, nor sound, nor both
in balance; but people communicating with people.

Rouben Mamoulian, Director

I was not part of the transition from silent to sound films, because I started making films after sound came in. I never made a silent film. But I'd like to point out something that I think is generally misunderstood. No one ever made silent films, because one always had a piano or an organ playing. Even then the eye was not enough; the ear had to be satisfied as well. In those days filmmakers also had dialogue in a way. Instead of being spoken out loud, the film was interrupted by titles which you read - but it was still dialogue.

The advent of sound not only enriched the medium but gave it a more comprehensive and aesthetically pleasing form, because sound helped to sustain the continuity of imagery on the screen. In the silent film you would present a scene; then boom, you would have a title; and then back to the scene. It was pretty much like the commercials now on television, but related to the story. The coming of audible dialogue and sound effects helped to eliminate that. The first benefit to my mind, therefore, of the coming of sound was that filmmakers were allowed to maintain the visual flow and continuity of the film.

Coming from the theatre, I obviously was accustomed to dialogue in my experience, so dialogue was no news to me. What was news to me was the camera, and I was thoroughly excited about its potential magic. At first they wanted me to help silent film directors handle dialogue, but I refused to do this because I thought it would be unenlightening

for me. I could do that on the stage. When I subsequently made my
first film, what intrigued me principally was the style and poetry of
the visuals. Coming from the theatre I was mainly attracted to the
visual values of the film; and, to me, dialogue always remained subser-
vient to the language of visual imagery. But I felt excited about the
possibilities of applying the same imaginative treatment to sound: to
dialogue, to music, to noise, and to the various other audible features
of the film! I felt strongly that sound did not have to be treated in a
merely naturalistic manner. This is what excited me about using dialogue in film.

When I began my first film, the soundman was the boss. There was
one microphone hanging in the centre of the stage. You would direct the
scene, and the soundman would come on like Caesar and say to the actors
'No, you have to stand there; you have to come closer; you can't open
this letter, because on the sound track it sounds like thunder. We'll
have to dampen the letter.' In those days the crackling of a newspaper,
or a letter, blocked the microphone! So we always had to use limp paper
(the kind Dali would paint!), which could be folded and opened smoothly.
There were strict technical rules about recording sound in the early
days.

There were also strange notions prevailing among cinematographers
at that time. I had a first-rate cameraman with me on my first film,
APPLAUSE, by the name of George Folsey. (He's still going strong and
looks as young as ever.) I said to Folsey, 'I want black shadows.' He
said to me, 'You can't have them, because Mr. Zukor and Mr. Lasky like
to see everything on the screen. They feel that if you pay for the actors, you've got to see them all!' It was not unlike the slight handi-
cap that D. W. Griffith, the greatest of us all, faced when he did his
first close-ups. His producers said 'You pay them full salary; give me
the full figure. Don't cut it off!'

Another example: one time I wanted to shoot an entire scene in one
shot, which meant moving the camera. In those days the studios took the
easy way out in everything. Having panicked when sound unexpectedly
arrived, they had bought up Broadway plays because the plays had dialogue

ad infinitum. All cameras, of course, had to be enclosed in a big bungalow in which one could actually suffocate. They would put three cameras on simultaneously, shoot two close-ups and one long-shot, and then
intercut them. The result was a 'talkie'. And they were well named -
they were mostly talk!

In this case, however, I wanted to shoot the scene in one shot by
trucking forward and then backward into close-up, medium-shot, and long-
shot. The only way to get movement, of course, is to move something!
I got the camera movement I wanted by moving the bungalow - the whole
thing! This bungalow was like a house on tiny rubber wheels. It weighed tons, and took about eight husky men to keep it from shaking from the
inadequacies of the studio floor and to keep it moving. The director,
the cameraman, the assistant, and what not, had to be inside the camera
booth during the shot - and after two minutes everyone began to suffocate! So Folsey said 'That's impossible, you can't do it!'

Then I had another idea. Since the essence of each art is to do
what is impossible in other arts, it occurred to me that what is impossible on the stage or in real life should be possible and desirable on
the screen because of the magic of sound recording, just as the things
that are possible with camera are impossible on the stage. In one
scene, therefore, I wanted a young girl, recently come from a convent,
to be whispering her prayers while Helen Morgan, her mother and a burlesque queen, was singing a burlesque song. With only one microphone,
however, you could hear the song but not the whispered prayer! So I
told the soundman, 'Why don't we have a microphone under the pillow for
the whisper of the girl, and another for the song of Helen Morgan. Use
two channels, recording it on two strips of film; put them together; and
balance it so that you'll hear both the whisper and the song.' The
soundman said 'Impossible, we've never done it, it's going to be a mess.'
(To complete the situation, the wardrobe man brought Helen Morgan onto
the set dressed beautifully and looking glamourous, when she was supposed to be a fading burlesque queen! I wanted her to look bedraggled.
The wardrobe man said 'Impossible: she's a star, and a star must be
glamourous and beautiful.')

Together, these obstacles got my goat! I ran upstairs where the
mogols happened to be having a meeting. Zukor, Lasky, everybody was
there. I walked in and must have looked a bit like Mr. Hyde, because
the secretary went pale and said 'You can't go in there, they're having
a meeting!' I said 'Oh yes I can', banged the door open, and walked in.
'Now look', I began, 'I have a contract to direct this film, and nobody
does what I want them to do.' 'Why not?', they asked. 'I don't know',
I said, 'they think it's impossible.' 'Maybe it is', the mogols replied.
'I don't think it is', I said. So they asked, 'What exactly is the
trouble?' I said, 'Call everybody up here! I want to speak in front of
them.'

So up came Folsey, the soundman, and the wardrobe man. I said,
'Folsey says one thing, and the soundman says another, but I want something else! I want to relieve them of all responsibility for this film.
If I'm wrong, then I am at fault and you can fire me. But they've got
to do it my way first!' Folsey said, 'You know, I respect Mr. Mamoulian
as a stage director, but I've been in the movies a long time. What he
wants is impossible!' (It was quite understandable for him to say this,
because I had spent five weeks learning the technique of filmmaking by
asking Folsey silly questions about lenses! I would say 'What does this
do?', and he would explain it to me. Now I was telling him what to do,
so obviously he felt it wasn't quite right.)

Then the soundman chimed in, supporting Folsey, and adding 'I'm
trying to save the studio money!' Now that's a formidable argument!
It's difficult to answer, you see. They all brightened up at the
thought of saving money. And then the wardrobe man repeated that stars
are supposed to look glamourous.

The big bosses were in an embarrassing position. Finally I said,
'Look, either it's done my way or I quit right now'. (I'm a great
quitter when I don't like things.) So they said, 'All right! Everyone
is to do what Mr. Mamoulian wants done'. I turned to Folsey, and said
'And you've got to do it with a smile! Don't scowl at me!' Folsey,
a charming Irishman with blue eyes, replied 'I'll smile as long as they

know it isn't my responsibility'. I said 'Fine'.

We went down to the studio, and I must say that they were a little
cruel to me. They just stood around gleefully waiting for directions.
Folsey said 'All right, how do you want me to <u>light</u> it?' We had to use
an enormous amount of lighting in those days, and coming from the theatre this blaze of light was like a blinding sun in the Sahara to me. I
couldn't judge the relative values of light, semi-light, and so on. It
was very difficult. But Folsey just stood there and said 'You tell <u>me</u>!'
Well, I told him! Then we started to rehearse the camera movements, and
I told the soundman 'You're recording on two channels!'

Then I got cold feet! I thought to myself 'This is the end of me,
because it'll probably turn out to be a mess. They're probably right.'
Anyway we did this and that and by 5:30 we had done the scene! We almost
died in that bungalow because the scene took over three minutes in one
shot. But we did it! (All the moving shots in the film were eventually
done that way - by moving the bungalow!) I went home that evening, and
I didn't sleep all night. I kept saying to myself 'This is the end of
me'.

The film was being shot in New York at the Astoria Studios. They
had a marvellous doorman at the Studios, a tall enormous Irishman with
plenty of gold braid. He looked like Lord Mountbatten, and didn't know
me from Adam. Every morning I would sneak into the studio, and the doorman would say 'Wait, hold it! Where are you going? What do you do?'
I would reply 'I work here'. He'd look very suspicious, but would eventually let me go through in a very patronizing manner.

When I arrived at the Astoria Studios the morning after my showdown
with Folsey and the others, I got out of my taxi and walked up the steps.
Suddenly this mountain of gold and glory bowed in an Oriental salute,
took off his cap, and said 'And good morning to you, Mr. Mamoulian, sir!'
I said to myself 'My God, what's going on here?' I walked into the studio, and one of my three assistants grabbed me (the one I had brought
from the stage to have at least one soul near me who knew my work) and
said 'This could have been your last day in films, you know, because the

boss ordered your scene to be developed last night! They all came here
at 8:00 o'clock in the morning – Zukor, Lasky, everybody – and looked at
it. If it hadn't come out, this would have been the end for you. But
they liked it! They're sending it to Kansas City to a convention of
salesmen to show them what their next year's product is going to be.
And the order from on high now is 'Give Mamoulian what he wants!' '

I walked onto the set, and there was Folsey whistling 'It's never
been done in one shot before!' The soundman was singing 'This is a
breakthrough – two channels!' They were both so happy I gave in to a
foible: revenge is out of fashion, but I thought I might as well play a
little 'Monte Cristo' with those guys. Folsey asked 'Where do you want
your camera today?' I said 'Today I want four cameras'. He said 'But
we only have three here'. 'Well', I said, 'get the fourth one!' 'Where
do you want them?', he asked. I replied 'One up there on the ceiling,
the other over there, the third one over here, and the fourth one six
feet below the level of the floor'. He said 'Now wait a minute! You
know, Mr. Mamoulian, that the Astoria has no basement. It's got a concrete floor – three feet of concrete – and you can't dig a hole like
that.' I said 'Look at the New York streets and those big guys with
electric drills. Get six of them and dig me a hole ten by ten and six
feet deep.' And I added 'George, you're going to handle this camera
lying on your back like Michaelangelo!'

Within about two minutes six guys walked in with electric drills
and were about to ruin the property of Paramount when, of course, I
stopped them and said 'That's my revenge, you see?'

In APPLAUSE, unfortunately, the traffic noises had to be made on
the set. It was pathetic, and it still is pathetic when I hear it. But
for the subway scenes we got permission to shoot in the subway. Those
sounds were authentically recorded. We also shot in Pennsylvania Station, and did a scene on the top of a skyscraper by breaking the law.
I was fortunate and wasn't sent to jail only because they couldn't locate me at the time.

Not everyone, of course, was happy with my innovations. Although the New York press was highly eloquent on the subject in my favor, a lot of people in Hollywood thought that I shouldn't be allowed into a studio. One trade paper wrote: 'Mr. Mamoulian doesn't realize that the camera is created to stand on a tripod, not to move around'. And Walter Wanger sent me a wire saying 'I suppose you'll make your next picture when we figure out how to put a camera into a tennis ball'. Indeed, I wish they would solve that problem!

My main interest in sound, as I said, was in dialogue. But my concern must not be misunderstood! I believe that you should first of all construct your script architecturally in visual imagery. Then, when you need words, put them in. The less dialogue the better the film, from my point of view, for the imagery itself talks to you: color, props, actors' faces talk to you. When all of these are not enough to express the thought and ideas, then you need words. When you are stopped, and you cannot express it visually, then you put in words.

My second priority was to use sound from a psychological rather than a realistic point of view. I have always been excited about using sound in a psychological manner. To give you one example: in LOVE ME TONIGHT the aristocrats discover that Maurice Chevalier is not a baron but a tailor. The three aunts dash downstairs where the whole clan is assembled, and Elizabeth Patterson announces the discovery. Someone says 'What?!', and she says 'He's a common tailor!' As she utters these words, she makes a gesture and knocks a tiny vase onto the floor. As the vase hits the floor, I dubbed in the sound of an enormous bomb exploding because that is the psychological effect of the sound! Film people, of course, thought I was crazy, but the audience loved it, because it conveyed the inner meaning of something that would be plain noise otherwise.

LOVE ME TONIGHT is probably the most stylized film I've ever made, because nothing is real there. The whole film was preconceived. It's a modern fairy story, and I used every kind of device, like slowed-down or speeded-up motion. You see, for example, a horse galloping full speed yet making a circle around a tree. All the singing in LOVE ME

TONIGHT, except the orchestral music, was done on the set and on the
actual locations. Not a single song or part of a song was dubbed.
Sometimes during a song I would use a muffled piano which would later
be covered by the louder sound of the orchestra. All the music was
recorded to the beat of a metronome to coincide with action, because
the whole film is rhythmic. Even the dialogue rhymes, so I used a metronome when recording it. The film people thought I was absolutely crazy,
but the audience understood it and loved it. So long as they love it,
why not be 'crazy'?

I don't take credit for the screenwriting, but naturally I build
the film in my mind visually. I know what sequence I want to follow
another sequence, and where I want dialogue and where not, and what it
should be about. This is an extension of the way I work on the stage.
No matter what script it is, you must go through a long process of re-
vision and rewriting. By the time you open on Broadway there's a tremendous difference between the original script and what the people see,
and hopefully it's better.

The process of writing for films is a process of one or two writers
and a director working in very close consultation. A lot of changes
must be made, because writers deal with the written word and often
don't know what's ultimately going to appear on the screen. Sometimes
the most astonished people upon seeing the final film are the writers.

I remember doing BECKY SHARP, the first full-length color film.
The script was written by Francis Ferrago in collaboration with me.
When I finished the first cut I thought I would show it to him, but with
a surprise! There is a scene in the film where Miriam Hopkins kisses
Alan Mowbray on a couch. I said to my cutter 'When they kiss, put in a
title, dissolve, and then put in all our outtakes - all the cutoff ends
of film showing what occurs after you've cut the scene (the stuff where
you see the cameraman or carpenter or electrician, or a stagehand car-
rying water or lamps, and so on)'. I said 'Give me about 400 feet of
that, and then put in another dissolve and come back to the two kissing'.

When we got Francis Ferrago to the preview, he sat next to me. We,

of course, were eagerly awaiting his reaction. The sequence came on,
and you cannot imagine Ferrago's response! For the longest time he kept
repeating 'Maybe it's something marvellous, but I don't get it'. After
awhile I said 'It's a joke!' He said 'Thank you, I thought I was losing
my mind!'

But there's a difference with executives and producers. They never
know what's in your mind! RKO had a convention in Hollywood, and they
asked me if I would allow them to show my rough-cut of BECKY SHARP. I
agreed, and told my cutter to bring the cut to them. He did, and they
ran it. My cutter was there, and as the picture began he suddenly realized that he hadn't taken out the 400 feet of out-takes! He was dying!
He thought he was going to get fired! Well, when the thing was over,
the executives and producers got up and said 'By God, you gotta hand it
to Mamoulian - he sure knows those effects!' Those effects indeed!

A director, however, must be able to predict audience reactions.
A director is no good unless he combines two persons within himself, one
subjective and the other objective. To give a lofty comparison, consider a cook. He cooks a dish; but then he has to taste it, and if it
doesn't taste good, he must re-cook it. Similarly, a director must be
on the one hand a director; but then, immediately after that when he
looks at his film, he must objectively become the audience, completely
divorced from his former role. Frequently you do something you are
thrilled about as a director, and then you sit back and you say 'Nope,
that's not right'. An actor who is in the film, especially a leading
actor, cannot possibly fulfill the role of an audience, because we never
see ourselves as we are. (I, for instance, think I am the youngest,
most handsome man in the world; unfortunately, most people don't agree.)

The greater the star and the better the talent, the more joy it is
to work with them. I find the greatest stars the easiest to work with,
because they not only have a talent but enough common sense, profes-
sionally, to know what's good and what's better. For example, I had a
scene in CITY STREETS in which Gary Cooper comes to visit Sylvia Sidney
in prison. She wants him to stay away from the gangsters, but he's already joined them. When he walks in, she is terribly happy to see him;

but later on, when he tells her that he's joined the gang, she's very
unhappy. Sylvia Sidney is one of our best actresses, and she did the
scene beautifully. She laughed and smiled when he came in, and then
cried when he told her he was a gangster. I, however, said to her
'Sylvia, it's good - but how would you like to try something that is
better, if you can do it? Reverse the procedure! When you see him, cry
with joy; and when at the end he tells you that he's a gangster, don't
cry at all but rather smile with the kind of smile that transcends sor-
row'. Being a very talented actress, she took up the challenge - they
love a challenge - and did the scene beautifully. It was much more
interesting than doing it the orthodox way.

What happens in the movie hierarchy is not the same as in the hierarchy in an army. A general gives an order and you must execute it,
whether you like it or not. But if you ran a film crew that way you
wouldn't get good results. So the first problem of a director, and his
first aim, is to win the confidence of his actors. I'll go even further:
the director must win the <u>affection</u> of his actors. There are great
stars who have power, position, glamour, glory, and certain faith in
what they're doing and what they think is good and what they think is
bad. This applies to all the best actors, cameramen, soundmen - to
everybody. The whole point is that you are not dealing with inanimate
objects. The idea is to catch their interest, their affection, and suggest to them something that is better than what they had in mind. When
they realize this, then of course their confidence in you become limit-
less.

I'll give an example which may amuse you. When they asked me to do
a film with Greta Garbo (QUEEN CHRISTINA), I had reservations because I
had been told that whenever Miss Garbo came to do an intimate love scene,
she usually asked her director to go for a cup of coffee and sandwich
while she did the scene with the cameraman and the actor. After that
the director could come back. I said to Miss Garbo 'I can't work that
way, you know. I've got to be there every minute of the time'. She
said 'Well, I'll agree in this case'. But I didn't know that she had
yet another idiosyncrasy!

The dialogue in QUEEN CHRISTINA was written by S. N. Behrman, who
was one of our distinguished playwrights. Garbo had speeches to make.
Not just lines like 'Leave me alone', or 'Give me a glass of water'. In
those kinds of films she sailed on the strength of her glamour and fas-
cination. But this was different. So on the first day on the set I
said to Garbo 'Well, now we are going to rehearse'. She said 'Rehearse?
Oh, I can't rehearse!' I said 'What do you mean?' She said 'I never
rehearse. You rehearse the other actors, then you tell me where you
want me to be, where to go, where to sit down, and I do it. My first
take is the best.' I said to myself 'If this is true, I am the happiest
man in the world. I'll shoot this picture in three weeks!' So I said
to her 'All right, let's try it your way'.

I rehearsed the two male actors for an hour-and-a-half. Then Garbo
came in, and I told her what to do. We made one take, and as she was
coming off the set towards me I said 'How do you feel about it?' She
said 'Fine, fine'. I just sat! She did a double-take, and said 'Well,
how do you feel about it?' I said 'Very bad, very bad - it just isn't
there'. She went pale and said 'This isn't going to work out'. I
said 'No, it won't - not this way it won't. Look, Miss Garbo, we did it
your way. How about doing it once my way?' She replied 'Well, if you
rehearse me I'll be no good; I'll be stale. If you make several takes,
each will be worse than the other.' I said 'I'd like to take the chance;
and I promise you one thing: when I get the take I like, I will have
your first take printed, too. You can come to the projection room in
the morning at 8 o'clock. You can be there alone and look at the two
takes, and whichever take you prefer I'll use in the picture. Isn't
that fair?' She said 'All right, if you want to waste time!' I said
'OK, I want to waste time'.

So I rehearsed her for an hour, until she said 'I'm through, I'm
dead, I'm empty, empty'. Sometimes, you know, an actor or actress does-
n't realize the progress he or she is making because the more you demand
of them the more they feel they're failing. They don't realize how much
they've advanced. After an hour's rehearsal I made takes two, three,
four, five, six, seven, and eight. Then I said 'That's it - print take

eight and take one, and get them into the projection room tomorrow at 8
o'clock'. Garbo started to come off the set, and as she was passing me
by she leaned down and whispered 'Please, do not print take one!' So
she felt it, too!

Directors have differing attitudes about rehearsing. I was in
Paris some years ago when the Moscow Art Theatre was there with Nemiro-
vitch Daneshenko, a great director who worked with Stanislavski. I had
lunch with him, and asked 'Do you still direct together with Stanislavski as you used to?' He said 'No, we can't. Stanislavski is very slow.
He hates to open a show, but he loves to rehearse. He needs five years
of rehearsals. Me? I work fast. To me, two-and-a-half years is plenty!' I was thinking: 'Here on Broadway we do plays with four weeks rehearsal!'

There is no rule on how long you rehearse. You rehearse as long as
you need to achieve all the values you can imagine the scene having. No
actor can give you all the potential of a scene at a first reading, or
at a first rehearsal, or at a first take usually. There are basic things
that an actor develops, and then there are the refinements which make
the thing excellent. The difference is this: to me acting is the art of
appearing spontaneous. A good actor is the one who gives you the feeling of spontaneity - and if you can get it on the stage after thousands
of performances of the same play, that takes professional acting. You
don't get spontaneity simply because you haven't rehearsed enough. As
a matter of fact, you just get a bad performance.

When I was doing the film SUMMER HOLIDAY, I was rehearsing the
great actors Walter Huston, Frank Morgan, Agnes Moorehead, and Mickey
Rooney. I kept at it for three hours. Finally I said 'All right, we've
got it'. Walter Huston said 'Please, Rouben, I beg you: let me do it
once more'. I said 'Look, you've done it well. Sit down'. Then I rehearsed a love scene between Gloria DeHaven, who was just a young girl
at the time, and Mickey Rooney. I said to her 'All right, let's begin'.
We went through the scene, and I said to myself 'My gosh, I need three
months to work on this girl!' So I thought I would start with the basic
things. I said 'Gloria, go through it again, and bear in mind this one

thought - just this one simple thought'. She agreed, and went through
it. Then I said 'Now, Gloria, add this second thought to it'. She
stopped and said 'Mr. Mamoulian, if you rehearse me again, I will be
stale!' The audience of professional actors, of course, simply guf-
fawed! From then on we kept asking 'Gloria, are you getting stale?'

My point is this: an actor or actress never gets stale as long as
a new incentive is given. Obviously if you keep on repeating, making
identical takes, and not giving the actors a new challenge, then they
will become stale. But if you achieve with each take greater refinement
and depth of emotion, then each take is a challenge. Finally you hit
the top, and that's when the director says 'All right, that's it -
that's the top'. Then you stop, because after that you may go down!

Julius J. Epstein, Screenwriter

I needn't tell you how I broke into screenwriting if you've read the book <u>What Makes Sammy Run</u>, for there's a story in the book about a ghost writer, Julian Blumberg. I am Julian Blumberg! Blumberg in the book is a great big schlemiel. I'm still a schlemiel.

I came to Hollywood as a ghost writer, and stayed in the closet for one or two pictures. Then I wrote an original screenplay called LIVING ON VELVET, which later starred Kay Francis and George Brent, and I came out of the closet. I sold the story to Warner Brothers, but didn't get one penny for it. Instead, they gave me a contract for one hundred dollars a week, with a clause stating that they could fire me after the first week. Upton Sinclair was running for governor of California on the Epic-Socialist ticket at the time. When I got my first salary check I noticed it was for $86, not $100. I said, 'Where's the $14?' 'Well', they replied, 'we're fighting Upton Sinclair, and that's your contribution'.

When I came to Hollywood in 1933, sound hadn't been around for very long. My brother, Philip, and I did a picture with Raoul Walsh, and Walsh would continually say, 'Too many titles, cut the titles'. He kept referring to the dialogue as titles! (My brother and I are still noted for writing a lot of dialogue, much too much and too weighty.)

When sound came in, Hollywood raided every field of literature. The trains were full of playwrights, novelists, short story writers,

poetry writers, people who wrote home for money - anybody who could put
a word on paper. Warner Brothers had 75 writers under contract, week
to week; Metro had about 125 to 150 writers; Paramount had about 100
writers; and so on. There were little cubicles in the writers' building, and each writer had his own little cubicle.

There was one man who became head of a studio at a very young age,
and who, when presented with a finished script by one of his 75 writers,
wouldn't read it, but would say immediately 'Give it to another writer'.
His theory was simple: it mightn't help, but it couldn't hurt! (Like
the enema story!) That was his standard practice, and the reason why
there were so many names on a script in the old days.

On present-day pictures, I think, you will see many more solo credits than you saw in the old days, simply because there aren't many writers under contract any more. In those days it didn't cost the studios
any more to put another writer on a script. Nowadays if they put another writer on a script, it's going to cost them. It's a matter of economics.

I learned my lesson about the status of screenwriters very early,
probably my first week in Hollywood. I remember picking up a trade
paper and reading a story on the front page in a black box (I think I
remember it almost verbatim). It was two short paragraphs which went
something like this:

> "Paramount executives are throwing their hats in the
> air over the script, So Red the Rose, handed in by Maxwell
> Anderson on Stark Young. Never in the history of motion
> pictures, say they, has a script so intelligent, so lucid,
> so articulate, and so wonderful been handed to a studio."

End of paragraph. Second paragraph:

> "William Slavins McNutt is now doing a polishing job."

A second point about the status of the screenwriter! My brother
and I did FOUR DAUGHTERS with Curtiz. It won an Academy nomination and
was a big success. Naturally the studio wanted a sequel, but my brother

and I fought against the idea. There's never been a sequel that anywhere approached the original. But the studio insisted upon a sequel,
so we sat down and made up a story for the sequel called Four Wives.
They then said, 'Can't you bring back Garfield?' Garfield was a suicide
in the original picture! He was one of the first losers, a musical
arranger who wrote three notes - that's as far as he got in the concerto.
He married Priscilla Lane, who really belonged with Jeffrey Lynn, a
really good musician. Garfield realized that he was ruining her life,
and being a good boy committed suicide!

We said, 'How can we bring back Garfield? A dream sequence?'
Finally we insisted: 'Look, let him rest in peace'; and they decided to
let him rest in peace.

Then somebody hit upon the idea of having Jeffrey Lynn, who was
also a musician, take those three notes Garfield had written, expand
them, and finish the concerto. The studio said to us, 'We want a big
scene at Carnegie Hall with the audience getting up and applauding, and
a close shot of the hands clapping'. We said, 'Is that not a cliche?
Won't the viewers expect it? Since he was a loser in the first picture,
how about if Jeffrey Lynn writes the concerto from his three notes, and
the concerto is terrible, so he's a loser in death too?' To our great
surprise, the studio said, 'That's great, marvellous!' So we wrote the
script that way.

Then came the budget conference with everybody in attendance, and
in walks Max Steiner. His name was on every Warner Brothers' picture,
'Music by Max Steiner'. Steiner throws the script down on the table and
says, 'Do you mean to tell me that it's going to say on the screen,
"Music by Max Steiner", and the concerto is going to be a failure?' So
we had to change the story back to the concerto being a success! If we
hadn't done it, another writer under contract would have done it (and
they had 75 writers under contract). This story illustrates the relative
importance, in those days, of a writer as compared to a composer.

Everything's a matter of economics, a struggle with studio heads
and producers. I was with Warner Brothers under contract for nearly

thirteen-and-a-half years. I free-lanced for a while, and then came
back and worked in a different capacity for another four years. It was
a fight from beginning to end with Jack Warner.

And not only at Warner Brothers! My brother, Philip, and I did
some work on the MGM version of THE BROTHERS KARAMAZOV. When we were
signed we were brought in by the story editor to meet Louis B. Mayer,
the head of the studio. It was a perfunctory meeting: we exchanged
amenities and left. Mayer then turned to the story editor and said,
'Tell me about the brothers'. The story editor, thinking he meant the
brothers Karamazov, said 'Well, one was a drunkard and a gambler, another
one was a religious fanatic, and they plotted to kill their father'.
Mayer said, 'And they seemed like such nice boys!' And we weren't nice
at all!

I've worked with some very fine producers, though - and the finest
producer is the one who leaves you alone. In forty years I have myself
produced four movies, each of them from a script that I wrote. On my
last two pictures I've been the producer, though I am only the screenwriter on the script on which I am now working. If you read the trade
papers, especially in television, there's a new word·in Hollywood called
the 'hyphenate': the writer-producer, the writer-director, the producer-
director. What's the function of the <u>producer</u>? It's like your appendix - it's there but it serves no purpose. Unlike the old days, nobody
knows now why a producer is really there. The head of the studio in
New York, or the executives somewhere else, or now the conglomerates
really control the purse-strings.

Often a producer will tell you, especially if the book you're adapt-
ing is a best-seller, 'Look, it's a best seller! Put in the scenes that
made it a best seller!' Yet I've done a lot of adaptations for movies,
and have had much more success with flop plays or novels than with great
big hits, because often a director or producer is afraid to make changes.
That wasn't the case with Frank Capra and ARSENIC AND OLD LACE, however;
Frank realized that changes had to be made. But lots of times producers
will say, 'Keep it just as it is', because it makes them feel more secure. Why do they insist on buying hit plays and best-selling novels?

It gives them a feeling of security. They figure, 'People have liked it once; they'll like it again'. And lots of times they're wrong.

Of all the writers brought out to Hollywood when sound came in, the best screenwriters were former playwrights because of their skill in using dialogue. Some novelists, of course, were very good; you can't make a broad generalization. But if a novelist comes to a difficult emotional moment in a story, and it's too much for him to put in dialogue, the temptation is to skip the dialogue and put it in narration. But you can't do that on the screen! If you have a problem to talk out in a picture, then you have to talk out the problem. You can't say, 'They talked out their problem'. So the best screenwriters, I think, came from the playwrights.

On the other hand, some dialogue won't work in pictures. Take Hemingway, for instance. I once read a play of Hemingway's; all dialogue. It was dreadful, and was never produced. It was full of Hemingway dialogue - the repetitiveness and terseness - and on the printed page was just marvellous. But it was no good as a play.

Another example: I once did a script of Fitzgerald's BABYLON REVISITED. He had written the screenplay many years before, and it was absolutely unusable. Now, I'm a lazy writer. If somebody else writes a script and there are things that I can use, I say 'Well, why not? It's less work for me'. But there wasn't one line of dialogue of Fitzgerald's script that could be used.

There's a great difference between dialogue for the printed page and spoken dialogue. I don't know why that is. I think perhaps it may be because a novel's dialogue can be surrounded with prose - embroidered with prose - and you can't do that on film. On film it's naked dialogue and each word is important. It's not a broken phrase, and then a prose sentence, and then another line of dialogue. It's all dialogue. One line has to lead to another. You can't skip a difficult moment.

I recall a little trick I used to use when beginning to write. The terrible thing to every writer is facing a blank piece of paper each morning. So I'd never finish a scene at night! Even though I'd know

what the next two lines were going to be, I'd never put them down on
paper. When I got up the next morning, I'd start with the two lines
I thought of the previous evening, and I was off! I never had to face
a blank piece of paper!

In the early days our custom was to notate the technical things
in the script as we wrote it: long shots, medium shots, things like
that. It's not done this way anymore at all. Now we just write master
scenes, and the directors do all the technical things with the camera.
This is now the director's job - his portion of the movie. If there's
a specific story point that demands a close-up shot, then of course you
write it in. But nowadays a screenwriter basically writes only master
scenes. I wouldn't presume to tell a director about the use of the
camera and everything else, unless it's a story point - and that happens very rarely.

I've had good luck with directors. Especially today, when so few
pictures are made and you have more directors to choose from. You no
longer have the old studio system where they not only had 75 writers
under contract, but probably 50 directors under contract as well. They
made 60 pictures a year, each major studio - A and B pictures - and you
got your director not because he was right for that picture, but because
he wasn't doing anything else at the time. If he was on salary and
being paid but not doing anything, he was assigned to your picture.
Most of the time you took pot luck.

I, myself, have no wish to be a director. I tried directing a
screen test once for a picture I did. The test was made with William
Holden, who had just come from finishing a picture with Billy Wilder
whom he idolizes (and rightly). Holden came on the set and gave me a
look that said 'I dare you to tell me what to do!' I was absolutely
paralyzed. The distance from the sound stage to the executive office
was exactly a quarter of a mile, and I think the world's record for a
quarter mile was 47.6. Holden did it in about 45 seconds, and probably
said 'Get this bum off the picture!' I've never even tried to direct
again!

My brother, Philip, and I did about six pictures with Michael Curtiz, a very fine director although he never learned the English language.
Curtiz was marvelous on the visual side of directing. He knew just when
the cigarette smoke should curl backwards; when to move; when not to
move. He was marvelous in that way. He always said to the actors,
'Give me the tear in the eye'.

Curtiz had a dialogue director, Irving Rapper, who later became a
big Bette Davis director. Rapper would take the actors aside and rehearse a scene while Mike was doing everything else on the set. We all
knew, of course, that the night before the story conferences Mike would
get his directions from his wife, Bess Meredith, who was one of the
great silent screenwriters, and then come in and tell us what Bess had
said. But sometimes Mike would forget what to say! I wish I had a
tape recording of those story conferences! We were under contract
(everybody was under contract in those days), and Wednesday was payday.
Curtiz would refer to my brother and me as 'You goddam Wednesday bums!'

(Let me add, parenthetically, that in the silent days the giant
screenwriters - many if not most of them - were women: Frances Marian,
Zoe Akins, Bess Meredith. Today lots of women have found their way into
screenwriting. Screenwriting is wide open for women writers.)

My brother and I did CASABLANCA with Curtiz, writing as we went
along. We started with very little in the way of a story. There wasn't
much of the unproduced play that could be used. We were just beginning
to write when Hal Wallis, the producer, said to my brother and me, 'Go
to Selznick and sell him the story, because we want to get Ingrid Bergman for the picture'. Bogart was under contract, and practically everybody else, including Claude Rains, but not the leading lady! So we went
to Selznick to tell him the story. He was in his office having his
lunch - his soup on his desk. He never looked up from his soup as we
started to tell what little story we had. I soon realized that we had
told less than a half-hour of story and were floundering. Ingrid Bergman's character hadn't even come into the picture yet, and we wanted her
for the starring role! So I said 'Oh hell, it's going to be a lot of

crap like ALGIERS. A lot of cigarette smoke and guitar music'.
Selznick said 'You've got Bergman!'

After we had been working on the story about a week or so, my
brother and I went to Washington with Frank Capra to work on the WHY WE
FIGHT series. We came back in about four weeks. We were way behind,
and Ingrid Bergman kept saying to us 'Who do I go off with at the end,
Henreid or Bogart?' We kept saying 'We haven't made up our minds yet'
- and that was absolutely true! We didn't know, and we didn't know until the very last. I know the exact spot on Sunset Boulevard, just
below Beverly Glen Boulevard, where we were driving to the studio, about
five days before the ending was to be shot, when the ending came to us.

I must go back to silent pictures for a moment. One of the great
influences on my life in writing for motion pictures was Robert Sherwood, the great playwright. Sherwood, before he was a playwright, was
movie editor of Life when it was a humour magazine. He wrote movie
criticisms. I shall never forget reading, when I was in high school, an
article he wrote in which he said that 90% of all movies can be called
'her sacrifice'. I and my brother said 'We're never going to write such
a movie. If we ever veer towards a story where it's going to be 'her
sacrifice', we'll stop. We'll never do that kind of movie'. Well, if
you examine CASABLANCA, it could be called 'his sacrifice', since
Bogart sends Bergman off with Henreid. It was Bogart's sacrifice.
That was the only time, I think, we violated a good rule.

CASABLANCA is one of my least favorite pictures. I'm tired of
talking about it after 30 years. I can explain its success only by the
Bogart cult that has sprung up after his death. I can recognize that the
picture is entertaining and people love it. It's fun and romantic. But
it's a completely phony romance, a completely phony picture. For instance, nobody knew what was going on in Casablanca at the time. Nobody
had ever been to Casablanca. The whole thing was shot on the back lot.
There was never a German who appeared in uniform in Casablanca for the
duration of the entire war, and we had the Germans marching around with
medals and epaulets. Furthermore there were never any such things as
letters of transit around which the entire plot revolved.

The movie is completely phony! I've gotten the most acclaim for
it, but I say honestly that it's one of my least favorite pictures. It
was one of the few pictures on which we had terrible fights with Curtiz,
the actors, and the producers because of the tension and suspense we
induced by not finding an ending for the film until very close to the
completion of the shooting schedule. The delay caused a lot of arguments; they never knew if they were going to have an ending at all!

When the picture came out it was not a financial blockbuster by any
means. I don't know where on the list of top grossers it falls, but way
down, I imagine. Most of the money from the picture is made now from
television, playing it again and again and again. In the theatres it
was a nice, profitable picture, but certainly not a blockbuster. Then
the Bogart cult came up - a kind of magic. They were such an impossible
romantic pair: the tough Bogart, a petrified forest, and the regal Bergman. Such a romantic pair had a certain chemistry, and I think this
applies to the success of the picture. When it plays in New York now,
there's a capsule review which always appears in the New Yorker magazine:
'Not really a very good movie, but a lot of fun'. This is accurate, I
think.

Many more movies have gone by which were not successes, but of
which I'm much more proud. I'm prouder of LIGHT IN THE PIAZZA, which
nobody ever sees, than I am of CASABLANCA. I'm prouder of PETE 'N TILLIE
I think there's much better writing in PETE 'N TILLIE than there is in
CASABLANCA. The picture that nobody ever saw that we did in 15 days for
$300,000 called TAKE A GIANT STEP, which was way ahead of its time - one
of the first black pictures - is much better than CASABLANCA.

But I'm very happy to work with good directors like Curtiz. In the
old days writers weren't allowed on the set. We weren't even allowed to
go to our previews. It took a strike to win that right. One of the
provisions in an early strike contract was that writers were to be noti-
fied and allowed to go to their previews. Prior to this, my brother and
I were always trying to get out of our contract and attend the previews.
Once we went to the prop department and got two raggedy, hillbilly beards
that tied around the head with a rubber band, put them on, and went to a

preview, while the entire staff was hanging around the box office
waiting for the picture to open.

Why was attending previews important to screenwriters? Because
otherwise your follow through efforts on the film were terribly limited
in most cases. Today, of course, it's an entirely different story.
They welcome a writer going through a picture. In the old days, however,
you seldom had a director assigned to a picture before the script was
finished. Then a director would come on, and you'd have to start all
over again with the director because of the changes he wanted. Now,
most of the time, you start from the beginning with the director. On
the script on which I'm now working, I started with the director right
from the beginning. We know what we're doing, and it's a real collaboration.

But, again, I have no talent for directing, and I admire and envy
directors, because film is a director's medium. The director is king.
Even though you can't possibly make a bad picture without a writer and
a script, much less a good picture, film is still a director's medium.
And that's the way it should be. (I've said this at Writers' Guild
meetings, and it makes me very unpopular with my fellow Guild members.)

I'm often depressed about the present situation in motion pictures,
because the producing organizations will try to make as many carbon
copies of the latest box office success as they can. I think this was
probably always true, but even more so today. Unfortunately today the
pictures with the greatest amount of violence are the most successful -
exploitation pictures, Kung Fu, that type of picture. They're tremendously successful, and there's a whole slew of them coming out. I find
this a depressing situation, although it may change as the box office
drops.

The good side of what's happening now is that there are many more
independent producers, or even filmmakers who don't use producers. They
are their own producers, making the pictures they want to make - such as
the filmmakers who made MEAN STREETS. It's a very impressive picture,
even though the filmmakers were unknown when the film was made. AMERICAN

GRAFFITI is another example. No major studio would make it until Francis Ford Coppola put his imprimatur upon it by agreeing to put his name on it as producer. It's been a tremendous success, even though it was made by a couple of recent graduates from film school.

Now, of course, I suppose we'll see copy after copy of MEAN STREETS and AMERICAN GRAFFITI, with ever more violence and sex. It's doubly unfortunate that so much effort is put into trying to copy success, for so many fine original scripts await production. I have a script I've had for 15 years that I would love to make. Nobody wants to make it because it's about good Germans, and they say people don't want to hear about good Germans. I would love to make it. I go around peddling it time after time again. I think it's my favorite script of all the scripts I've written, and I can't get it produced! But that, too, is what it means to be a screenwriter!

Walter Reisch, Screenwriter

I started as a writer of titles for a director who didn't speak the language in which we made our picture. He was a very fine Hungarian director by the name of Michael Curtiz who came from Hungary to Vienna as a refugee from the communistic revolution after the first World War. He was a sensational director, although he never spoke any language properly! The American press later unloaded all Mike Curtiz anec-anecdotes about the abuse of the English language on Samuel Goldwyn, but Goldwyn could never have demolished the language as Mike Curtiz did. Curtiz was just unbelievable, even though he was not unaware of it. His own wife, a fine American writer, could tell him hundreds of times that he was speaking improperly, and he'd continue to talk the same way as before.

Right after World War I, when I was a young student in Vienna looking for work, Curtiz came to Vienna and was discovered as a director. He had an enormous gift for directing action. I don't have to remind you that he not only directed CASABLANCA, YANKEE DOODLE DANDY, and FOUR DAUGHTERS, but practically every Errol Flynn picture. He was a master of the medium, both in silent days and with sound. I never wrote a picture for him, but I was his assistant title translator!

When Curtiz first came to Vienna, I was told that I didn't have to speak his language. There was no need to speak his language, for he demonstrated everything with his hands. On the way into Vienna from

Hungary, while riding in a car with a gypsy, Curtiz had with him a
little dictionary which had a page on which all the verbs that express
motion were enumerated: 'to go', 'to walk', 'to leap', 'to climb',
'to jump'. He learned them by heart, and whenever he later had to tell
an actor what to do, he would use all the verbs. Not just the verb
which was appropriate, but all of them! If he wanted to tell an actor
'You go to this door', he would say 'You go, jump, leap, walk, crawl to
this door!'

I began my career in the silent days of the cinema translating
titles for Curtiz, and was still in Europe when sound came. Its coming
was more of a revolution there than here. Here in America it was principally a great commercial upheaval, but in Europe it was part of a
much larger artistic revolution.

In Europe, in 1926-27, the greatest silent picture ever made
appeared, after being locked for two years in the censorship archive:
the Russian picture POTEMKIN by Eisenstein. Until that time motion
pictures in Europe were just 'movies', as a rule, with few exceptions:
the films of Chaplin, some by King Vidor, and the Lubitsch pictures, of
course. But all of a sudden POTEMKIN appeared, and the greatest literary personalities of Europe dedicated pages and pages in the press
announcing that a new medium had been found. I think they were truly
right. In Paris the newspapers Le Soir and Le Matin dedicated a
whole week to POTEMKIN. In Germany they never stopped talking about it.
In Switzerland and in Scandinavia it was an absolute revelation: the
discovery that an artistic medium practically without words had been
found. (I disregard completely the political angle, of course. At that
time it was very difficult to praise the Russian revolution. I'm talking only about the artistic achievement.) Great writers like Ferenc
Molnar, who wrote the original Liliom, and Lesley Storm, and John van
Druten, who was a very young writer at the time, wrote open letters to
the Times. It was a great upheaval. A new medium had been found.

Right after this an Austrian colleague of mine, a fellow countryman
named G. W. Pabst, also released a silent picture. It was the first
picture Greta Garbo made outside Sweden, JOYLESS STREET, again a master-

piece that expressed everything in terms of silent motion pictures only
- drama, emotion, tragedy, comedy. All of a sudden everybody knew that
the days of 'Kino' were over. We had to pitch in and try to arrive at
masterpieces in the sense of Eisenstein and Pabst.

At that time there were hardly any sound motion pictures from
America, except for a few shorts. THE JAZZ SINGER hadn't appeared as
yet, because the motion picture theatres in Europe hadn't as yet installed sound systems. There was enormous litigation going on between
Tobis Film and Sound in Germany and Pathé in Paris and London. American sound pictures, therefore, came two or three years late to Europe,
and then played only in special movie houses. And by that time, the
revolution was already on. Everybody thought the movie business was
dead, but the producers still had an audience, and the companies knew
they had an audience. They also knew that the sound systems in Europe
had a peculiar problem: film music was absolutely flawless, but you
couldn't understand spoken dialogue. You couldn't make the actors on
the screen talk and have it come out of them clearly.

Once the producers and the companies realized that music would
work (especially UFA, the great German equivalent to MGM), they went one
step further and decided that they could never go wrong with Viennese
music! So we simply wrote scripts with Viennese music. Instead of the
lovers saying 'I can't say how much I love you', they would say 'But I
can sing it to you!' If we put five songs in a film, it was a hit!
Once the Viennese music took over, sound was established, and we just
wrote as if nothing else had ever happened - as if no POTEMKIN and no
JOYLESS STREET had ever been made. The transition was flawless!

In Europe you couldn't buy great plays. If a play was good, whether written by a Russian, Swiss, or Hungarian, it went to America. Every
play in any language that had any value, i.e. that had any chance on
screen - was purchased immediately by one of the five or six studios
in Hollywood. So we had no choice. We had to write originals! We
wrote our scripts from the word 'go', and when sound came we just put
in music.

Don't forget: we started with music! When Joe von Sternberg came to
Vienna he made what I would call - in a loose sense - a musical: THE
BLUE ANGEL was a story with music. Marlene Dietrich sang six songs and
three of them became world-famous. Emil Jannings had to listen to Marlene singing, because music was the only workable medium. Dialogue
wouldn't go. Later, of course, dialogue recording was perfected as
well.

In Europe, therefore, we wrote original scripts. Once in Hollywood, however, we did more adaptations. For example, the cast of characters in the film GASLIGHT was entirely different than in the stage
version. There were no English people in it anymore! How did this
come about? Angel Street, the play that inspired GASLIGHT, was a kind
of mystery, and very British. The leading lady was a fragile Bronte
type - Ophelia in 1950. The cliched British villain was a perverted
English gentleman; you never knew exactly if he was a fag or Jack the
Ripper. And that's how we wrote the original script.

But one day David Selznick, the producer of the picture, intervened.
Selznick, I do not hesitate to say, was the greatest producer of motion
pictures ever, and at that time the most powerful man in Hollywood. He
had just finished GONE WITH THE WIND, REBECCA, and SPELLBOUND. He had
had six world successes in a row - but we were at MGM, and he was not
at MGM.

One day, however, Selznick heard that the next George Cukor picture
- based on the play Angel Street - would commence shooting in about three
weeks, and he just walked into his father-in-law's office (his father-
in-law being Louis B. Mayer) and cast the picture! The charming, fragile
Bronte-type of the leading lady became the Nordic goddess, Ingrid Bergman. The decayed British gentleman who never could make up his mind
whether he was a fairy or a murderer, became Charles Boyer. And to
top it all, the typical British commissar - established throughout
the one-hundred years of British detective writing - became Joseph
Cotten. Why? Simply because David Selznick had these three people
under contract and had no picture for them! Charles Boyer had just
finished a picture, and they didn't have another for him. Ingrid

Bergman had just made INTERMEZZO, and neither did they have another picture
for her. Jennifer Jones, who was also under contract to Selznick, had
had a big success in DUEL IN THE SUN, and since he couldn't unload her
on GASLIGHT, he married her! Anything not to pay the salary!

   George Cukor, of course, is a man who won't go onto the set with
a script that isn't completely finished. The script has to be polished,
the sets have to be completed; he would permit no improvisations. So at
that moment he had a choice: was he going to make a picture or was he going
to throw the cast out? But he couldn't change that cast for anything in
the world! So he called us in: John van Druten, who was British, and
myself - and we worked right on the set.

   Selznick himself had nothing to do with the revisions; all he did
was to write pages and pages, stacks and stacks, of memos. Jennifer
went to bed very early at 8 o'clock in the evening, and he went to bed
at 4 o'clock in the morning. What did he do from 8 to 4? He wrote
memos. When the memos came, Arthur Hornblow, the producer, would say to
Cukor, 'Now George, you read that, you know'. George would say,'Of
course', and then give it to van Druten, who wouldn't read it for anything but would give it to me, and I still have them at home.

   At 8:30 every morning Ingrid Bergman would come and say that she
was quitting the picture - that the part was not 'her'. Finally she
played her scenes and, of course, won an Academy Award. Charles Boyer,
like all Frenchmen, stayed in his dressing room counting his money.
Joseph Cotten didn't have time to find out what it was all about anyway,
since he was still mentally with his radio programs and only learning the
lines for the night!

   But we writers worked on the set - we were members of the medium.
We were troupers, we did it, and 40 years later GASLIGHT is still a
success. It is unimportant, you see, who plays what, but very important
that sometimes it works. If the material is good and if the enthusiasm
gets in and if everybody does his share, in the end it is a good picture even without the Bronte heroine, or Oscar Wilde, or the British
commissar.

This is what it's like being a screenwriter. We dig out the story, the conflict; and in contrast to Dostoevsky, we just begin the story and we end it. Once you have an understanding with the studio, or with the producer, about what they want – whether they want a comedy or a detective story or an adventure story or science fiction – you go home and there's the typewriter and paper. You sit and you figure-out that next week is the first installment due on the property tax, so bang – off you go. You've got to write! If you are one week behind, they are asking 60% more, so you write! There is no first moment; there is no last moment. It's a job. And, as the greatest American in that department, Thomas Edison, once said, 'It's one percent inspiration and 99% perspiration'.

Around 1950 the second floor at the new Irving Thalberg building in Culver City was the writer's floor. Every writer had his tag on the door: Ben Hecht, Charles MacArthur, Alice Dur Miller, Anita Loos, S. N. Behrman, Robert Sherwood, Jack Hilton, John van Druten, Walter Reisch – an almost endless series of the American Hall of Fame of writing. My office was opposite a door on which was written the name 'James Cain'! James Cain, a wonderful guy, was hired for $3000 per week (which is easily the equivalent of $6000 per week today), and he got a 52-week contract through his agent, Bert Allenberg. He came with his secretary from the East. Every day he would arrive for work at 9:00 o'clock as the contract stipulated, and would be surprised to find me already at work, because I am an early riser who would get there at 8:15 and start typing. Cain had a contract for one year with two optional years after that, always with a raise. Now in the three years that James Cain was in Hollywood, he didn't write one script – not one page! Nobody knew that he was under contract! He wrote three novels, some of which were later filmed by Warner Brothers. He had two divorces in these three years, and had a hangover every morning. He was there from 9 to 6, but nobody ever knew that James Cain was on the lot!

The point is that when a famous novelist came to Hollywood it meant nothing. It was much more important to have a man of whom it was known that he could write a hundred and twenty-five pages of script with a beginning and an end and a middle between. A novelist didn't mean anything to Hollywood, unless - like Ben Hecht or Charlie MacArthur - he could write screenplays!

On the other hand, there are many examples of smash movie successes made from novels which were faithfully translated, like William Wyler's WUTHERING HEIGHTS. I don't think he changed one line. In GONE WITH THE WIND there were only a few chapters left out. When they made the first version of PEYTON PLACE - a damned good picture and a terrific success - they photographed the book, leaving out only a few chapters.

But generalizing is impossible. Jerry Wald (the producer of PEYTON PLACE) next made a movie from a book by Scott Fitzgerald, and changed everything in it. The film of Cain's Double Indemnity used next to nothing from the novel, inventing the rest, and it was a great picture.

There are great, great books. And if they are great, they oughtn't to be changed. Don't change Les Miserables, for example. Valjean must be there, and the commissioner. Don't change the classics!

I've enjoyed screenwriting. I don't have any frustrations about not getting proper screen credit or being brushed aside. This is an internal and eternal fight between writers, directors, producers, actors, etc. The problem is different with writers, of course. Very few producers come onto the set and say, 'We are going to fix the lights now'. Few try to compose the music. I don't think most really want to act. But certainly they all have pencils at home, and they all write! But once you know this, and you fight it, you realize that this is a purely professional, esoteric, internal fight. Later the Screen Writers Guild takes over, and only your aunt suffers when a picture which you wrote has two more names on it.

In the end - and I say this without any blushing - if a picture is a success then everybody who had some sort of credit on it is a success. If the picture is a failure, it is better if your name is not on it! Then it is nobody's failure but the studio's! In the many years that I've been screenwriting (it's almost half a century now), I've had a lot of trouble. I've had a lot of fights. But it's nobody's business but

my own. In the last analysis we are facing two groups when a picture
is completed: the public and the press. But the public doesn't care.
They have absolutely no interest whether there is a writer on the film,
or two writers, or three writers, or what their names are. It is not
bitterness but experience from which I speak. Nobody can tell me that
it makes any difference if a picture has arrived with your name on it
as screenwriter, as well as the names of two guys who didn't do anything.
So what? It's only a question of attitude. I have no frustrations, and
I'm willing to go on with this kind of mishmash of credits - arguing about
'who wrote what' - for a long time to come.

    Nobody, I think, should be discouraged from going into this wonder-
ful medium of screenwriting because of the credits. I say in all hon-
esty that anybody who goes into films must know that filmmaking is
exclusively team work. Only one personality at one point gives real
color to the whole thing, whether he is a director or a great actor. When
you go into motion pictures you know that that's the way you will be
treated. A movie is not just a play by Bernard Shaw or any other
wonderful playwright. Everything's done in collaboration. There were
a lot of actors who contributed wonderful lines and never got credit
for it. I worked for many years with Ernst Lubitsch, who contributed
an enormous amount to every story, but his name was never on the titles
as screenwriter. Irving Thalberg never had his name on the picture as a
producer.

    If you know that this is the kind of medium it is, then I for one
say: Try to get into it! It's a wonderful medium, and a pleasure to
work in. I take all the shadowy days in stride with the sunny days.
If some of my pictures had not been successful, we wouldn't now be discussing pictures I wrote thirty years ago. But they are still remembered. I'm proud and delighted to pass on to anybody who wants to go into
screenwriting the advice: Go ahead! Don't worry about the credits.
Make a good picture. Make your contribution, that's all.

Bernard Herrmann, Composer

My subject is film music. I should like firstly to indicate how
the sound film was an ideal back in the days of classical Greece. I
should like secondly to say something about the contemporary use of music in films. And I should like to conclude by discussing with you sections of the scores of three films that I had the pleasure of composing:
Welles's CITIZEN KANE, Truffaut's FAHRENHEIT 451, and Hitchcock's PSYCHO.

Drama, as we know it, began with the Greeks. Less well known is
the fact that the Greeks projected and kept alive a vital part of the
theatre which they called the 'melodram'. The melodram was theatre with
the spoken word accompanied by music.

Unfortunately we know very little about Greek music, except that
whatever music they did create must have been of great simplicity: perhaps some harps, some string sound, some woodwind sound and some choral
music. But in the melodram the Greeks encountered a problem that has
remained with us from that day to this: whenever people get on the stage
and start to talk, and some instrument in the pit begins to play, you
can't hear what the people are saying. This has been one of the great
recurring problems in theatre, and we shall see how it was solved.

Although modern drama really doesn't have music in the pit (it's
been done away with), the idea of using music with drama has persisted
since the time of the Greeks. The notion was essentially reborn with
Monteverdi, whose first attempt at what we now call 'opera' consisted

in deciding that the voice could speak at specific pitches which could
be accompanied and underlaid by sound. That was the beginning of opera
as we know it - the opera which, departing from melodram by taking another direction, soon left the word and became more interested in music.
But the idea of drama with accompanying music (melodram) still remained.
In the 18th century Gluck worked at melodram, Mozart attempted it, and
it persisted through the 19th century in little isolated works. Even
in the present day certain works by Carl Orff might be considered melodram, while a great part of Berg's "Wozzeck" is really a melodram rather
than opera.

But along the way in the early part of the 20th century Claude
Debussy became fascinated by the concept of melodram. He faced the same
problem as the Greeks, but he, of course, created the form of his kind
of vocal music - as evidenced in "Pelleas" - which is practically spoken
drama with music. Debussy's dream was to write pure melodram, and he
lived long enough to see some early examples of the cinema! He saw early
experiments in the cinema in which an orchestra sat behind the screen and
played specially composed music. He felt that this was the art of the
future. Debussy said that the cinema would allow the perfect creation
of poetry, vision, and dreams. If Debussy had lived long enough into the
era of the sound film, who knows what he would have created. Who knows
what we've lost.

With the invention of the sound film, the problem of the Greeks was
solved; for by separately recording music and sound and voice, we are
able to mix them together at the proper volume. The speaking voice and
the music can achieve a perfect balance. That is the greatest contribution of the genuine sound film.

Nobody attempted to write music for silent films. They simply play
existing music, good or bad. And when early sound came in, they could
only draw upon what had been commercially viable in the past in the theatre. This was the situation until a film called THE BROTHERS KARAMAZOV
was made by the Soviet director Fedor Ozep working in Germany in 1931.
The film starred Fritz Kortner and Anna Sten. Ozep employed a composer
by the name of Karol Rathaus who did the score. This, to me, was the

first great realization of the dream of melodram. Rathaus, who remains
relatively unknown, was to become a refugee in New York and to teach at
Queen's College. Nobody gave him an opportunity to write any further
films. But the music of THE BROTHERS KARAMAZOV is one of the most imaginative achievements in sound film.

What did Rathaus do? He treated for the first time the music of a
film as an integral emotional part of the whole, not as decoration. Because the film deals with one of the Karamazov's falling in love with a
prominent harlot and visiting her in her establishment wherein a gypsy
orchestra plays, the music of the picture begins with a gypsy orchestra
simply playing Russian gypsy music. But as the picture progresses and
the brother becomes more and more involved with the harlot, the music
stops being ornamental and becomes an emotional mirror of him. It becomes more and more tragic and more and more hysterical. It reaches its
greatest moment, I think, when the brother hysterically drives a troika
through a raging blizzard accompanied musically by a great battery of
percussion instruments. Remember: this was done way back in the early
1930s! It is one of the great genuine achievements of using music for
the first time as an integral emotional accompaniment - not as decoration, and not to achieve the sale of phonograph records!

I don't know why, today, a film has to cost 4 million dollars to
push a record costing 70 cents, but it does! Film music ought not to be
written so that people going to cocktail parties can say 'Play me that
bit'. Music for film should no more be noticed than the camerawork. If
you sit and admire the camerawork of a picture the first time, there's
something wrong. And the music of a film oughtn't to be admired either.
Cinema is only one thing: an illusion of many arts working together.
The minute one aspect begins to dominate, and subordinate everything
else to it, the film is doomed. I know personally some great directors
who've gotten to the point where they don't even need a camera!

The use of music in films is a completely unstudied territory. In
the old days there used to be atlases of the world with unexplored regions
marked in white and labeled 'unknown'. Well, that's still what cinema
music is like. Some of the most sensitive directors are complete igno-

ramuses concerning the use of music in their own films, while sometimes
an inferior director will have a great instinct for it. Whatever music
can do in a film is something mystical. The camera can only do so much;
the actors can only do so much; the director can only do so much. But
the music can tell you what people are thinking and feeling, and that
is the real function of music. The whole recognition scene of VERTIGO,
for example, is eight minutes of cinema without dialogue or sound effects
- just music and picture. I remember Hitchcock said to me, 'Well, music
will do better than words there'.

Remember also, whenever speaking of music in the cinema, that the
ear deludes the eye as to what it is seeing. It changes time values.
What you think is long may be only four seconds, and what you thought
was very short may be quite long. There's no rule, but music has this
mysterious quality. It also has a quality of giving shape to a mundane
stretch of film. Let me explain that to you.

You can cut a scene ABA, or CBA, or BCA - any way you like. But if
you put music from one point in a film to another, there is no alterna-
tive to that music as it is in itself. Music is a kind of binding veneer
that holds a film together, and hence is particularly valuable in the use
of montage. It's really the only thing that seals a montage into one
coherent effect. That's why it was used in the newsreel in its most
primitive form. (Have you ever watched a newsreel without music? Try
it!) This sort of binding is one of the mysterious things that music
can do.

The other thing that the sound film permitted music to do for the
first time is to give a musical close-up (analogous to the way the camera
can give a visual close-up). Let me explain this to you. A lone clari-
net playing one note in a concert hall means nothing; but given the way
you can manipulate its sound on a sound track, it can be made to take
over the whole auditorium. This is another valuable way of using music.

There are some directors who say 'We can make a film without music
- we don't need it'. A wonderful example of this attitude was Richardson's MADEMOISELLE, a film with Jeanne Moreau. Jeanne Moreau, I believe,

portrays a school teacher who's a pyromaniac. As great an actress as
she is, however, she couldn't do anything to give the audience a sense
of her inner turmoil. Mr. Richardson (who was so sure that he'd gotten
it all on film) had no score prepared, and so the picture went no place.
When you saw Moreau's face in the film while her emotions supposedly
burnt within her, you heard just silence and some crickets. But with
the proper score that would have been a most moving and exciting film!

There's no reason why you can't have a film with sound effects and
no music. THE GRAPES OF WRATH, A TREE GROWS IN BROOKLYN, and DIABOLIQUE,
for example, had no music. Every once in a while there's an exception –
a good film without music. But generally the odds are against it. I've
been associated with so many films whose music pulled them through. Not
only me, but many colleagues of mine have saved films in a similar way
by making them acceptable for an hour or two.

Music really is something that comes out of the screen and engulfs
the whole audience in a common experience. It isn't something away from
the screen. I've spent a long life in films, trying to convince people
of this. They don't see it. It's partly because making a film is a
cooperative effort of many talents and gifts working together. But, you
see, at the present time there's this hysterical cult of the director.
No director can make a film by himself. No one man can do it. The
nature of the cinema requires cooperative pulsation. And I, having had
the privilege and pleasure of working for many great directors, can tell
you: the ones who have the greatest humility in this way achieve the
greatest films!

I have the final say about my music; otherwise I refuse to do the
music for the film. The reason for insisting upon this is that all
directors – other than Orson Welles, a man of great musical culture –
are just babes in the woods. If you were to follow the taste of most
directors, the music would be awful. They really have no taste at all.
I'm overstating a bit, of course. There are exceptions. I once did a
film, THE DEVIL AND DANIEL WEBSTER, with a wonderful director, William
Dieterle. He was a man of great musical culture. Hitchcock is very
sensitive: he leaves me alone! (Fortunately, because if Hitchcock were

left by himself, he would play "In a Monastery Garden" behind all his
pictures!) It depends on the composer, and I'm not making a rule about
it. But for myself, personally, I'd rather not do a film than have to
take what a director says. I'd rather skip it, for I find it's impossible to work that way. Many years ago Kubrick asked me to write the
music for LOLITA. When I agreed to do it, he said 'But there's one
thing I've forgotten to tell you: you've got to use a melody of my
brother-in-law'. So I told him to forget it.

It shows vulgarity, also, when a director uses music previously
composed. I think that 2001: A SPACE ODYSSEY is the height of vulgarity
in our time. To have outer space accompanied by "The Blue Danube Waltz"
and the piece not even recorded anew! They just used gramophone records.
The best you can come up with for the whole epic of outer space is to
play "The Blue Danube Waltz"! They even had a Howard Johnson's in the
film! (DEATH IN VENICE is a different kind of thing altogether.)

There are directors and directors and directors. Some are so ego-
tistical that you can't say anything to them, while others are sensitive
to anybody's opinion and want to hear it. For example, you must never
tell Hitchcock about a book you think would make a wonderful film. If
you do, it's dead. What you should suggest, rather, is that he sent you
the book and that you think it's great. Then it's got a chance!

Hitchcock generally was very sensitive about the use of music. He
sometimes said to me 'I'm shooting this scene tomorrow. Can you come
down to the set?' I'd come to the set and watch, and he'd say 'Are you
planning to have music here?' I'd say 'Well, I think we should have it'
'Oh good', he would say, 'then I'll make the scene longer; because if
you were not going to have music, then I would have to contract it'.
Some directors are considerate about things like that. Hitchcock, at
least, likes people to work with him through the shooting of the film.
So do Welles and Truffaut. But there are many directors whom I never
even met until the picture was completely shot. They're not even interested enough to care.

Of course there are disappointments in this business, but most are
unintentional. Things just don't fuse together sometimes. People go

off in different ways. Generally what happens is that somebody's ego
(usually the director's) is so great that everybody else becomes super-
fluous to him. His attitude becomes 'I can do it without you'. This
attitude has been the reason for some of Hitchcock's greatest films, and,
unfortunately, one of the reasons why Hitchcock and I don't get along
any more.

Today the cinema has become a medium for young people's ego expression. I wish they'd just make films and forget about their egos. I
recently went to talk to a director who was making a film, and I suggested that one of the things we should do was to go to one of the great
cathedrals of England and record the diapason stop on the organ. He
said 'No, I don't want no Catholic instrument in my film!'.

There are no fixed rules in this business. There is nothing, for
example, in the nature of a film that says we should use what they call
an 'orchestra' on the sound track. An orchestra was a device developed
over several hundred years - an agreed representation of certain instruments to play a certain repertoire. If you wish first to play the music of Haydn at Esterhazy, and then to play it in Paris, you have to
use the same kind of instruments. But music for film is created for
one performance - for that one film - and there is no law that says it
has to be related to concert music. As a matter of fact, such an opportunity to shift the complete spectrum of sound within one piece has never
before been given to us in the history of music. You can't do this in an
opera house. I know! If you write an opera and you request something a
little unusual, they say 'Well, we can't do Wagner if we do yours'. Or
'For Puccini we use this, why can't you use that?'. But not with film!
Each film can create its own variety of musical color.

The screen itself dictates musical forms: the way a picture is cut,
or the way it's shaped. I myself am very flexible to the demands of the
screen itself. I don't think, for example, that one can do a film score
that has the musical vitality of, say, a work by Richard Strauss, and
get away with it. I mean that in all seriousness! If you could do a
score for a picture, and really play Strauss's "Don Juan", no one would
watch the picture! The music would completely sweep you away and the

film would not be seen. Sound and music, after all, are only part of
the illusion which is cinema, not all of it. Filmed opera, therefore,
won't work because film is primarily visual, while opera is not primarily a visual art. Film aims at melodram, not opera - at an integration
of all the arts, not one in isolation.

You may have noticed that the tempi of the gramophone recordings
of my film scores frequently differ from the tempi of the soundtracks
themselves. Why? The tempo of the music on the film is dictated by the
film itself; on a film everything is dictated by the screen. But the
tempo of the music on a record is dictated by musical reasons which have
nothing to do with cinematic reasons. After all, there is no 'right'
tempo for a piece of music. Even with great classic music there is a
difference of opinion concerning tempi. (I hate to think what Toscanini
would think of Karajan's tempi!)

Now I must discuss a terrible thing, namely, most of the people who
write music for films! I would say (and I'd go to the gallows for saying it) that roughly 98 out of every 100 persons making film music would
have no more interest in making films if it weren't for the money. Only
about 2% are interested in the cinema, and the cinema is a very demand-
ing art form. The rest have figured out how to cheat. Most film music
is created by assembly line: one fellow sketches it, another fellow com-
pletes it, another one orchestrates it, and yet another adapts it. Consequently the music is dissipated; it has no direction. Then some man
of the lowest denomination says 'It'll be a hit!' I don't see what
merit this approach has for the creation of a film, but that's the way
it is.

There is enormous pressure to write film music which can be exploit-
ed afterwards. Out of every 100 film scores we make, the producers
would want a gramophone record of 99 of them. DR. ZHIVAGO is a good
example. Notice: nobody ever talks about the film. David Lean said
recently in London that without its wonderful music his film would have
been nothing. If that's what he feels about his film, too bad! But do
you see what a terrible and really revolting circle it is? What does
that piece of harmless legitimate music have to do with a big saga of

the ending of the aristocracy in Russia? Nothing! But to the studio
it's great!

I have a friend who was denied a film music contract from a studio
and asked for the reason. 'Oh', they said, 'we're using so-and-so. His
music sold over a million records.' My friend replied 'But I've sold
three-quarters of a million records!'. 'Yes', they said, 'but it wasn't
a million was it!'. This is what I've hated all my life. The cinema
is a great vehicle for contemporary expression, and a contemporary art
form. Yet I was recently in the Museum of Modern Art (the museum called
'the Museum of Modern Art'!), and the people working there are not interested in music for the cinema at all - not at all. One museum after
another is devoted to the contemporary cinema, yet uninterested in film
music. And they're proud of it, too, because they don't understand.
Even the people who should understand cannot comprehend what's happening
to them. I've spent my entire career combating ignorance.

I shall say no more about this. I want to speak about cinema, not
the way people abuse cinema and make it rubbish. Let me, therefore,
discuss some of my scores, beginning with CITIZEN KANE.

CITIZEN KANE

CITIZEN KANE originally had no main title. When it was initially
shown, there was no 'RKO' or 'CITIZEN KANE' title, just a black screen.
The first thing you saw was the pan up to the sign 'No Trespassing'. I
remember at the premier that people shouted all over the place 'lights,
sound, sound, sound, projection, sound', because they could not accept
a film that started in complete silence. Since the studio couldn't put
sound in, they unfortunately added a trade mark and a title instead.

Imagine the opening of KANE if it were silent, without music. That
is the way it was turned over to me. Does the sequence seem long to you,
imagined without music? This was the first sequence I scored. If I remember correctly, I didn't have the idea of a 'Rosebud' theme, nor of a
'Destiny' or 'Fate' theme. Both themes sort of automatically presented
themselves to me. You don't write music with the top of your mind; you

write it from a part you don't know anything about. Anyway, I was very lucky in the first hour of composition: I hit on two sequences of sound that could bear the weight of this film. (I was just in luck; if I had not had that luck, it might have been a disaster for me.) The picture opens with a motive I call 'the Motive of Destiny', of Kane's destiny. Later in the film the permutations of this theme become a can-can, jazz, all kinds of things. Then, when Kane sees the flickering snow, we hear for the first time the motive of 'Rosebud' around which the whole picture pivots. This second theme tells everybody what Rosebud is, even though they soon forget about it. But the music has told them, right away.

This opening sequence also uses an unconventional orchestra of eight flutes (four being alto), four bass flutes, very deep contrabass clarinets, clarinets, tubas, trombones, deep lower percussion, and a vibraphone.

Imagine now the sound track to the opening sequence alone, without the visuals. Decide for yourself whether or not you think the music by itself is too long. I think the music's too long. I, of course, had no choice about its length. The director gives you the visuals because this is his vision. Sometimes one can go to a director and complain, feeling that things are disproportionate and should be changed - but certainly not in a film like this!

Imagine now the full opening sequence, visuals and sound together. Do you still feel that the sequence is too long? I think not - and that's one of the great mysteries of the power of music in cinema! Without the music the picture is incomplete, and the time scale is skewed.

Why didn't I use percussive or rhythmic effects rather than music here? CITIZEN KANE is a romantic picture. It's about a man obsessed by a little gadget called 'Rosebud'. Percussive sound effects would have been inappropriate in the opening, and wouldn't have worked later on either, for similar reasons. As a matter of fact, later on in the film Kane picks up Susan in the street, and says 'I was on my way to the warehouse to look at some things my mother left me'. The reason he responds to the girl is that she faintly resembles his mother - and the orchestra

gives out the 'Rosebud' theme! Nobody's ever caught it, nobody's ever
written about it. They don't have to because it's there! Sometimes
with a subject this romantic you must do romantic things.

On the other hand, there is a great picture, A WOMAN IN THE DUNES,
which was all done with electronics, with the most marvelous use of
electronics. Every picture is unique. I'm not implying that there's
only one way to score a picture, because there are many ways providing
imagination is used. But I doubt whether one could have substituted
percussive effects for music in a picture like KANE, a kaleidoscopic
picture. A certain greyness would settle over it.

The opera sequence in CITIZEN KANE presented a very great problem.
Perhaps you have read Miss Pauline Kael's book about the making of the
film. I would like to say publicly that she never wrote me or approached me to ask about the music, even though she has included pages of
spurious wisdom about it, including the purported 'fact' that we evi-
dently were so poverty stricken that we couldn't afford to use Massenet's
"Thais"!

Why did we have to write an opera for this sequence? Kane's girl-
friend, Susan, is partially modeled on a friend of William Randolph
Hearst; but she is also partially modeled on Ganna Walska, the lady
friend and later wife of Harold McCormick whose former wife, Edith Rockefeller, was instrumental in getting Samuel Insull to build the Chicago
Opera House. Our problem was to create something that would give the
audience the feeling of the quicksand into which this simple little
girl, having a charming but small voice, is suddenly thrown. And we had
to do it in cinema terms, not musical ones. It had to be done quickly.
We had to have the sound of an enormous orchestra pounding at her while
everyone is fussing over her, and then - 'Now get going, go!' - they
throw her into the quicksand.

There is no opera is existence that opens that way. We had to
create one. But this doesn't stop Miss Kael from saying that we could
not afford "Thais", with its lovely little strings, which we could have
afforded any time. The point is that it wouldn't have served the emo-

tional purpose. I didn't particularly care to write an opera sequence
like this, but KANE demanded it. Not Welles, but KANE. It was the
only way, from a cinematic point of view, that we could convey the terror that this girl was in.

How could we achieve this effect musically? If Susan couldn't
sing at all, then we know she wouldn't have found herself in this position. But she had something of a little voice. So I wrote this piece
in a very high tessitura, so that a girl with a modest little voice
would be completely hopeless in it. (Later on, singers like Eileen
Farrell would sing it to great effect.) We got a very charming singer
to dub Susan's voice, explaining to her the purpose of the effect. Notice: the reason Susan is struggling so hard is not that she cannot sing,
but rather that the demands of the part are purposely greater than she
can ever meet.

One should note this opera sequence carefully, because this is a
case where the music had to be created for the film, and it's my conten-
tion that no other approach could have solved the problem. Had we played the last scene of "Salome", we'd have gotten the same effect, but it
wouldn't have shown Susan starting the opera. (The beginning of "Salome"
anyone can sing.) The problem was: can Susan survive the beginning?
That was the problem the film posed.

Look and listen to Susan in her music lesson. In this case the
music was written before the scene was filmed; the scene was photographed
to a playback. If you think about it, you'll understand why a conventional opera wouldn't have worked. It wouldn't have worked because there
doesn't exist that terror-in-the-quicksand feeling at the beginning of
any conventional opera.

It's discouraging to see an eminent critic dispose of the problem
by saying that we couldn't afford to use "Thais". People think that
Pauline Kael is the gospel. That's how falsehoods are perpetrated. If
this is how good she is about the music, I hate to think how good she is
about anything else. I happen to disagree with the premise of her whole
book on KANE, because she tries to pretend that Welles is nothing, and

that a mediocre writer by the name of Mankiewicz was a hidden Voltaire. I'm not implying that Mankiewicz made no contribution: the titles say so on the screen, and Orson says that Mankiewicz did make a valuable contribution. But without Orson all of Mankiewicz's other pictures were nothing, before and after. With Orson, however, something happened to this wonderful man. (He was a wonderful man in a way, except that his life was very disappointing to him. But he could not have created KANE.)

There are so many people interested in trying to pretend that Orson didn't do anything. This is in great vogue today: to pretend that all the great masters of the past and of today really didn't do anything. It was the bootblack who did it for them!

This gets me into the realm of authors and authorship. There's nothing that says a film should be like the novel from which it's adapted, or that a visualization of a piece of music has to resemble the music, and I think people who think that are wrong. If you don't like movies and think that the picture they are making is distorting your novel, then don't let them make a film of your novel. But if you like their money, just take it and shut up! I'll tell you a great story about Stravinsky. Selznick asked Stravinsky to do the score for a film, and Stravinsky agreed. Selznick asked his price. Stravinsky answered '$100,000'. Selznick retorted 'We don't spend that kind of money for music!'. 'Ah', Stravinsky replied, 'it's not for the music. That's cheap. It's for my name!'

The next part of KANE I'd like to consider is the little marriage breakfast scene in Kane's first marriage. Imagine the visuals alone, without the music. This is what I was given. The popular music of this period corresponding to the images would have been a romantic waltz. So each change in mood and each cut was designed to be a variation on a basic waltz theme. The structure of the sequence is therefore simple: a series of waltz variations in absolutely classic form, giving unity to the scene and making it whole.

The ending of KANE gave me a wonderful opportunity to arrive at a

complete musical statement, since the ending contains no dialogue with
the exception of perhaps one or two lines. I wished at the end of the
film to summon forth and draw all the dramatic threads together. This
last musical sequence is played by a conventional symphony orchestra.
I used a full orchestra for the simple reason that, from the time the
music of the final sequence begins to the end of the film, the music has
effectively left the film and become an apotheosis of the entire work.

    I was fortunate indeed to start my cinema career with a film like
CITIZEN KANE. It's been a downhill run ever since! I receive all kinds
of requests from producers, most of whom say 'I want you to write a
score like you did for KANE'. I reply 'Do you have a picture like KANE?'
They don't realize that you can't write another KANE, or PSYCHO, because
there's only one KANE, or PSYCHO. People always tell me how difficult
Welles is to work with. I would say about my own career that the only
people I've met worth working for were difficult people, because they're
interested in achieving something. Just spare me the charmers! Welles
in every other way of life may be difficult, but when it comes to making
artistic decisions he's a rock of Gibralter.

                              FAHRENHEIT 451

    I should next like to consider a film I made with the French direc-
tor Francois Truffaut. I speak no French, and Truffaut speaks no English, but we found a way to work through an interpreter. When Truffaut
spoke to me about doing the score for the film, I said to him 'Why do
you want me to write you FAHRENHEIT? You're a great friend of Boulez
and Stockhausen and Messaien, and this is a film that takes place in the
future. They're all avant-garde composers. Why shouldn't you ask one
of them?' 'Oh, no, no', he said, 'they'll give me the music of the 20th
century, but you'll give me the music of the 21st'. Well, it sounds
funny, but I had explained to him my belief that the music of the future,
of the period of FAHRENHEIT 451, will achieve a serenity, and that people's lives will be so devoid of any kind of feeling that music will
serve to restore and retain a classic concept of serenity and beauty.
This picture gave me an opportunity to expand this idea.

The people of FAHRENHEIT 451 have little feeling about things as
we understand them, and the film was constructed to reflect this. If
you were to see this film without music, I don't know if it would achieve
the effect. The film was photographed around Ealing and Shepperton in
England, and no attempt was made to hide either the contemporary archi-
tecture of the place or the people in it. The only thing that takes
them into the future is the action of the picture and the kindergarten
outfits they are wearing.

Consider the opening of the film. Like KANE, it has an unconventional main title sequence - the titles are spoken. Then we go to the
opening sequences which have to do with fire engines, in which the music reflects an interest in toys and the complete lack of feeling of the
police and bystanders. But notice: nothing happens in the music. There's
a kind of greyness about it, and this was purposely done. The first time
that we really achieve any feeling of human contact in this picture is
when Montag learns to read and discovers Dickens. The second time occurs
in the little scene where he interrupts his wife and her television on-
lookers, and reads Dickens to them. Here, for the first time, the music
takes on a bit of humanity.

If we now go to the conclusion of the film, where the principals
come to the people who are bookreaders and memorize books, one can see
where I had the wonderful and unique opportunity in the film to use the
orchestra to convey a full song of humanity. We were lucky with this
sequence. When they came to photograph it, they found that there had
been a terrific snowfall, although no one had planned on having one.
Truffaut took advantage of the event, shot the sequence outside at Shepperton, and the whole unplanned wonderful ending of the picture resulted.
Believe it or not, one of the powerful executives of the studio wanted
to hire a pop singer to sing a pop tune over the whole last sequence.
He didn't get his way, of course, but that's what he would have liked
to have done. This same executive also said to Truffaut, in my presence, 'I don't like your picture at all'. Truffaut replied 'I didn't
ask your opinion, did I?' Such rare integrity is seldom encountered.
It is difficult to find two people who stick together on a film.

Although FAHRENHEIT 451 received poor notices, particularly in
America, it's been commercially successful throughout the world. It's
shown all the time; it never stops. One day, I suspect, it'll come into
its own and achieve critical success as well.

PSYCHO

I wish, lastly, to discuss some parts of PSYCHO by Hitchcock. In
film studios and among filmmakers, there is a convention that the main
titles have to have cymbal crashes and be accompanied by a pop song –
no matter what! The real function of a main title, of course, should be
to set the pulse of what is going to follow. I wrote the main title
music for PSYCHO before Saul Bass even did the animation. They animated
to the music. The point, however, is that after the main title nothing
much happens in this picture, apparently, for 20 minutes or so. Appear-
ances, of course, are deceiving, for in fact the drama starts immediately
with the titles! The climax of PSYCHO is given to you by the music right
at the moment the film begins. I am firmly convinced, and so is Hitchcock, that after the main titles you know that something terrible must
happen. The main title sequence tells you so, and that is its function:
to set the drama. You don't need cymbal crashes or records that never
sell! (The only orchestra used, incidentally, is a string orchestra,
the same kind of orchestra with which one plays Mozart. I mention this
because people have all kinds of ideas about the instrumentation used,
including a wonderful new study of PSYCHO which says I wrote wonderfully
for woodwinds!)

When I was first shown this film, Hitchcock was depressed about it.
He felt it didn't come off. He wanted to cut it down to an hour television show and get rid of it. I had an idea of what one could do with
this film, so I said 'Why don't you go away for your Christmas holidays,
and when you come back we'll record the score and see what you think'.
(Hitchcock always goes away for 5 or 6 weeks for Christmas.) 'Well', he
said, 'do what you like, but only one thing I ask of you: please write
nothing for the murder in the shower. That must be without music.'

When Hitchcock returned we played the score for him in the mixing and dubbing studio (not at a recording session). We dubbed the composite without any musical effects behind the murder scene, and let him watch it. Then I said 'I really do have something composed for it, and now that you've seen it your way, let me try mine'. We played him my version with the music. He said 'Of course, that's the one we'll use'. I said 'But you requested that we not add any music'. 'Improper suggestion, improper suggestion' he replied.

Many people have inquired how I achieved the sound effects behind the murder scene. Violins did it! People laugh when they learn it's just violins, and that's interesting to me. It shows that people are so jaded that if you give them cold water they wonder what kind of champagne it is. It's just the strings doing something every violinist does all day long when he tunes up. The effect is as common as rocks. (The soundtrack on THE BIRDS is another story. It was all done electronically. At that time the only place which possessed the equipment to do the sound was in West Berlin, so we went there. I worked with a chap named Rennie Gassman at the West Berlin Radio Workshop. The whole score is electronic.)

I wish also to explain something interesting about the murder scene itself in PSYCHO. The final shot, which appears to be a pan and zoom shot into the drain hole of the bathtub, was the most expensive and difficult aspect of the entire film. Every frame was printed separately and enlarged gradually, millimeter by millimeter. People think it's an ordinary zoom shot, yet every frame was enlarged, one by one, by Eastman. To get that effect took the longest time and cost more money than any other aspect of the production of the film.

There's a rumor that PSYCHO was shot in color, but released in black and white. This is only a rumor, for PSYCHO was not made in color; it was made as cheaply as possible. The whole picture was shot by a television crew in a little under three weeks, and was purposely shot in black and white. That's one of the reasons why I use a string orchestra; I wanted to get a black and white musical color. It never was shot in color. Don't believe everything you read!

Conclusion

The cinema is a great contemporary art form. I believe that when
we're all gone, people in the 21st century will be interested neither
in our literature nor in our music but only and completely in our cinema. That will be our legacy to them. (Just think if we could see a
film made in 1870!) The people, therefore, who view the cinema as a
hack way of making money are betraying one of the greatest means of
expressing themselves completely and fully - a means directly related to
that ancient Greek ideal of melodram because it consists of spoken drama with music. I admit that there have been other attempts to change
the function of cinema, but essentially it retains this ideal, and the
ideal will persist.

I don't think that it's possible to advise up-and-coming young
composers on special areas of training which will enable them to become
expert film composers. Creators of film music must have it in their
bones, and their imaginations must be triggered by working in films.
Many people have their egos stimulated by working in films, but they
haven't got much imagination. Ego stimulation is no rarity, but to have
a fertile imagination is quite another story. Mozart once said that
whenever he saw a piece of music paper and thought of the word 'aria',
he got excited! By an empty piece of music paper and an idea! That's
how one has to feel about cinema. Nobody ever starts out to make a bad
piece of film. Everybody starts wanting to make something good, but
there's a long road to be traveled to make it good, and it requires a
certain flexibility. I myself don't feel that film music is of much
interest divorced from the film. Many people disagree with me, but to
me it seems like playing the accompaniment to a song without the melody

I don't know how you begin to understand the function of film musi
You can study counterpoint all you like, and then write a piece of musi
for you've been studying the rules of composition. But rules and sensi
tivity can be miles apart. Hundreds of films have died for lack of a
sensitive musical score, though written by men who knew the rules. Jea
Cocteau once made a fine remark concerning sensitivity in film music.

He said that a film score should create the sensation that one does not know whether the music is propelling the film, or the film is propelling the music. This use of cinematic music is so mysterious that I can actually say, after surviving 60-odd films, that I don't know much about it myself. I know instinctively about it, but I don't know intellectually. I have to leave that to my superiors.

The European Influence
on the Coming of Sound
to the American Film, 1925-1940:
A Survey

by Gerald F. Noxon

The European influence on the coming of sound to the American film was both varied and profound. It stemmed from conditions existing within the world film industry, from political and economic events in Europe, and from the international nature of the history of film production.

To assess comprehensively this influence is beyond the scope of a short essay. I shall therefore confine myself to a brief examination of its more obvious elements, and a few less obvious ones which seem – in hindsight – to have been important. Furthermore, I shall attend only to human elements and not to intellectual abstractions, for I have chosen to focus only upon those elements manifest in the motivations, thoughts, and actions of selected persons involved in the production of American films during the transition from silent to sound films (1925 – 1940).

To impose order on disorder, I have sorted the persons involved into three categories unclearly distinguished:

> A.   Persons of European origin whose education and experience in film production were acquired in Europe during the silent era, but who came to America, and established significant reputations in U. S. production, prior to the coming of synchronous sound.

> B.   Persons already prominent in synchronous sound production in Europe, who came to the U. S. during the transition period specifically to lend their talents to the production of sound films.

C.   Persons who do not fit neatly into categories
A or B, but who have contributed so much of a European
nature to the development of the sound film in America
that their omission in this survey would be nonsensical.
(E.g., persons of foreign origin whose training and
experience in film production were obtained in the U. S.,
but whose foreign backgrounds remained an essential influence upon their film work in this country; or persons
of American or Canadian origin whose contributions to
the sound film manifest a close association with European
ideas in general and with styles of European film production in particular.)

Having paid tribute to didactic propriety in establishing these categories, I shall ignore them quite frequently in the remainder of this essay. For it is rarely possible to evaluate a creative individual without taking into account his relationships with other individuals engaged
in the same kind of work. This fact tends to erode the validity of cat-
egorical distinctions, but in no way destroys their value as useful
markers along the road to enlightenment.

Category A

I shall begin by giving a representative listing of persons in
category A: Ernst Lubitsch, F. W. Murnau, Paul Leni, Alexander Korda,
Maurice Tourneur, Robert Florey, Paul Fejos, Michael Curtiz, Victor
Sjostrom, and Mauritz Stiller. These men are known predominantly as
directors, but most of them also worked as writers and actors in both
theatre and films in their early days in Europe. Most of them successfully made the transition from silent pictures to sound films in the
U. S. film industry, and even those who were only partially successful
in the transition, or were deemed to have failed in it, contributed
valuable ideas to the development of an American way of sound film production.

One of the most important of these directors is Ernst Lubitsch.
He was the first of a contingent of Austrian and German born, European
trained, directors who were to form so powerful and long-lasting a force
in American film production. Of all the obvious influences from Europe

on the birth and development of the American sound film, Lubitsch was
the most pervasive, the strongest, and the most durable. He sat astride
an important sector of U. S. production before, during, and long after
the coming of sound, never losing this dominant position throughout the
whole period from his earliest silent pictures made in Hollywood to the
very end of his career. And, quite apart from his own constant activity
as director and producer, Lubitsch was responsible for bringing many
other gifted European film people to Hollywood, helping them to establish themselves rapidly in the U. S. industry. If the so-called 'Lubitsch Touch' in directing can be considered important in terms of his
own art, Lubitsch's ability as an importer of film talent for the entire
production industry was of equal or greater importance to the development of the American film.

Lubitsch's story is indeed prototypical. He started as an actor
under the stage director, Max Reinhardt, in 1911, and remained an actor
from 1912 until his debut as a director of film comedies in 1914. In
Germany in the next six years he directed about 50 films of widely differing kinds, from Italian-inspired spectaculars to so-called 'sophisticated' (and certainly satirical) comedies, some of them little known
outside of Germany.

In 1923 he came to Hollywood at the behest of Mary Pickford to
direct ROSITA, and stayed to introduce his own particular brand of European, lightweight, boulevard comedy to the American film industry with
conspicuous success. He was right there on the spot for the coming of
sound, and, quite unlike most established Hollywood directors, was ready
and waiting for it. His stage experience, as well as his long and successful career in the silent film, gave him great prestige in Hollywood
where the coming of sound brought extraordinary problems and great disorder. In this unique situation, Lubitsch, who was in a position to
direct any kind of film he fancied, showed shrewd perspicacity. Instead of merely adding spoken dialogue to the kind of successful silent
comedies he had been making, such as KISS ME AGAIN and SO THIS IS PARIS,
he decided to indulge his penchant for the Viennese mode of romantic
musical comedy which he discerned to be a format peculiarly suited to

the exploitation of the new sound film. His first excursion into sound
was THE LOVE PARADE made in 1929. In this notable film he combined the
visual freedom of the silent camera, which he preferred not to surren-
der, with a new, though theatrically derived, stylistic approach to the
integration of music and dialogue. This formula was to have a mighty
and long-lasting effect on the American sound film.

F. W. Murnau, too, had been a student of Max Reinhardt, and a stage
director in Berlin before directing his first film there in 1919.   In
1922 he acquired a world-wide reputation with NOSFERATU, and extended it
in 1924 with THE LAST LAUGH.   Three years later, on the very brink of
the sound revolution, William Fox brought Murnau to Hollywood where,
without studio interference, he made his last major silent picture SUN-
RISE.   Despite its intrinsic merits, SUNRISE was a costly commercial
failure, and Murnau's subsequent career in the U. S. was soured by the
excessive studio interference to which he was thereafter subjected.

After breaking with Fox, Murnau formed an association with Robert
Flaherty for the joint production of a South Seas location film TABU.
Flaherty left the production before the film was completed.   Murnau
finished TABU himself, but died in a car accident before it was publicly
shown.   Ironically enough, TABU turned out to be a considerable financial success.   It was released with a music track added, but was neither
designed nor produced as a sound film.

Murnau, therefore, was not one of the notable directors who made a
successful move into sound film production.   This may have been due principally to his difficulties with William Fox after the ill-fated SUNRISE,
particularly in connection with his third film for Fox, OUR DAILY BREAD,
made as a silent picture in 1928.   By the time shooting was completed
and the material edited for OUR DAILY BREAD, sound films had come to
dominate Hollywood production, although many silent films were still
being made in Europe.   Fox, determined to have a sound film to market,
but against Murnau's wishes, cut the film from 2 hours and 17 minutes to
1 hour and 7 minutes, added a sound track, and finally released the hy-
brid in 1930 under the title CITY GIRL.   Obviously this unfortunate affair gravely prejudiced Murnau's chances of making a successful transi-

tion into sound film production. In this he was the victim not only of
the questionable judgement of William Fox, but also of his own untimely
death. Had he lived after TABU, he might well have proved to be as successful in sound production as he had been in the best of his silent
pictures. Certainly he possessed a wealth of talent and experience
which would have served him well.

Regardless, Murnau exerted a considerable influence on subsequent
U. S. sound film production through the artistic impact of THE LAST
LAUGH and SUNRISE, as revealed in the work of a number of successful
Hollywood directors. Frank Borzage was prominent among them. His films
THE RIVER (1929), LILIOM (1930), and A MAN'S CASTLE (1933), among others,
give strong indications of Murnau's influence.

Murnau's influence lived on in Hollywood in the work of another
director, Edgar Ulmer. Ulmer was born in Vienna in 1900. Like Lubitsch
and Murnau, he collaborated with Reinhardt and became a set designer and
assistant to Murnau on THE LAST LAUGH, TARTUFFE, and FAUST. Although he
had not directed a film on his own, Ulmer came to Hollywood in the midst
of the sound revolution with some useful credentials. They were not,
however, sufficiently impressive to lead him immediately into the direction of major sound films. He was assigned to direct second features,
some of them exploitation pictures; but even under these conditions he
maintained a standard of production artistry which revealed his European
roots and training, including his work with Murnau on some of the latter's best films. Never a major figure in Hollywood, Ulmer nevertheless
extended and reinforced European influences on the general run of production in the thirties, forties, and fifties.

In connection with Murnau's influence on both Borzage and Ulmer, it
is interesting to note that when Borzage died in 1961 during the production of ATLANTIS, THE LOST KINGDOM, Edgar Ulmer was chosen to complete
the film. By rights, Ulmer does not fit correctly into our category A
of directors, since he was not an established director in Hollywood or
elsewhere prior to the arrival of sound. But his close identification
with Murnau, whom he outlived by so many years, makes some mention of
his work logical at this point.

We come next to yet another of the German directors who worked
originally with Max Reinhardt, Paul Leni. Leni, born in 1885, was active in Kammerspiel and expressionist theatrical productions in Germany,
and directed his first Kammerspiel-influenced film BACKSTAIRS in 1921.
He followed this with several successful silent films, climaxed in 1924
by WAXWORKS - an artistically notable work and a commercial success on
an international scale. This film brought Leni an invitation from Carl
Laemmle of Universal to come to Hollywood where, in 1927, he made THE
CAT AND THE CANARY, an immensely successful horror film and a prototype
for works of this genre to the present day.

Leni was not only an outstanding director of films, but a trend-
setting art director. He designed the sets for all his own films in Germany before coming to Hollywood, and also worked as a designer for such
well-known European directors as Joe May, E. A. Dupont, Karl Grune,
Alexander Korda, Michael Curtiz, and Arthur Robison. Although Leni did
not take credit for the art direction on his films for Universal in Hollywood, he was certainly a major influence in this aspect of production,
and indeed a major influence on decor, lighting, and cinematography in
Hollywood in general. His sudden death in 1929 brought Paul Leni's
career to an untimely end, just after he had completed THE LAST WARNING,
another excellent horror film which met with great success in both silent and sound versions.

Unlike Murnau, Leni seems not to have had serious difficulties with
his Hollywood boss, Carl Laemmle. The sound version of THE LAST WARNING,
for instance, is slightly longer than the silent version, in contrast to
the violent truncation of Murnau's OUR DAILY BREAD in the sound version
released by Fox. Paul Leni was only 45 at the time of his death, but
all the evidence indicates that, had he lived, he would have continued
his successful move into sound films and might well have become an important director in Hollywood. Despite his brief activity in the sound
film, Leni's influence on the American film continued to be significant
long after his death.

Another European director with whom Leni, in the capacity of art
director, had been associated in Germany came to Hollywood in 1927. He

was Alexander Korda, later to become Sir Alexander as a result of his
subsequent production activities in Britain. It is for these latter
activities that Korda's name is generally remembered, but his influence
on U. S. production during the critical years of transition from silent
to sound films cannot be ignored.

Korda was born 'Sandor' Korda in Hungary in 1893. His two younger
brothers, Zoltan and Vincent, were also to have careers in film production - the former as a director, the latter as an art director. Both
were moderately successful, but never achieved the prominence of their
elder brother. Alexander Korda began as a film director in his native
Hungary in 1916, working successfully until 1919 when he moved first to
Germany and then to Austria. He continued to make competent and successful commercial films. It was on one of these, DER TAINZER MEINER FRAU,
made in 1925, that Paul Leni collaborated as art director.

Korda came to Hollywood in 1927, and his second film in Hollywood,
made during his first year there, laid the foundation for his subsequent
career. The film THE PRIVATE LIFE OF HELEN OF TROY, from the book by
John Erskine, was an unexpected critical and financial success in the
U. S. and in Britain. This success carried Korda through the transition into sound films, and enabled him to direct half a dozen acceptable
sound films in Hollywood during the years up to 1930. His films showed,
if not great talent, a definite ability to adapt European dramatic ideas
and forms to the tastes of U. S. and British film audiences. This ability was not ignored in Hollywood. Indeed Korda's influence on the development of the American sound film seems to have been greater than the
intrinsic worth of his Hollywood films.

With his considerable Hollywood experience behind him, Korda returned to Europe in 1930 where he settled first in France. There he
directed two films, one of which was MARIUS - the first and by far the
best screen version of Marcel Pagnol's play, with script by Pagnol himself, and with Raimu and Pierre Fresnay in leading roles. This famous
film, known and loved in countries throughout the world, greatly enhanced
Korda's reputation as a director, even though Pagnol was the important
factor in the whole production.

MARIUS and its two sequels, FANNY and CESAR, were productions of
Paramount Pictures in France, and the fact that Korda had directed the
first of them strengthened his influence on trends in the development of
the sound film in the U. S.   MARIUS was one of the first great international hits of the sound film era, despite the specifically local
character of its subject matter and its length of 2 hours and 5 minutes.
Both the subject matter and the length of the film were virtually pro-
hibited by the Hollywood thinking of the day.   Rene Clair's SOUS LES
TOITS DE PARIS, another great international sound film hit from France,
had preceeded MARIUS by only a few months, and with its visual emphases,
musical integration, and minimal dialogue had provided an equally strong
challenge to the 100%-all-talking Hollywood concept of the sound film.
These two French hits, one directed by Korda, served to underline the
approach to the sound film adopted by Ernst Lubitsch in THE LOVE PARADE.
All three of these films made big money at the box office, and, what was
perhaps more important to Hollywood, made it in the international film
market.   As the 1930s began, the question of whether or not the Hollywood sound film could command the great international acceptance which
U. S. silent productions had achieved and maintained was giving Hollywood producers many sleepless nights.   THE LOVE PARADE, SOUS LES TOITS
DE PARIS, and MARIUS gave reasons for optimism in connection with the
appeal of the sound film internationally, but also gave serious reasons
to doubt the validity of the heavily dialogue-oriented films which had
generally dominated Hollywood production since the first days of sound.
Both the optimism and the doubts stemmed largely from European examples,
and Alexander Korda was a considerable factor in the deliberations of
the time.

Korda could have returned to work in Hollywood had he wished to do
so, or he could have continued to make films in France or elsewhere on
the European mainland.   But he had other ideas.   He went to England to
found London Films, a production company organized largely by and for
himself, and dominated by him as director and producer for a decade.
This move did not curtail Korda's influence on the development of the
American sound film, but rather accentuated it.

In 1933 Korda produced and directed for London Films THE PRIVATE
LIFE OF HENRY THE EIGHTH, inspired by the success some six years before
of his Hollywood silent film THE PRIVATE LIFE OF HELEN OF TROY. HENRY
THE EIGHTH had a marked and somewhat alarming effect on Hollywood, not
so much because it was so successful critically and financially in Britain and throughout Europe, but because it proved to be a unique box
office hit in the U. S! It was, indeed, the first British sound film to
achieve a major financial success in the U. S. Although it was made in
Britain, it was not just another British film, but the combination of
British talent with that of the European continent. It was the first
British film to emulate successfully the Hollywood technique of assem-
bling talent from a number of countries to exploit the film internationally while maintaining a domestic financial base.

Hollywood was quick to realize the potential threat that appeared
in THE PRIVATE LIFE OF HENRY THE EIGHTH. The script of the film was by
Lajos Biro, an Hungarian, with an important assist from Arthur Wimperis,
a British author. The decor was by another Hungarian, Vincent Korda;
the music by Kurt Schroeder, a German; and the brilliant cinematography
by Georges Perinal, a Frenchman. The excellent cast provided the British contribution of thoroughly stage-trained but film-conscious professional actors. HENRY THE EIGHTH was probably the film by which Korda
exerted the greatest influence on the development of the American sound
film, both for its intrinsic entertainment value in the international
market, and for the implications which the adoption of the international
talent policies of London Films held for the future.

Apart from Korda's direct influence on Hollywood production, the
direction of growth which he gave to London Films, with the support of
important British financiers, was the cause of a more general but serious
concern to Hollywood producers. As a producer, Korda sponsored the first
specifically international English language film by Rene Clair, THE GHOST
GOES WEST, with a script by the American Robert Sherwood. Korda likewise
engaged William Cameron Menzies in 1936 to direct the well-remembered
version of H. G. Wells's THINGS TO COME. Menzies was a well known Hollywood art director who had been strongly influenced by the German ex-

pressionist school of film decor ever since working with Lubitsch in
1923 on the latter's first U. S. film ROSITA. In 1937 Korda introduced
the famous Belgian director, Jacques Feyder, to the English language
sound film by bringing him to London to direct KNIGHT WITHOUT ARMOUR;
and in 1940 he produced the first English language film LYDIA by the
well known French director, Julien Duvivier.

The advent of war in Europe ended the threat that London Films and
Alexander Korda had presented to Hollywood. Clair, Duvivier, and Feyder
came to the U. S. to make films, and Korda himself returned to Hollywood, where in 1942 he produced TO BE OR NOT TO BE for United Artists,
directed by Ernst Lubitsch. It seemed at that time that Korda had been
re-absorbed into his Hollywood past, but there was still some life left
in London Films. After the war Korda returned to Britain where he produced, in 1948 and 1949 respectively, THE FALLEN IDOL and THE THIRD MAN,
both directed by Carol Reed and scripted by Graham Greene from his own
stories. These two films are generally regarded as the best produced
by Korda, the best directed by Carol Reed, and the best film versions of
Graham Greene originals. But, ironically, they marked the virtual end
of Korda's long career. He produced only two more films of lesser interest before his death in Hollywood in 1956. Clearly, however, in many
ways other than the directing of films, Alexander Korda's influence on
the birth and development of the American sound film was far greater
than his lack of artistry and weakness for ostentatious vacuity might
suggest.

So far we have dealt chiefly with directors and producers of Austrian, German, and Hungarian origins, sharing to a great extent a common
background in the German cinema. We now consider a Frenchman, Maurice
Tourneur, whose earliest experience in film was obtained exclusively in
the French film industry, but who came to the U. S. in the very early
days of the silent cinema. He was born in Paris in 1876, but his influence on the American film was so broadly based and lasting that it
has carried over from the silent era into sound and cannot be ignored in
this study.

Maurice Tourneur began as an artist, a pupil of Puvis de Chavannes and Auguste Rodin. He became a stage director under the famous Antoine, then a film actor and director for the Eclair Company in Paris. In 1914 he came to the U. S. to head the Eclair Studio in Tucson. He made about 60 films in the U. S. before deciding, in 1927, that supervisory inter- ference with his work in Hollywood was becoming unacceptable. Returning to France, he made at least 20 more films of variable quality but rea- sonable success. He was seventy-two when he made his last and one of his best films IMPASSE DES DEUX ANGES.

Although Tourneur made his successful transition from silent to sound films in France, it was by the narrowest of temporal margins. His long and active career as a director in the U. S. covered the develop- ment of the American cinema from the first years of its gradual ascent to a position of world dominance right up to the coming of sound. Dur- ing this period Tourneur worked with many persons destined to prominence in film production in the U. S. His effect on many of them was so pro- found that his influence carried over into the development of the sound film in Hollywood long after he himself had returned to France.

Tourneur's early association with the American scenarist, Jules Furthman, who wrote the script for Tourneur's version of Stevenson's TREASURE ISLAND in 1920, made a lasting impression on the man who was to become one of the best of U. S. screen writers of the thirties and for- ties. Furthman worked principally with von Sternberg on such films as UNDERWORLD, THE DOCKS OF NEW YORK, MOROCCO, and SHANGHAI EXPRESS; but also with Howard Hawks on COME AND GET IT, THE BIG SLEEP, and other Hawks films; with Paul Fejos on BROADWAY; with Raoul Walsh on BODY AND SOUL; and on films for Howard Hughes, Edmond Goulding, and Richard Fleischer. Tourneur's influence on American directors from D. W. Grif- fith onwards was also major. In the silent days perhaps Rex Ingram owed most to Tourneur, followed in the sound era by Clarence Brown. Brown was Tourneur's co-director on THE LAST OF THE MOHICANS in 1920, and the experience marked his whole future as a director.

But Maurice Tourneur's influence on the American film went far be- yond the aspects manifest in the work of particular directors. He brought to U. S. production generally the then-novel conception of film

as an art in whose service cinematography, dramaturgy, decor, and acting
must be fused into an entirely new form of human communication. He
brought this conception with him to the U. S. in 1914. It derived from
his own experience and training in Europe, and stemmed not only from
Puvis de Chavannes and Rodin, but from Mayakovsky, Antoine, Jacques
Copeau, Max Reinhardt, and Stanislavski.

Perhaps, however, it is Tourneur's influence on the selection of
story material for American films that has proved to be the strongest
and most durable. He never ceased to urge American directors and producers to look to the modern classics in literature for their stories,
and he practiced what he preached in his own American films: THE BLUE-
BIRD from Maeterlinck and A DOLL'S HOUSE from Ibsen in 1918; THE WHITE
CIRCLE and TREASURE ISLAND from R. L. Stevenson in 1920; VICTORY from
Conrad in 1919; and THE LAST OF THE MOHICANS from Fennimore Cooper in
1922. These were the kinds of story material that he consistently ad-
vocated as a base for the development of the American film, and not without effect. Clarence Brown was probably the American director whose
work as a whole and whose choice of story material was most strongly influenced by Maurice Tourneur. Among Brown's better films of the sound
era we find story materials which were in close accord with Tourneur's
ideas of what should be selected for worthwhile American films: ANNA
KARENINA from Tolstoy and AH! WILDERNESS from O'Neill in 1935; THE HUMAN
COMEDY in 1943 from William Saroyan; THE YEARLING in 1947 and INTRUDER
IN THE DUST in 1949 from William Faulkner. The latter film, coming almost 20 years after Tourneur's THE LAST OF THE MOHICANS, seems to fulfil
admirably with its stark realism the cinematic requirements of a film
version of a modern American literary classic. This notable screen
adaptation seems, in fact, a kind of tribute to the ideals of film art
so long proclaimed by Tourneur in the U. S. and elsewhere. The film was
released just a year after Tourneur's retirement from active production
in France.

Another Frenchman, Robert Florey, arrived and settled in Hollywood
in 1921. Before his move to the U. S., Florey had been an assistant to
the French film pioneer, Louie Feuillade, one of the most prolific and

original of the early European filmmakers. In Hollywood Florey worked
first as an assistant to Louis Gasnier, a veteran director of serials
who was the first head of production for Pathe Freres in America, and is
remembered today chiefly as the man who made both THE PERILS OF PAULINE
and THE EXPLOITS OF ELAINE. Late in the 1920s Florey made several experimental shorts in collaboration with the Serbian artist Slavko Vorkapich. Vorkapich arrived in Hollywood about the same time as Florey,
working first in film as an actor. Later he became a specialist in the
creation of montage sequences for the major studios and a well known
teacher of film at the University of Southern California and elsewhere.

The chief importance of Florey and Vorkapich in the context of this
study lies in the fact that they brought with them to Hollywood a sophisticated knowledge and appreciation of contemporary European art,
particularly the Dada and Surrealist movements that were little known in
the Hollywood production establishment of the day. It was not until
much later indeed, after World War II, that the significant relationship
between the films of Feuillade and Gasnier and Surrealism was generally
remarked upon, and the status of these and other early directors favor-
ably noted.

Robert Florey did not find the going easy in Hollywood in the 1920s.
He did, however, eventually find work as an assistant to several prominent American directors, including King Vidor and von Sternberg. Florey,
although achieving no great conventional success in Hollywood, exerted
a strong and enduring influence going far beyond that which his list of
screen credits might indicate. He and Vorkapich were among those extremely rare individuals who succeeded in challenging to some degree the
commercial or pseudo-artistic attitude which dominated Hollywood in the
1920s. They did so not simply by talking, but by making short experimental films on shoe-string budgets. At least one such film is still
remembered, LIFE AND DEATH OF 9413, A HOLLYWOOD EXTRA, made on the brink
of the transition to sound in 1928.

Unlike Vorkapich, his collaborator, Florey did not go into film
teaching, but remained constant in his search for success as the director
of theatrical film features. He got his first genuine chance in Holly-

wood, appropriately enough, as co-director of the Marx Brothers' film
COCOANUTS. Thereafter he was relegated to a miscellany of second features until, in 1947, he became associate director with Charles Chaplin
on MONSIEUR VERDOUX. Florey had to wait many long years to get to work
on the kind of film he really appreciated. But his presence, and his
fund of enthusiasm for American films in general over those long years,
have not been forgotten in Hollywood. Florey has written several books
about Hollywood, including a recent volume dealing with the earliest
days of filmmaking on the West Coast, Hollywood, Annees Zero, published
by Seghers in Paris in 1972. He was ever a civilizing influence on the
American film, silent and sound.

A somewhat later, but quite extraordinary, arrival in Hollywood was
Paul Fejos, another recruit from Hungary. Fejos was born in Budapest in
1898, and died there in 1963 after one of the strangest film careers
imaginable. He started in his native land as a director, turning out a
series of 'quickies' made on shoe-string budgets in an average shooting
time of one week per picture. The subject matter of these films was
extremely varied, ranging from an adaptation of Oscar Wilde's THE CRIME
OF LORD ARTHUR SAVILLE to THE LAST ADVENTURE OF ARSENE LUPIN. This
whirlwind activity continued from 1920 until 1923, when extreme economic
difficulties forced Fejos to abandon a film in mid-production and leave
the country in search of a career elsewhere. He made his way to the
U. S. via Vienna, Berlin, and Paris. There is some evidence that he
worked for both Max Reinhardt and Fritz Lang along the way.

He arrived in New York in 1924 without money and unable to speak
English. As a youth he had studied medicine, which enabled him to get
an $80-a-month job at the Rockefeller Research Institute as a laboratory
assistant to a Japanese professor who was also short on English. At the
same time he contrived to work as a kind-of stage manager-advisor on a
Theatre Guild production of Ferenc Molnar's THE GLASS SLIPPER. By 1926
Fejos had saved enough money - $40 according to the legend - to drive
across the country to California in an old Buick.

He finally arrived in Hollywood where, after a difficult period, he
teamed up with Leon Shamroy who was trying to get established as a young

cameraman. By what can only be termed a 'miracle', they managed to bor-
row $5000 from a Mr. Edward Spitz, and with that money Fejos directed,
with prodigious ingenuity, his first American film THE LAST MOMENT. It
was completed in 1927, and shown to Hollywood's critic a la mode, Welford
Beaton, who praised it to Chaplin. Chaplin, in turn, found it excellent,
as did Mary Pickford and Douglas Fairbanks. The immediate result was
that Fejos received a contract to direct for Universal.

In 1928 Fejos completed his second American film, the silent LONE-
SOME, an even greater success than THE LAST MOMENT, and termed by Beaton
"a work of genius". Within a couple of years, Fejos had jumped to the
top of the Hollywood heap through his own talent, courage, and ingenuity,
and aided by rare good luck. What is more, he had done it by directing
two excellent and highly original films. This sequence of events is
probably without parallel in the annals of Hollywood.

Fejos made the transition from silent to sound films in 1929 with
BROADWAY, an adaptation of a stage piece with music by Philip Dunning
and George Abbot. The adaptation was by Edward T. Low, Jr., and Charles
Furthman, brother of Jules Furthman whom we have mentioned above. (The
surname keeps surfacing in the main stream development of the American
sound film.) Hal Mohr was responsible for the innovative cinematography,
including a final sequence in Technicolor. BROADWAY had a million dollar budget, about twice what an average Hollywood picture cost at that
time. After spending $5000 on THE LAST MOMENT, and an adequate but
modest amount on LONESOME (which had included some sound sequences),
Fejos found himself commanding all the resources of the largest sound
stage in Hollywood, including a new $25,000 crane built especially for
the film and sufficiently silent in operation to permit a wide variety
of camera shots during the sound takes. In spite of the fact that
BROADWAY was not the kind of subject that Fejos might have chosen for
himself at this point in his career, he did a satisfactory job and demonstrated some of his inventive drive and inherent originality. The
commercial success of the film was practically assured by the fact that
the stage original had run for over two years in New York, and had been
staged by road companies all over the U. S.

While directing his next film for Universal, CAPTAIN OF THE GUARD, a musical fantasy about the French Revolution, Fejos suffered an injury by falling from the scaffolding of a huge set built for a scene representing the storming of the Bastille. He was in bed for 6 weeks, and John Stuart Robinson took over the direction of the film for which he, rather than Fejos, received direction credit.

A disagreement with Carl Laemmle Jr. over his next directing assignment for Universal, THE KING OF JAZZ, resulted in the termination of Fejos's contract with the studio. Fejos then signed with MGM, accepting as a first assignment the direction of the French and German versions of THE BIG HOUSE in 1930. The scenario was by Frances Marion, another name that keeps cropping up whenever the best of the early American sound films are discussed. THE BIG HOUSE, directed in the English version by George Hill and starring Wallace Beery, was a tremendous success, marking a new step forward in the evolution of the sound film in Hollywood. The French and German versions were judged to be equally good, and Paul Fejos was given full credit for excellent work on both. He had some superior helpers: in addition to Frances Marion who did the scenario, Ernst Toller worked on the German dialogue, and Douglas Shearer created a sound track which was technically far above Hollywood standards for the times.

Thus, Fejos worked with the best creative and technical talent available in the U. S. at the time on his last direction assignment in Hollywood, THE BIG HOUSE. Both Frances Marion and Shearer won Oscars for their work on the film. Fejos certainly learned a great deal from his Hollywood experience, but he had far more to give in return than the industry was capable of absorbing in those early days of sound. His kind of personal film, marked with his own brand of direct human warmth and tenderness, expressed with the aid of his great natural gift for lyric cinema, and tempered by his ever-present delicate irony and the economy of his cinematic style, could find no broad base of support in the Hollywood industry of the day. So, without actually breaking his contract with MGM, Fejos in 1931 accepted an invitation from Pierre Braunberger to make sound films in France.

Although Hollywood could not provide Fejos with the means of making
his own kind of film, many of Hollywood's most talented and creative
film people were moved and inspired by his work, and his influence was
more profound than could be realized and understood at the time. Indeed, it was not until after the end of World War II, when the great
Italian neo-realist school of cinema came into being, that the promise
of Fejos and LONESOME was fulfilled and world-wide acceptance of his
kind of film came about.

In the meantime Fejos continued his extraordinary career as a filmmaker, directing dramatic films for commercial distribution in France,
in his native Hungary, in Austria, and in Denmark. After 1935 his interest turned to documentary, in particular to anthropological films,
which he made for Danish and Swedish producers in Madagascar, the East
Indies, Siam, and Peru. In 1939 Fejos returned to the U. S., not to
make films in Hollywood, but rather to settle in New York where he was
to become an outstanding research anthropologist before his death in
1963.

Yet another Hungarian director of considerable importance to this
study was Michael Curtiz, who was born in Budapest in 1888, ten years
before Paul Fejos, and died in Hollywood in 1962. Curtiz left his native land for Denmark in 1913, then a leader in world film production.
It is claimed that in Denmark he worked with both Stiller and Sjostrom,
and became assistant to August Blom on ATLANTIS (an extraordinarily advanced film cinematically) in which Curtiz also acted. Having benefited
by his Scandanavian experiences, he returned to Hungary where in the
next 5 or 6 years he made dozens of films. His nigh-incredible capacity
for work, and his ability to apply himself to any kind of subject matter
with acceptable results, had already established his value as a commercial director of note by the end of World War I. In 1919 the economic
woes of Hungary forced Curtiz to leave for Vienna, as had both Korda and
Fejos before him. Curtiz made at least a score of films in Austria before moving to Berlin, where he managed to make at least 4 films in less
than a year. In 1926 he was hired by Warner Brothers and went to Hollywood. With his usual immediate application to the work at hand, Curtiz,

despite language difficulties and a completely new environment, made 10
silent films in two years, including the super-spectacular NOAH'S ARK
to which some sound was added. Warner Brothers had brought Curtiz to
Hollywood to make this high budget feature, designed to out-class C. B.
de Mille at his own game, but first assigned him to direct the other
silent pictures to familiarize himself with Hollywood production methods.
By 1928 he was ready for the big one. The flood scenes in NOAH'S ARK
surpassed anything that had been previously seen in any de Mille production, thanks to all concerned - including Hal Mohr, the chief camera
operator, who had worked for Curtiz on some of his first Hollywood silent films.

With NOAH'S ARK Curtiz had reached the pinnacle of silent film production in the Hollywood style. It must be remembered, of course, that
Curtiz, unlike Fejos, had some 60 silent films to his credit and a truly
international reputation before he was brought under contract to Hollywood. But apart from past experience and reputation, Curtiz was by
nature singularly well-geared to the Hollywood production line techniques for turning out films continuously and in rapid succession. In
fact, Hollywood had nothing to teach Curtiz about speed in production.
If anything it was the other way around. Nor did he have much to learn
about assessing the box-office value of story materials or stars. He
could and did work with an amazing variety of subject matter, and with
all kinds of star players - old ones, good and bad, and many new ones
whom he created himself as he went rolling along at top speed. When it
came time for Curtiz to make the full transition from silent to sound
production, he was more than ready. He waited until 1930 to make MAMMY
with Al Jolson, an all-talking-singing picture in Technicolor that showed
a surprising feeling for a typically American brand of nostalgic myth.
It showed an equally surprising degree of sophistication in the design
of the camerawork, the contrapuntal manipulation of sound, and the integration of vocal numbers. In this, his first complete Hollywood sound
film, Curtiz contributed many valuable and influential techniques. MAM-
MY is not simply a photographed stage musical, but an even more cinematically perfected work than (e.g.) Lubitsch's LOVE PARADE.

After the success of MAMMY, Curtiz made no less than 67 films for
Warner Brothers over a period of 23 years. In addition he made 15 pictures for other Hollywood producers including 20th Century Fox, Paramount, and MGM. At the time of his retirement in 1961 Curtiz had made
97 features in Hollywood, of which 10 were silent and the rest sound.
He died in 1962.

If only for the number of commercially acceptable films that Curtiz
made, and the variety of subject matter that he successfully treated in
them, his influence on the development of the American sound film must
be rated as considerable. And that influence was fundamentally European!
The majority of his films have a quality that is neither easily described
nor precisely evaluated. It seems, however, that the Curtiz 'touch' has
most to do with his surprising capacity to enter into an instinctive understanding of, and sensitivity to, a wide range of important American
myths, while at the same time retaining a perspective on the subject
which derives from his European point of view. Perhaps for these reasons Curtiz is more highly valued in Europe for his artistic achievements
than in Hollywood, where he is remembered chiefly for the extraordinary
consistency of his commercial success.

Passing from foreign directors whose influence on the American film
was predominantly German, Austrian, French, Central European, or an amal-
gam of all four, we come to the Scandinavians. First and foremost among
them is Victor Sjostrom, born in Sweden in 1879. He began as a stage
actor and manager, and then became a screen actor with the Swedish Bio-
graph Company in 1912, appearing in one of Stiller's films. He soon
moved into directing, and, working with great speed even for those days,
completed some 50 silent films of which THE PHANTOM CHARIOT is probably
the best known. He came to Hollywood in 1923 and made half-a-dozen silent pictures, of which THE SCARLET LETTER was the best, before finally
making THE WIND, now recognized as a _film a clef_ in the coming of sound.

THE WIND, begun in 1927 for MGM, was intended to be a silent film,
and a silent version was in fact released in Europe in that same year
when very few European theatres were equipped for sound. In Hollywood
MGM was anxious to have a sound film to market, and, although Sjostrom

did not supervise the sound version, the nature of THE WIND lent itself
to the addition of post-synchronized sound effects. The film seems almost to call out for the kind of sound track which MGM added, and its
success helped greatly to establish the cinematic validity of natural
sound effects as distinct from synchronized dialogue. Unfortunately,
MGM also changed the ending of the film in the sound version from tragic
to happy. Even so, the sound version stands up remarkably well today.

After making THE WIND, Sjostrom returned to Sweden, where he directed only two more films before devoting himself exclusively to acting.
He thus failed, for unclear reasons, to complete a successful transition
from silent to sound films in Hollywood or elsewhere. But he left THE
WIND as a transitional monument that seems to grow in importance with
the years.

Another great Scandinavian director, Mauritz Stiller, was in Hollywood during the transition to sound. Unfortunately, he never made a
sound film there, and his stay in America was not a great success (unlike that of his protege, Greta Garbo). On the whole the direct influence of the Scandinavians on the coming of sound to American films
was surprisingly slight, considering their great natural talent for the
cinema. Their influence, however, ought not to be ignored, if only on
account of THE WIND.

Frances Marion (of whom we have spoken before in connection with
Paul Fejos and THE BIG HOUSE) was the screenwriter for Victor Sjostrom
on both THE SCARLET LETTER and THE WIND, and for Frank Borzage on HUMOR-
ESQUE in 1920. Her long career in Hollywood well illustrates how the
influence of foreign directors on the American film extended far beyond
the effect of the films for which they were personally responsible. As
a result of the efforts of American scenarists like Marion and Jules
Furthman, cinematographers like Gregg Toland and Hal Mohr, and art directors like Cedric Gibbons and Van Nest Polglase, all of whom worked
for top directors of both European and American origin, the influence of
European ideas on all aspects of production spread pervasively through
the U. S. studios. At no time was this influence more important than
during the transition from silent to sound production.

We come now come to two film artists, both natives of Austria, whose impact on the development of the American film, silent and sound, is so important and so widely recognized as to require only brief and confirmatory mention in this study. They are Eric Oswald Stroheim, born in Vienna in 1885, and Joseph Stern, born in the same city in 1894. Each of them added a 'von' to his name, and Stern changed his name to 'Sternberg' as well. Both had complicated careers in the film industry which make it difficult to fit them into our categories accurately, but this is probably the best place to discuss them with a brevity in no way proportionate to their importance.

Von Stroheim came to the U. S. some time before World War I, and made his first appearance in the film industry as a Hollywood film extra in 1914. His career as a film director began as an assistant to D. W. Griffith, but it was his excellence as a screen actor which drew the attention of Carl Laemmle at Universal, who gave him his first opportunity to direct on BLIND HUSBANDS.

Von Stroheim completed few films, and none of them with a finished sound track by him. His monumental silent film GREED, however, set standards for realism in the American film which are as valid today as they were in 1924 when the film was made. Although all of Von Stroheim's work as a director was done in the U. S., his lasting influence on film production in the U. S. was overwhelmingly European in content. He himself said that European writers of the 19th century realist school (Dickens, Zola, and De Maupassant prominent among them) were the sources of his cinematic style.

Von Sternberg's importance, however, is more clearly related to the development of the sound film than that of Von Stroheim's, if neither so great in scope nor perhaps so obvious, and his career is more complicated in an international sense. He was brought to the U. S. by his parents at the age of 7, who then sent him back to Vienna to complete his schooling. He returned to the U. S. and served his film apprenticeship with the World Film Company in New York. During World War I he helped to make training films for the U. S. Army Signal Corps. Thus, although Austrian by birth and education, he obtained his first film experience in America. Von Sternberg's first participation in a feature film in the U. S., however, was as an assistant director to a Frenchman, Emile Chautard, on a film adapted in 1919 from a French original by Maurice Leblanc, THE MYSTERY OF THE YELLOW ROOM.

The next 4 or 5 years were difficult ones for Von Sternberg. He worked intermittently and variously as assistant cameraman and scenarist in New York, London, and Hollywood. He picked up his first screenwriting credit on BY DIVINE RIGHT, a film directed by Roy William Neill in 1924 on which Von Sternberg also served as assistant director.

In spite of his initial film experiences in the U. S., Von Sternberg came to his first feature directing assignment with a viewpoint dominated by European film ideas and screen techniques. Although, therefore, he had never directed a silent feature in Europe, his first silent picture THE SALVATION HUNTERS, made from his own scenario for distribution by United Artists, was fundamentally a European work. It stemmed directly from the symbol-laden style of the German Kammerspiel dramas. Von Sternberg was thoroughly embued with the post-expressionist theories of the great German scenarist, Carl Mayer, and he readily adopted the unique mixture of realism and symbolic values which characterized Mayer's work as the leading exponent of Kammerspiel drama.

THE SALVATION HUNTERS was frankly experimental, and had no commercial significance. It was not until he directed UNDERWORLD in 1927 for Paramount that Von Sternberg began to achieve importance as a director of silent pictures in Hollywood. UNDERWORLD was the result of the application of the basic dramatic principles of Kammerspiel to the essentiall American sub-world of gangsterism, a subject matter which had up to that time been neglected by Hollywood. UNDERWORLD revealed gangsterism as an immensely rich vein of subject material for the cinema. The film was an enormous success in the U. S. and in Europe, and had a powerful influence on the production policies of Hollywood for many years to come. UNDERWORLD likewise secured for Von Sternberg a dominant position at Par amount which lasted some 8 years, during which time he directed 14 films One film, THE BLUE ANGEL, was made in Germany in collaboration with UFA studios and producer Eric Pommer in both German and English versions.

A detailed examination of the screen credits on UNDERWORLD is en-
lightening. It discloses an interrelationship of persons who were destined, both in themselves and in their interactions with others, to influence greatly the coming of sound to the American film. The directing
credit is, of course, Von Sternberg's, but he also receives an editing
credit for the film. The writing credits include three names in addition to that of Von Sternberg: Ben Hecht, Robert N. Lee, and Jules Furthman. For Ben Hecht, UNDERWORLD marked the beginning of a long career as
one of Hollywood's best and best-known screenwriters. His short gang-
ster-story outline, on which UNDERWORLD was to some extent based, won
Ben Hecht an Oscar and established a kind of Kammerspiel-gangster syn-
drome that influenced not only Hecht himself but many other screenwriters, directors, and producers for decades. This marriage of German
dramatic sensibilities and film techniques, as epitomized in the work of
Carl Mayer, with the characteristically violent elements of American
folklore, has proved to be one of the most durable of all Hollywood mar-
riages, and one of the most profitable to all concerned. It was even
fed back into the main stream of European film production of the late
1930s and onwards via the poetic-realist school of French cinema.

The second writing credit on UNDERWORLD went to Robert N. Lee, who
seems to have been involved more or less as a studio watchdog to guard
against any outrageous nonconformity with commercial aims on the part of
the as-yet-untested director. The third credit to Jules Furthman was
perhaps the most phophetic of the three, since he became one of Von
Sternberg's preferred screenwriters. He scripted 7 more films for Von
Sternberg, including some of the best of the Von Sternberg-Marlene Dietrich successes.

The credit for art direction on UNDERWORLD went to Hans Dreier, the
famous German who was to become an even more constant collaborator with
Von Sternberg than Jules Furthman. Dreier designed at least a dozen
films for Von Sternberg, and his sense of decor played an unusually important part in the success of Von Sternberg's films. He brought to
Von Sternberg exactly the kind of visual background needed to support
the developing opulence of the latter's style as he moved from symbolic

realism to an ever greater indulgence in the exotic and imaginative ba-
roque. Through his association with Von Sternberg, Dreir became firmly
installed at Paramount. He brought his Germanic talents to the service
of a wide range of Hollywood directors from Ernst Lubitsch to Preston
Sturges, with whom he collaborated on HAIL THE CONQUERING HERO! in 1944.

Von Sternberg, aided by both Jules and Charles Furthman as screenwriters and Dreier as art director, made a satisfactory if not brilliant
transition from silent to sound films with THUNDERBOLT in 1929. This
debut in sound, however, was entirely eclipsed and forgotten the next
year by the overwhelming success of THE BLUE ANGEL, a film introducing
Marlene Dietrich (and, incidentally, the only sound film directed by an
essentially Germanic director in Germany up to that time).

Whatever may be thought of the quality of Von Sternberg's work as
a whole, his influence on the coming of sound to the American film was
European in nature, and one which proved itself to be both profound and
lasting.

Category B

We come now to our second category of filmmakers: persons already
firmly established in sound film production in their respective countrie
before coming to the U. S. In most cases these persons possessed world-
wide reputations in their areas of expertise, and were invited to come
to Hollywood expressly to lend their talents to the development of U. S.
sound film production. They accepted, or in some cases solicited, these
invitations for a variety of reasons. Some simply wanted the opportunit
to work in the world's foremost center of film production, to learn what
they could from the experience, and to make more money than they could
elsewhere. Others came as refugees from political persecution in their
homelands, and in anticipation of worse conditions yet to come as a result of the outbreak of war in Europe.

Among these persons were producer Eric Pommer; directors William
Dieterle, Max Reinhardt, Fritz Lang, G. W. Pabst, E. A. Dupont, Anatole
Litvak, Rene Clair, Julien Duvivier, Jean Renoir, and Jacques Feyder;

cinematographers Karl Freund, Rudolph Mate, Eugen Schufftan, Boris
Kaufman, and Franz Planer; and art directors Hans Dreier, James Basevi,
and Eugene Lourie. These people of varied talents came to Hollywood
mostly in the mid or late 1930s, after the initial imperfections in
sound recording techniques had been remedied, and a considerable degree
of mobility had been restored to the camera. It was, therefore, because
of their artistic achievements in what had become a stabilized technical
process of filmmaking on an international scale that these people were
brought or made their way to Hollywood. They came not so much as pioneers in a new medium, but as leaders in an established one.

Fritz Lang must, I think, be considered as the most important of
the above listed directors in the context of this study. Apart from his
long and distinguished career in the German silent film, Lang's highly
effective use of natural sound and minimal dialogue in M made him a director of the greatest potential interest to Hollywood producers. His
difficulties in Germany with the Hitler regime made him look with favor
on working abroad, first in France and then in the U. S. He came to MGM
to make his first American film FURY in 1936. It was an extraordinary
achievement in that he was able to sustain in it all the quality of his
best European work. Fritz Lang directed more than a score of films in
Hollywood, of which at least half-a-dozen are of truly superior quality.
His work in Europe and America is so well known in general, and so many
of his films are still in distribution, that his great influence on the
American sound film in its most sensitive and formative period needs no
emphasis here. Despite mixed verdicts on his work from critics and sometimes the box office, we need only look at FURY, THE WOMAN IN THE WINDOW,
and WHILE THE CITY SLEEPS, or almost any other of the 19 films directed
by Lang currently available in the U. S. in 16mm distribution, to grasp
the extent to which he still participates in the mainstream of development of the American sound film.

G. W. Pabst, another German director with a career in European silent and sound films at least as distinguished as that of Fritz Lang
(and in some ways far more interesting), did not fare nearly so well as
his compatriot in Hollywood. He came in 1934 and directed only one film,

A MODERN HERO, which was unsuccessful. He returned to Europe forthwith.
Nevertheless, his three German sound films, WESTFRONT 1918 made in 1930,
and DIE DREIGROSCHENOPER and KAMERADSCHAFT made in 1931, are landmarks
in the early development of the sound film, and exerted powerful influence on Hollywood productions.

Somewhat similar to Pabst's experience in Hollywood was that of E.
A. Dupont, another established German director. His work cannot compare
in scope or quality with that of Pabst or Lang, and the many silent
films he made for the UFA producer, Eric Pommer, were run-of-the-mill
except for one picture VARIETY made in 1925. This starkly realistic
work, starring Emil Jannings, was such a tremendous critical and box
office success, particularly in the U. S., that it influenced Hollywood
producers well through the coming of sound. Dupont never made another
film half as successful as VARIETY, either in Britain where he made the
transition from silent to sound films, or in Hollywood where he arrived
in 1936 to make a few undistinguished films. All his influence stemmed
from VARIETY, and that film remains the only one available in the U. S.
today in a 16mm version.

One of Dupont's proteges, William Dieterle, had better luck than
his patron in Hollywood, although he started out there by co-directing
a gradiose flop. His co-director on the financial fiasco A MIDSUMMER
NIGHT'S DREAM was the famous German stage director, Max Reinhardt. It
was the latter's first and last excursion into sound film. The film was
generally recognized as a grotesque blunder, and its impact was entirely
negative. Reinhardt returned forthwith to Germany.

William Dieterle, however, stayed on in Hollywood to make a distinc-
tive niche for himself in sound film production by developing and directing a series of biographical films which came to constitute a readily
identifiable and successful Hollywood genre: THE STORY OF LOUIS PASTEUR,
THE LIFE OF EMILE ZOLA, JUAREZ, and DR. ERLICH'S MAGIC BULLET. These
were not films of cinematic innovation, but they introduced and validated
commercially a subject matter which, although treated in a simplistically
popular vein, was still a cut above the norm of Hollywood production in
the 1930s. The fact that many of these titles are still available today

in the U. S. in 16mm versions shows that they had, and still have, a
valid claim to importance in the development of the American sound film.
Apart from these biographical films, Dieterle made a number of successful commercial films in Hollywood, including SATAN MET A LADY, the second of three versions made in Hollywood within a decade of Dashiel Ham-
mett's novel The Maltese Falcon, and notable for a particularly skillful
performance by Bette Davis. Dieterle seemed to run out of steam after
the end of World War II, but he stayed in Hollywood making routine films
until 1958 when he returned to Germany. His influence on Hollywood is
important, but it was largely confined to the biographical films of the
1930s.

Other directors from other countries came to Hollywood as well.
Anatole Litvak, born in Russia in 1902, worked as director in Germany,
France, and Britain before coming to Hollywood in 1937. He contributed
substantially to Hollywood production from the late 1930s through the
1950s, directing films of differing kinds, most of them superior to the
norm: films such as BLUES IN THE NIGHT, THE BATTLE OF STALINGRAD, THE
SNAKEPIT, and SORRY, WRONG NUMBER. Litvak retained a stronger European
flavor in many of his Hollywood films than most transplanted directors,
but he was more of a component in Hollywood's development than a seminal
influence on it. He supplied the kind of European flavor already in
demand.

Jacques Feyder, another famous director, Belgian by birth but
French by adoption, arrived in Hollywood in 1929 in the midst of the
sound revolution. The immediate cause of his departure from Europe was
the banning by the French government of his silent satirical comedy
LES NOUVEAUX MESSIEURS made in 1928. Feyder accepted an offer from Hollywood to direct Greta Garbo in THE KISS (1929). The film was a taste-
ful and intelligent, if somewhat uninspired, piece of work, which is
more than can be said of the rest of the films he directed during the
four years that he stayed in Hollywood. There was simply nothing in his
Hollywood films to recall the brilliance of his silent films made in
France: L'ATLANTIDE, CRAINQUEBILLE, and the great version of Zola's THE-
RESE RAQUIN (now unfortunately a 'lost' film).

Feyder and Hollywood were mutually incompatible, a situation which
was not due to a loss of talent on Feyder's part. This fact was soon
confirmed by the quality of the films he made on his return to France.
In collaboration with an old friend, the screenwriter Charles Spaak,
Feyder directed 3 films in 2 years, LE GRAND JEU (1934), PENSION MIMOSAS
(1935), and LA KERMESSE HEROIQUE (CARNIVAL IN FLANDERS). It is the latter film, completed in 1935 but still a favorite on U. S. screens, which
justifies Feyder as an influence on the sound film in Hollywood and on
the making of historical films everywhere. After this great success
Feyder's talents seemed to fade. He worked spasmodically in Britain,
Germany, and Switzerland, where he died in 1948.

Two other famous French directors, Rene Clair and Jean Renoir, came
to Hollywood to work during World War II - Clair in 1940 and Renoir in
1941. Their work in the U. S. does not, therefore, fall within the time
frame of this study. Both of these men, however, had an important influence on the development of the American sound film because of the
films they had made in France during the 1930s.

Of the two, Rene Clair was the more closely and specifically related to the initial development of the sound film. His SOUS LES TOITS DE
PARIS, made in 1930, was a world-wide success and marked a unique advance
in the art of the musical film drama. His next two films, LE MILLION and
A NOUS LA LIBERTE, continued in the same brilliantly innovative style.
Clair's influence on Hollywood production stemmed from his first three
sound films, not from the films he made in Britain for Alexander Korda
or those subsequently made in Hollywood. In a way, however, Rene Clair's
whole career as a director has been marked by a degree of taste and
cinematic elegance that has permeated to some degree the entire art of
filmmaking in his lifetime in both Europe and America.

Almost the same thing is true of Jean Renoir. It was primarily the
films that he made in France before coming to the U. S. that have con-
stituted his most important influence on the American film, above all
LA GRANDE ILLUSION, that extraordinarily appealing and durable work of
art that compelled the attention of the international film-going public
and the producers of Hollywood and Europe alike. In the five years he

spent in Hollywood from 1941 to 1946, Jean Renoir made 4 films, at least one of which, THE SOUTHERNER, achieves the quality of human understanding and deep psychological perception that marked his best work in France. Directed by Renoir in 1945 from his own scenario, it was based on a novel by George Sessions Perry and is probably the best film by any French director working outside of his native country in a cultural context characteristically American. Unlike Rene Clair, Renoir's influence on the development of the sound film in America has little to do with innovations in cinematic narrative technique per se. Despite the originality and sometimes experimental quality of Renoir's style (or styles) of filmmaking, his high position as a director stems directly from the warmth of his personality, from the scope and depth of his understanding of people of all kinds, and from the feeling of compassionate realism which pervades almost all of his work.

Although the achievements of another French director, Julien Duvivier, are on a lower level than that of Clair or Renoir, some mention should be made of him since he directed 5 films in the U. S. between 1938 and 1943. Duvivier's influence on the American film stems from films he made in France in the 1930s, especially PEPE LE MOKO. As I have stated, the American gangster theme was originally introduced by Von Sternberg in UNDERWORLD as subject matter for treatment in the German Kammerspiel manner. Duvivier's PEPE LE MOKO reimported the gangster theme back into Europe. It was directed in 1936 from an excellent script by Henri Jeanson characteristic of the French school of poetic realism. The tragic death of the 'hero' in this film, played by Jean Gabin, established a new kind of 'hero' and a new kind of 'tragedy' in popular screen drama. In PEPE LE MOKO the protagonist, an admitted criminal in hiding from the police in the Algiers Casbah, is given a completely sympathetic treatment. He dies while attempting to escape from the Casbah in the company of the woman with whom he has fallen in love, and his death is conveyed to the audience as a truly tragic ending rather than as the inevitable final retribution for his criminal career. Both the theme and the characterization in PEPE LE MOKO, and especially the concept of the anti-hero, were to have a great impact in Hollywood and elsewhere – an influence quite disproportionate to Duvivier's overall importance as

a director. Hollywood remade the film twice, first in 1938 as ALGIERS,
a rather feeble imitation of the French original with Charles Boyer instead of Jean Gabin, yet almost a shot-by-shot copy of it; then later in
1948 as CASBAH, another feeble version in the form of a semi-musical.

Thus far we have been concerned primarily with film directors. But
European cinematographers, writers, art directors, and outstanding actors
and actresses had an influence which in some cases far exceeded the value
of the immediate activity in which they were engaged. Given the scope of
this essay, I shall mention only a few of them.

Karl Freund was one of the most important of the cinematographers
who came to Hollywood with established reputations in their native lands.
He was born in Bohemia in 1890, and died in Hollywood in 1969. Starting
as a newsreel cameraman in Germany in 1908, he photographed his first
feature film in 1910. After that he rapidly achieved the position of a
leading cinematographer in the German film industry. He photographed at
least 7 silent films for Murnau, including DER LETZTE MANN (THE LAST
LAUGH) in 1924 and TARTUFFE (1925); for Paul Wegener he did at least 3
films, including THE GOLEM (1920); for Fritz Lang, part two of DIE SPIN-
NEN (1920) and, in collaboration with Gunther Rittau and Eugen Schufftan,
METROPOLIS (1926); for Paul Czinner, DONA JUANA (1927) and FRAULEIN ELSE
(1929); for Carl Dreyer, MICHAEL (1924); for E. A. Dupont, VARIETY (1925)
and for Walter Ruttman, SYMPHONY OF A BIG CITY (1927). In Germany he
collaborated at various times with other famous cinematographers such as
Rittau, Schufftan, Fritz Arno Wagner, Rudolph Mate, and Franz Planer.
He also acted as assistant director on a number of films.

Preceded by this great reputation, Freund came to Hollywood in 1930
in the early days of sound. For some 20 years thereafter he worked with
many of the leading Hollywood directors: for Lewis Milestone on the famous final sequence of ALL QUIET ON THE WESTERN FRONT (1930); for Rouben
Mamoulian on DR. JEKYLL AND MR. HYDE (1931) and GOLDEN BOY (1939), with
Nick Musaraca; for Tod Browning on DRACULA (1931); for Robert Florey on
THE MURDERS IN THE RUE MORGUE (1932); for George Cukor on CAMILLE (1936);
for Sidney Franklin on THE GOOD EARTH (1937); for Clarence Brown on MARIE
WALEWSKA (1937); for James Whale on GREEN HELL (1940); for Jules Dassin

on A LETTER FOR EVIE (1945) and TWO SMART PEOPLE (1946); for Vincente
Minelli on UNDERCURRENT (1946); for Fred Zinneman on SEVENTH CROSS
(1944); and for John Huston on KEY LARGO (1948).

Karl Freund's credits have been given in some detail because it is
only by such specific information, albeit incomplete, that the extraordinary range of his activity as a cinematographer can be indicated,
and the source of his influence on the American film understood.

Rudolf Mate, another famous European cinematographer, was born in
Cracow in 1898 and died in Hollywood in 1964. His career was similar to
that of Karl Freund. In fact, he made his debut as a cameraman as assistant to Freund on MICHAEL, directed by Carl Dreyer in 1924, although
he had done some work prior to that for Alexander Korda in Hungary.
Mate stayed with Carl Dreyer as cinematographer on THE PASSION OF JOAN
OF ARC (1928) and VAMPIRE (1931). In 1934 he worked for Rene Clair on
THE LAST MILLIONAIRE and for Fritz Lang on LILIOM. Mate made his Hollywood debut as a cinematographer in association with John Seitz on the
film BEAUTY'S DAUGHTER for the veteran Hollywood director Allan Dwan,
and then served as cinematographer on a long list of films, many of them
by Hollywood's best and most prominent directors: he worked for Wyler
and Hawks, in association with Gregg Toland, on COME AND GET IT (1936);
for Wyler on DODSWORTH (1936); for Robert Florey on OUTCAST (1937); for
King Vidor on STELLA DALLAS (1937); for William Dieterle on BLOCKADE
(1938); for Leo McCarey on LOVE AFFAIR (1939) and MY FAVORITE WIFE
(1940); for Alfred Hitchcock on FOREIGN CORRESPONDENT (1940); for Alexander Korda on THAT HAMILTON WOMAN (1941); for Rene Clair on FLAME OF
NEW ORLEANS (1941); for Ernst Lubitsch on TO BE OR NOT TO BE (1942); and
for Charles Vidor on COVER GIRL (1944).

In 1947 Mate switched from cinematography to direction, directing
about a dozen pictures in Hollywood of which none were more than run-of-
the-mill in quality and certainly did nothing to enhance his overall reputation as a film artist. His work as a cinematographer, however, was
distinguished by the excellence of the directors for whom he worked and
by the high level of the films produced.

It is interesting to note that Freund and Mate worked with approxi-

mately the same number of prominent directors in Hollywood - 12 are
listed above for Freund and 11 for Mate. Yet there is only one director
listed for whom both worked, Robert Florey. Thus Freund and Mate, between them, worked with at least 22 of Hollywoods most prominent directors over a period of 18 years from 1930 to 1948. Their combined European influence was considerable.

This influence was augmented by the presence in Hollywood for brief
periods of Eugen Schufftan, a celebrated European cameraman of German
origin whose best work was done in France for G. W. Pabst on L'ATLANTIDE
(1932), and for Marcel Carne on DROLE DE DRAME (1937) and QUAI DES BRUMES
(1938). Schufftan first came to the U. S. in 1939, but despite the excellence of his reputation in Europe he found it difficult to obtain work
as a cinematographer (possibly because of union objections to his employment). In 1943, however, he worked for Rene Clair as 'technical director' on IT HAPPENED TOMORROW, an American, Archie Stout, receiving credit for the cinematography. Although he did little work in Hollywood,
Schufftan's presence in the U. S. between 1939 and 1949 was not without
significance, for his long and distinguished career as a cinematographer,
and his invention of the famous 'Schufftan Process', made his opinions
and advice valuable to many U. S. film people. He returned to Europe
after his period of relative inactivity in the U. S. to resume his career as a cinematographer. He worked for Alexander Astruc on LE RIDEAU
CRAMOISI (1952), and for Georges Franju on LA TETE CONTRE LES MURS (1958)
and LES YEUX SANS VISAGE (1959). He then returned to the U. S. to work
for Jack Garfein on SOMETHING WILD (1961), and for Robert Rossen on THE
HUSTLER (1961) and LILITH (1964).

The career in the U. S. of another prominent European cinematographer, Boris Kaufman, influenced the development of the American sound
film in ways rather different in kind from the three cinematographers
already mentioned. Boris Kaufman was born in Bialystok, Poland, in 1906,
the brother of Denis Kaufman (better known as Dziga Vertov) and Mikhail
Kaufman, the well known Russian filmmakers. As a boy he lived in Russia, but after the revolution he moved to Germany and then to France.
In France he began his career as a cinematographer with the directors

Jean Lods and Jean Vigo, working for the latter on the famous short film A PROPOS DE NICE (1930) and then on ZERO DE CONDUITE (1933) and L'ATA-LANTE (1934).

Kaufman came to the U. S. at the beginning of World War II. He experienced the same kind of difficulties in obtaining work as Eugen Schufftan, but apparently overcame them, for his list of credits for cinematography includes work on nearly 20 features between 1939 and 1945. Although Kaufman's major work in U. S. production did not really begin until he photographed ON THE WATERFRONT for Elia Kazan in 1954 (which lies beyond the scope of this study), he had an important influence on the American sound film even when not working or working on films of little distinction, for his documentary background and his personality enabled him to convey to others with clarity and force his original conceptions about filmmaking. Kaufman eventually came into his own through his work with Elia Kazan and Sidney Lumet.

What was it that these foreign cinematographers brought to the American film? One thing is certain: they did not attempt to impose on the films which they photographed in Hollywood a particular style of cinematography with which they might have been associated in Europe. Rather, they brought with them an acute understanding of the importance of style itself to the overall impact of film, and also artistic standards which they applied as fully as they were able to their work in Hollywood. They were unceasing in their efforts to improve these standards whenever they could. The technical possibilities which the big Hollywood studios offered them were generally superior to those available in Europe in the 1930s, particularly in the areas of lighting and camera mobility. The cinematographers who had worked in European studios (such as those of UFA in Germany), where almost all 'exterior' shots were photographed inside the studios, found that the huge backlots of the major studios of Hollywood, with their acres of established exterior settings, presented a wealth of untried cinematic possibilities. The California sunlight, and the availability on the backlots of the most sophisticated kinds of artificial lighting under conditions of studio-like control, was a combination which presented a new and exciting challenge to foreign cinematographers.

Foreign cinematographers exerted a lasting influence, as well, through their association with American cameramen while collaborating on the photography of various Hollywood films. Karl Freund, for instance, worked in collaboration with Arthur Edeson, J. Rose, William Daniels, Nick Musaraca, George Folsey, and other well known American cinematographers. Rudolph Mate worked with John Seitz, Gregg Toland, and others. Such close collaborations on the set, while not always immediately fruitful, had a cumulative and reciprocal effect on all concerned.

As important perhaps as the influence of European cinematographers was that of a few outstanding art directors. Reference has already been made to the work of Hans Dreier, but his influence on the look of Hollywood films, particularly in the period of the transition to sound, is important enough to justify more detailed examination here.

Dreier was born in Bremen in 1885. He worked for a time in South Africa, but by 1919 he was the assistant art director at the UFA studios in Berlin. He came to Hollywood shortly after the end of World War I to work for Universal. In 1923 he went to Paramount as head art director, where he began his long and intimate collaborations with Ernst Lubitsch and Joseph von Sternberg. Over the years he worked with many other well known directors, including Rouben Mamoulian, C. B. de Mille, King Vidor, Sam Wood, Billy Wilder, and George Stevens. Dreier's prominent position at Paramount, and his own work on such notable films as THE DOCKS OF NEW YORK, SHANGHAI EXPRESS, and THE BLONDE VENUS for von Sternberg, DR. JEKYLL AND MR. HYDE for Mamoulian, THE LOVE PARADE, TROUBLE IN PARADISE, and BLUEBEARD'S EIGHTH WIFE for Lubitsch, CLEOPATRA for C. B. de Mille, and FOR WHOM THE BELL TOLLS for Sam Wood made him one of the most influential art directors in Hollywood during the transition to sound, on a par with Cedric Gibbons at MGM.

Another notable art director who worked in Hollywood was Eugene Lourie. Born in Russia in 1905, Lourie achieved great success in France working first on decors for the Ballet Russe de Monte Carlo in collaboration with the choreographer Massine. His career as an art director for

films did not begin until 1935, and he did not come to Hollywood until
the beginning of World War II. His fame as an art director, however,
preceded him, thanks largely to Jean Renoir for whom he had worked on
THE LOWER DEPTHS in 1936, LA GRANDE ILLUSION in 1938, and LA BETE HU-
MAINE and LA REGLE DU JEU in 1939. Lourie came to the U. S. to continue
his work for Renoir on films which fall outside the time frame of this
study, but his European work for Renoir on the films previously mentioned was surely not without effect on the Hollywood scene.

James Basevi, an English art director, came to Hollywood at about
the same time as Lourie, and his work there lies outside the period under discussion. However, his work for John Ford on THE LONG VOYAGE HOME
in 1941, which marked the beginning of his extended collaboration with
Ford, had an impact on Hollywood which is worthy of mention here.

Category C

We come now to a group of individual film artists, some of American
origin and some of European birth, who do not fit neatly into either of
the first two categories. Some of them are so famous in world cinema
that they cannot be ignored in this study, yet need not be dealt with
here in detail.

Charles Chaplin and Alfred Hitchcock come immediately to mind.
Both were English by birth, yet are personifications of Hollywood itself; both are international figures and have influenced the development
of film on a worldwide scale; and both made films which were of particular importance in the first days of the sound film. Hitchcock's BLACK-
MAIL (1929), the first British 'talkie', displayed an altogether surprising degree of ingenuity and imagination in the use of sound, and opened
the way to future developments. Chaplin, with CITY LIGHTS (1931) and
MODERN TIMES (1936), questioned and resisted the then-current dominance
of dialogue as the major component in the sound film.

The theories of the Russian directors Sergei Eisenstein and Vsevo-
lod Pudovkin respecting the functions of sound were not without effect
on Hollywood and on the development of the U. S. sound film in general.

Eisenstein came to Hollywood in the midst of the sound revolution in
1929 with his collaborator, Alexandrov, and his cinematographer, Tisse;
and, although he never made a film in Hollywood, his concepts were widely discussed in the U. S. without finding immediate application. He
never completed QUE VIVA MEXICO!, which might have become a most influential film in America. Nevertheless, the impact of his visit to the
U. S. was substantial.

Pudovkin never visited the U. S., but his book Film Technique and
Film Acting was one of the first treatises on the theory of film to be
circulated in English. Over a period of years it had a considerable
circulation and influence among the cognoscenti in matters of film, as
great as any theoretical treatise ever written on the subject.

Two other men, less prominent in the world of film than those whom
we have just mentioned, are yet - in a rather strange way - of interest
in the context of this study. They are Robert Siodmak, an American born
in Memphis, and Fred Zinnemann, an Austrian born in Vienna. Their names
were linked at the outset of their unusual careers, as they were both
involved in the making of a film that has become quite famous, MENSCHEN
AM SONNTAG (PEOPLE ON SUNDAY), made in Germany in 1929. It is a social
documentary owing much to the work of Dziga Vertov, Alberto Cavalcanti,
and Walter Ruttmann. The director was Robert Siodmak. His two assistants were Fred Zinneman and Edgar Ulmer. The scriptwriter was Billy
Wilder, and the cinematographer was Eugen Schufftan. All of these
people eventually came to work in Hollywood, arriving there by very
diverse routes. Robert Siodmak stayed in Europe, making several good
films in Germany and France, before coming to Hollywood in the early
1940s. There he did not achieve real success until he directed THE KIL-
LERS in 1946. It was the best picture he made in his native land.

Fred Zinnemann gained his first film experience in Paris and Berlin.
He came to the U. S. in 1930, where he worked first as an extra in Hollywood, then as the director of a documentary LOS REDES made in Mexico
in collaboration with Paul Strand, the pioneer of U. S. documentary filmmaking. This was an historically important film, since it marked the
beginning of the organized activities of a group of American documentary

filmmakers who were to have considerable success until the outbreak of
World War II. Their work and its influence on Hollywood can be detected
in John Ford's important film THE GRAPES OF WRATH (1940). Zinnemann,
however, did not remain in documentary work. He went instead to Hollywood to make short films for MGM, and to act as assistant director on
many feature films. He also directed features on his own, including THE
SEARCH - a dramatized documentary of considerable quality made in Switzerland after the war. It was not until he directed HIGH NOON in 1951,
however, that Zinnemann achieved an influence on the Hollywood scene by
enlarging the psychological scope of the Western.

Neither Siodmak nor Zinnemann did anything spectacular to change
Hollywood, but each of them brought something of European thought and
experience to their work in the U. S., deriving from their earliest experience in working on MENSCHEN AM SONNTAG in Berlin. Later on Billy
Wilder was to bring a great deal more of the same kind of thing to Hollywood from the same point of origin.

Conclusion

Many other persons were working in Hollywood at the time of the
transition to sound whose education and training had been profoundly
European. Their number and their cumulative influence has never, to my
knowledge, been assessed. I refer, of course, to men like Hans Kraly,
who was Ernst Lubitsch's favorite screenwriter in Germany, accompanied
Lubitsch to Hollywood, and continued to work for him and other well
known directors such as Lewis Milestone and William Wyler; and Max Steiner, the Viennese composer and concert pianist, who came to Hollywood in
1929 to be musical director at RKO, and subsequently became one of the
most important formative influences in the creation of the Hollywood
style in film music.

The list of these and many lesser known Europeans is long, and some-
day perhaps it will be examined in detail and its significance justly
assessed in the interests of film scholarship. But for the purposes of
this brief study, we have heard enough names and seen enough evidence

of the European influence on the American sound film. It is time to
draw some conclusions. They will not be startlingly different from
those suggested elsewhere in the past, but they may be strengthened by
our extension of the range of the evidence available, and, in some instances, by our additions to the common knowledge of the subject.

First, it is clear that the "German Invasion", as it was called by
Richard Griffith and Arthur Mayer in their 1957 book The Movies, was in
fact an even more profound and far reaching combination of circumstances
than the two authors indicated, as far as Hollywood was concerned. The
German-Austrian influence on U. S. film production before, during, and
for a considerable time after the introduction of sound was the single
most important, pervasive, and durable factor in the development of
Hollywood production in the period from 1925 to 1940. It was not, to be
sure, a homogeneous influence, for it incorporated elements absorbed
from other European sources. But it was preeminently German in the
whole of the effect produced.

This German influence, I think, is most clearly summed up in the
work of one great film artist, Carl Mayer. Strangely, Mayer never visited the U. S., but his conceptual brilliance in matters of film theory
and his artistic achievements were widely demonstrated and propagated in
Hollywood by his many able ambassadors. He wrote the script for only
one notable film made in Hollywood, SUNRISE, directed by F. W. Murnau in
1927. It was not a commercial success despite the excellent script which
greatly improved the story by Herman Sudermann on which it was based.
Yet Carl Mayer, through the quality of his work over a rather short career (he died at the age of 50), introduced to the screen at least two
fundamental and important dramatic concepts, and saw them vividly presented in what are now classic films made from his scripts.

The first of these concepts embraces all the elements of German expressionist art, and is put before us in complete and concentrated form
in THE CABINET OF DR. CALIGARI, completed in 1919 from a script by Mayer
This film has become so famous that we are sometimes inclined to forget
the importance it has had as a model of film form and content, serving
the creators of fantastic, grotesque, and horror films to this day. Two

other German films of the period served to amplify and reinforce the
tenets of THE CABINET OF DR. CALIGARI, namely, the third version of THE
GOLEM (the only one now known to exist) directed in 1920 by Paul Wagener
from a script by Henrik Galeen, and WAXWORKS, directed in 1924 by Paul
Leni from another script by Galeen. It was the great success of WAX-
WORKS which brought Paul Leni to Hollywood, as we have described above,
where he introduced all the dramatic elements and screen techniques of
German expressionist cinema in THE CAT AND THE CANARY (1927) and, most
notably, in THE LAST WARNING (1929). These great popular successes initiated a new tradition of horror filmmaking in Hollywood which leapt the
barrier between silent and sound films with the greatest ease, and has
continued to defy the erosion suffered by so many film formulae over the
years with a persistence almost equal to that of the Western.

The second and more important dramaturgical concept applied to the
screen by Carl Mayer, and adopted by Hollywood, was that of the German
'Kammerspiel' theatre. The film in which the Kammerspiel theories were
so forcefully introduced to the U. S. producers and public was DER LETZE
MANN (THE LAST LAUGH) directed by F. W. Murnau from a script by Carl
Mayer in 1924. Although not a consistent example of all the theories of
Kammerspiel, this film admirably incorporates the most important elements: the concentration on a single theme, the studied realism reinforced by a brilliantly mobile and subjective use of the camera, and the
symbolic use of all visual elements. This combination produced an impact of a kind that had never before been experienced by the American
public.

THE LAST LAUGH was a great commercial success in the U. S., but
more importantly it modified the whole development of screen dramaturgy
in Hollywood just as sound was introduced. The most immediate result,
as we have noted, was that F. W. Murnau was invited to Hollywood to direct SUNRISE from a script by Carl Mayer. It was not Murnau, however,
who carried on the development of Kammerspiel concepts in Hollywood, but
rather Joseph von Sternberg as the director of UNDERWORLD, for therein
he applied Kammerspiel principles to essentially American subject matter.
We have already traced, in this regard, the pervasive influence of Kam-

merspiel dramaturgy on and through screenwriters such as Ben Hecht and
Jules Furthman, cinematographers such as Karl Freund, and art directors
such as Hans Dreier.

The Kammerspiel influence was also enhanced at this time by the
resurgence of Von Stroheim, who by reason of the box office success of
his version of THE MERRY WIDOW was able to follow it with THE WEDDING
MARCH in 1927, a film much more to his taste. Von Stroheim was never
directly involved with the theories of Kammerspiel as such, but his ob-
session with realism and his constant effort to enhance the psychological and symbolic values in film are coincident with Kammerspiel ideas as
demonstrated in THE LAST LAUGH. Stroheim's complete disregard for the
classic unities, of course, and his taste for elaborate digression,
place his work on a different and more cinematic plane than that of Kammerspiel, as generally interpreted. But on the whole Stroheim's work
derives essentially from European sources, with a strong emphasis on
German elements.

If we list some of the key films produced in the U. S. in 1927, we
can see the importance of the German influence on Hollywood just at the
moment when sound was being introduced: SEVENTH HEAVEN, directed by
Frank Borzage, a high point in the well established genre of the senti-
mental, romantic love story; THE FLESH AND THE DEVIL, a romantic melodrama and vehicle for Greta Garbo in typical Hollywood style, directed
by Clarence Brown from an original story by the Austrian novelist Herman
Sudermann; THE JAZZ SINGER, director Alan Crossland's second excursion
into sound and the first successful effort in the new medium; THE LAST
MOMENT, Paul Fejos's first experimental Hollywood film; THE CAT AND THE
CANARY, in which Paul Leni introduced German expressionist techniques;
SUNRISE, the first Hollywood film by F. W. Murnau, exponent of German
Kammerspiel concepts; THE KING OF KINGS, a major but typical Hollywood
spectacular directed by C. B. de Mille; CHANG, the second effort in a
new, interesting, but short-lived genre of dramatized travelogue; UNDER-
WORLD, Von Sternberg's first arresting application of German Kammerspiel
concepts to the American scene; THE DIVINE WOMAN, an undistinguished
Garbo vehicle directed by the great Sjostrom; THE WEDDING MARCH, mordant

realism and devastating satire in a return to top form by von Stroheim;
and A GIRL IN EVERY PORT, the first notable success of Howard Hawks,
directed by him from a script based on his own story, and ornamented by
Louise Brooks.

It is interesting to note that of the 12 films listed, 8 can be
termed 'innovative' by Hollywood standards, THE JAZZ SINGER, THE LAST
MOMENT, THE CAT AND THE CANARY, SUNRISE, CHANG, UNDERWORLD, THE WEDDING
MARCH, and A GIRL IN EVERY PORT; and in 5 of these 8 films, European and
overwhelmingly Germanic influences represent the innovative factors: THE
LAST MOMENT, THE CAT AND THE CANARY, SUNRISE, UNDERWORLD, and THE WEDDING
MARCH.

It is likewise interesting to see how these influences, which were
crucial in the transition from silent to sound films, were to develop in
the next few years. The German expressionist genre was continued in a
strong vein by Paul Leni with THE CHINESE PARROT (1927), and THE MAN WHO
LAUGHS and THE LAST WARNING, released in 1929 after his untimely death
brought a promising career to an end. His place was soon taken by other
directors of horror films, all more or less in the expressionist tradition, among them Tod Browning who directed DRACULA (1931), and James
Whale who directed FRANKENSTEIN (1931). The Kammerspiel influence pene-
trated broadly and pervasively a wide range of Hollywood dramaturgy. It
was continued with maximum concentration by Von Sternberg in THE DOCKS
OF NEW YORK (1928), and, of course, in THE BLUE ANGEL, made in Germany
in 1930. But directors other than Von Sternberg were deeply impressed
with the qualities of Kammerspiel, and began to incorporate them in their
work as evidence both in the selection of subjects for their films and
in their treatment of them. Frank Borzage with THE RIVER (1929) treated
an essentially romantic subject with a degree of realism and psychological insight far from the sentimentality of SEVENTH HEAVEN, although
Charles Farrell played in both films. Clarence Brown turned from the
Sudermann-inspired melodrama of THE FLESH AND THE DEVIL to psychological
drama with ANNA CHRISTIE, adapted from O'Neill's play, both Garbo vehi-
cles. Lubitsch briefly deserted his operettas (with and without music)
to make THE PATRIOT (1928) with Emil Jannings, a forgettable tribute to

that masterpiece of Kammerspiel, THE LAST LAUGH. Paul Fejos made LONE-
SOME (1928), a masterpiece stamped with his own brand of acute psychological understanding and matchless realism. King Vidor in THE CROWD
(1928) combined elements of German expressionism with the characteristically psychological and symbolic elements of Kammerspiel, and added
his own inspiration to make one of the best pictures of his career. Von
Stroheim was a sad loss to the roster of Hollywood's and the world's
directors when he was unable to complete QUEEN KELLY in 1928. Rouben
Mamoulian, a native of Armenia who had made a name for himself on Broadway before coming to Hollywood by his direction of Porgy and Bess, made
his first film APPLAUSE (1929), an astonishingly inventive blend of
European theatrical elements and camera mobility made possible by the
development of post-synchronous sound techniques. His second film CITY
STREETS (1931) was directly in the tradition of Kammerspiel and Von
Sternberg's THE DOCKS OF NEW YORK, and his third film DR. JEKYLL AND MR.
HYDE (1931) demonstrated that elements of expressionism and Kammerspiel
can be intensified by the novel atmospheric use of sound. Lewis Milestone's THE FRONT PAGE (1931), from the play by Ben Hecht, is itself an
excellent application of Kammerspiel dramaturgy to U. S. newspaper myth.
Even C. B. de Mille, in one of his carefully calculated intervals between
biblical spectaculars, indulged in some Kammerspiel-inspired drama with
THE GODLESS GIRL (1929), a film containing criticism of the U. S. penal
system. Howard Hawks with SCARFACE (1932), and Mervyn le Roy with LITTLE
CAESAR (1930) and I AM A FUGATIVE FROM A CHAIN GANG (1932), carried on
the development of Hollywood realist drama firmly based on Kammerspiel
principles and enlivened by the fast and violent action inherent in the
subject matter.

    In this way an entirely new dramatic genre was firmly established
in Hollywood within a few years. It has become a permanent resource,
strong enough to resist all the errors and misfortunes which have assail-
ed the U. S. production industry in subsequent years.

    Not all the concepts of screen realism came from Germany in the
1920s. Von Stroheim and Paul Fejos, for instance, had their own particular brands of realism which, although European in origin, were not

derived directly from Kammerspiel. Another sort of realism, in fact, had come to the U. S. from France as early as 1913 when Albert Capellani brought a copy of his remarkable version of Zola's GERMINAL to New York, a fine example of the power of the 'new naturalism' in film. This new kind of realism, conditioned not so much by psychological and symbolic values, but rather by social, economic, and even political ones, derived from the work of 19th century French novelists such as Flaubert and Zola, and from the work of painters such as Courbet. But it came to the cinema, in particular, via the theatrical productions of Andre Antoine.

Antoine was 60 years old when he began making films, and did not have enough time to learn how to put his original and prophetic views on the cinema into practice. But he inspired many other younger French directors of the day, such as Capellani, Zecca, and, most importantly for our purposes, Maurice Tourneur. We have discussed Tourneur at some length, but it is hard to overestimate the part he played in creating within Hollywood a degree of respect for the work of serious novelists and dramatists, whether classic or contemporary, as sources of story material for films. This respect for literary originals which Tourneur preached was far from universally accepted in Hollywood, but it did impress enough talented screenwriters, directors, and producers that eventually films would be made of such contemporary American writers as O'Neill, Faulkner, Hemingway, and Steinbeck.

The influence of two other great French directors on the development of the sound film in America was essentially a continuation of the precedent of Maurice Tourneur. The films of Rene Clair and Jean Renoir, despite their innovative cinematic techniques, were fundamentally inspired by literary concepts, both classic and popular. It is no accident that Clair is the only filmmaker ever elected to membership in the French Academy. Renoir, too, although his films have been inspired by a much wider range of interests and concerns than those of Clair, was embued by a profound respect for the classic realism of 19th century French novelists. Only a year or so prior to his coming to the U. S. at the beginning of World War II, Renoir reaffirmed his belief in the worth of the

French realist tradition by making an adaptation of LA BETE HUMAINE from
the novel by Zola. Renoir's natural affinity and respect for the work
and its author are evident in the quality of the film, one of his best.

Such were the principal European influences on the coming of sound
to the European film. I have mentioned many Europeans and have given
some evidence of their involvement in U. S. production. For the most
part their contributions fall into one of the two principal areas of
influence we have discussed: German expressionism and Kammerspiel, in-
corporating certain English and middle-European elements; and French 19th
century realism, involving respect for and utilization of literary originals.

What emerges from this study, brief and incomplete though it must
be, is the extreme complexity of the patterns of European influence on
American sound films. The countless threads of personal history, with
their innumerable interconnections, are worthy of far more study in
order to bring film scholarship to a level even remotely comparable to
that which has been achieved in the other arts over the centuries. Comprehensive and precise investigations of the historical events are surely
called for while many of the persons intimately connected with the events
under study are still alive.

One overriding fact comes out of this study: the European influences
on the coming of sound to the American film enabled Hollywood to become
not only a capital of a national cinema, but for a limited period the
center of world cinema, and thereby returned to the film something of
its pristine and unique character as the one truly popular international
art of the century.

Part IV:
Comparison
and Contrast

APPLAUSE:
The Visual & Acoustic Landscape

by Lucy Fischer

"Observation has proved that the combination
of word and picture aroused two kinds of reactions
in audiences. Some were quite incapable of getting
a united impression from picture and sound. The
people on the screen suddenly appeared startlingly
incorporeal, flat, shadowy and inanimate, while
from somewhere outside the picture and quite dis-
connected with it came the voices. Or else the
voice came from the mouths of these screen figures
and these, as though animated by the sounds, suddenly seemed more vivid, plastic and real than in silent
film." 1

These words were written by Rudolph Arnheim in 1933 as part of a
chapter on the sound cinema in his book Film. Although Arnheim's ulti-
mate purpose in the text was to warn us of the dangers of the soundtrack
- its tendency to bolster the realistic film illusion - he nonetheless
managed to point out something quite important about the sound-film
medium. For Arnheim's observation contains two crucial insights: that
both sound and image have particular spatial attributes, and that the
successful fusion of visual and auditory tracks is not as automatic
as is commonly supposed.

More deeply submerged in Arnheim's remarks is yet another assumption, one that may at first glance seem surprising. According to Arnheim it is sound, and not image, that carries the most emphatic sense
of spatiality. As he writes in another passage,

> ". . . sound arouses an illusion of actual
> space, while a picture has practically no depth
> . . ." 2

While one might reject Arnheim's final conclusion regarding the
incompatibility of sound and image, and question his assertion of there
being a qualified sense of depth contained within the image, his remarks
prove, nonetheless, extremely useful. For while other critics of the
period[3] seemed insensitive to the spatial quality of sound, Arnheim
immediately recognized its primacy. ("Sound", he said, "is very strongly indicative of space."[4]) And while other critics seemed to believe
that the fusion of sound and image was a quite automatic phenomenon
(some sanctioning, while others condemning that formal merger), Arnheim
sensed that the creation of a sound/image illusion was a highly tenuous
process, and one whose success revolved around the parameter of space.

It is from this theoretical perspective that the extraordinary
power of Rouben Mamoulian's early sound film APPLAUSE (1929) becomes
comprehensible. In watching and listening to APPLAUSE we are immediately struck by the difference between it and the standard sound-film fare
of the period. Whereas other films seem 'incorporeal' and 'inanimate'
(to use Arnheim's words from the opening quotation), in APPLAUSE sound
seems to function to make the image 'more vivid, plastic and real'.
Yet while we immediately sense the singularity of APPLAUSE, the reasons
for its perceived superiority are not so instantly clear. And it will
be the purpose of this paper to articulate and render them lucid.

APPLAUSE falls within the genre of backstage musical drama, and is
based on a novel by Beth Brown. It tells the story of an aging burlesque stripper named Kitty Darling (Helen Morgan) and her loving attempts to raise her daughter, April (Joan Peers). On the level of the
plot, APPLAUSE is pure formula and convention, transcended only by the
poignant and sublime performance of Helen Morgan. But plot is clearly
not what interests Mamoulian. Rather it is the depiction of atmosphere,
the rendering of the crass and seedy half-world of burlesque. As Mamoulian states in a 1971 interview,

"As a preliminary education [for the film] I went
to all the burlesque houses . . . what interested me
[was] . . . burlesque with its tawdriness, vulgarity
and sadness . . ." 5

Thus, in talking about the film, Mamoulian focuses not upon the
issue of dramatic structure, or characterization. Instead, he empha-
sizes the aspect of setting, of the material locale in which the narrative action unfolds. Significant, in this respect, is the fact that the
very first shot of APPLAUSE is that of an uninhabited space - an empty
street down which blow handbills for the arrival of burlesque queen
Kitty Darling.

It is this sense of a physical, corporeal universe that is everywhere apparent in the aural and visual mise-en-scene of APPLAUSE. Rather than simply employing a particular place of action, Mamoulian seeks
to 'build a world' - one that his characters and audience seem to inhabit. And that world is 'habitable' because Mamoulian vests it with a
strong sense of space. Unlike other directors of the period,[6] he recog-
nizes the inherent spatial capacities of sound and, furthermore, understands the means by which they can lend an aspect of depth to the image.

On the visual level, Mamoulian employs a variety of techniques to
create a world of palpable space; and the film can be seen as a virtual
tour de force articulation of the parameters of length, height, and
depth. A sense of length (or of the horizontal axis) is created largely
through camera movements, of both panning and tracking varieties. In
a remarkable shot toward the opening of the film we see the stage and
orchestra pit of a burlesque theatre. The camera begins focused upon a
drum, then pans right-to-left across the musicians' faces. It then move
up to the stage and executes a track in the opposite direction. Finally
it rests upon the women's faces, and reverses the direction of its
movement once more. In this highly intricate and peripatetic shot
(worthy of Jean Renoir) the horizontal plane has been emphatically introduced, only to be underscored again in later sequences.

Height is established in a somewhat more complex fashion. There
are, first of all, a series of vertical pans. To move from the feet to

the faces of the aforementioned chorus girls, the camera executes a vertical pan. On other occasions in the film the camera pans dramatically
from a character's feet to his or her face. One instance occurs when
Kitty's womanizing lover, Hitch (Fuller Mellish, Jr.) is seen standing
over Kitty, who is sprawled out on her living room floor. The camera
moves down from his head to his feet and then up again, stressing not
only the spatial aspect of height, but the psychological fact of his
dominance over her. Later in the film the parameter of height is again
strongly invoked by a dramatic camera pan up the side of the Empire
State Building, to find April and her boyfriend, Tony (Henry Wadsworth),
courting at the top.

But more subtle means of creating awareness of the vertical plane
are also utilized, although they are achieved without the aid of camera
movement. Mamoulian continually makes us aware of the various levels
on the vertical scale. Most often we view things from what may be
called normal eye level, but sometimes we view things from almost ground
level. The best example of this latter technique comes in a scene in
which Hitch bends down to tie his shoelace and peers voyeuristically at
April's legs. At other times (as in the shots of the stage from runway
level) we view things from a middle height.

Mamoulian also takes advantage of both extreme high and low angle
shots to reinforce this dimension. One thinks of the high angle shot
above Kitty on the dressing room sofa, as the chorus girls file around
her to admire her newborn baby; or of the high angle shot of Kitty
sitting on the living room floor singing "What Wouldn't I Do For That
Man?". Perhaps the most dramatic, however, is the extreme high angle
shot of the stage, as seen from the viewpoint of two men in the balcony.
The film also contains a series of assertive low angle shots: for example, the one (from Kitty's point of view) of the chorus girls circling
around her; or the Eisensteinian low angle shot of the vulgar, burlesque
manager whom Kitty calls on the telephone.

Various techniques are also employed to create the sense of depth.
The camera continually moves toward or away from objects, thus articu-
lating the space in between. The camera, for example, tracks into the

room in which Kitty is teaching the young April how to dance, or later
tracks in towards April and a nun at the convent school. The camera
also follows characters as they maneuver through space. In many scenes
the camera tracks behind someone as he or she advances through the dense
backstage area, or through a city crowd.

But there are also depth-creating effects that do not rely on camera movement. Even in shots in which the camera is stationary, there is
often a tremendous amount of background and foreground movement, all of
which makes us aware of the depth of the space. Whenever two characters
are talking backstage, there is a constant flow of movement on other
planes within the frame. In the background there may be a few girls
exercising; or on the diagonal a woman may be walking, fixing her garter

Mamoulian also employs the technique of rack-focus to create the
sense of depth. One thinks, for example, of the shot in which April and
Hitch are watching the outline of Kitty as she performs behind the stage
curtain, or of the shot in which Hitch peers lasciviously at April's
legs. Although not technically a camera movement, this device achieves
much the same effect, for through rack-focus it is as though we were
being pulled toward or away from an object, and thus made conscious of
the spatial distance that intervenes.

Often Mamoulian accomplishes a sense of depth by placing the camera in such a way that it must look through things in order to focus upon
its subject. In the convent scenes we often look at things through
trees or gates. In the backstage scenes we often peer through ropes,
flimsy curtains, or groups of people. At one point we see the burlesque
audience through the legs of the chorus girls; and at another, we see
the stage with our sight line obstructed by a pole. All of these are,
of course, not accidental. Rather, they are reminders of the density
of space that exists within the depicted environment.

In a manner similar to that of Josef von Sternberg, Mamoulian man-
ages to use decor itself as a means of evoking the tactile-spatial world.
We notice the depth of space in the frame partly because it is so clut-
tered. Kitty's room, for instance, is not experienced as a studio 'set',

because it is redeemed from the flatness and artificiality so prevalent
in film decor of the time. Chairs are strewn with clothes; walls hung
haphazardly with photographs; mantels filled with knicknacks; windows
draped with curtains. It is not so much that these touches are realistic. It is that, as used by Mamoulian, they give us the profound sense
of objects taking up space, existing within space. And the sheer number of objects that appear in the Mamoulian frame tends to dynamize
space itself. Even the costumes worn in the film (though dictated by
burlesque fashions) seem to be making a spatial-tactile statement, with
their layers of feathers and organza.

        Shadows in the film serve a similar function. In the scenes in
which they are used (Hitch's shadow on the wall, looming over April and
Kitty; Kitty's shadow on the backstage curtain) they serve not only as
tools of expressionism but as constant reminders of the three-dimension-
ality of space.

        This delineation of visual space in APPLAUSE would be noteworthy
in and of itself, if just for its extraordinary sense of palpable phy-
sicality. But it is all the more remarkable when one considers that it
was done in 1929, a year in which severe restraints were placed upon
camera technique as a result of the coming of sound. As mentioned earlier, much of the sense of depth created in APPLAUSE can be credited to
its virtuoso camera movement. Yet it is common knowledge that in the
first years of sound, camera movement was considered all but impossible.
Since the standard camera of 1929 had been designed in the silent era,
without consideration of its mechanical noise, it had to be soundproofed
for sync-sound filming. Until small 'blimps' were developed around
1931, cameras were encased in huge cabinets in which the director and
technicians were housed while shooting. Known ironically as 'iceboxes'
because of the degree of heat in their interior, these cabinets were
heavy and bulky, and made camera movement incredibly cumbersome.

        Mamoulian, however, refused to accept this technological limitation
and forced an unwilling crew to wheel the icebox around the set. As
Mamoulian recalls, in his discussion of one particular sequence,

"I wanted to do the whole scene in one shot
by keeping the camera moving. They had little
wheels on the bungalow and you had to have ten
men to move it and stop it. So I had the floor
marked, the focus set to change, the lights
ready, and . . . everybody going mad . . . we
made a take. I went home and was miserable. I
thought this could be the end of me in films'." 7

When one thinks of the awkwardness of the filming process, one is
even more impressed by such tracking shots in APPLAUSE as the one that
takes place during April's leave taking from the convent school. The
shot begins with the camera looking down a deep corridor. April and a
nun walk away from the camera towards a window at the end of the hall,
and the camera follows behind them. They then turn right and walk out
of view, but the camera pauses at the stained-glass window. It then
turns right and looks down another deep corridor which terminates in a
chapel. It then tracks down the corridor, hesitates once more, and
moves off to the left following the nun.

Clearly Mamoulian's use of camera movement dynamizes the viewer's
sense of visual space. And it makes one consider that perhaps Arnheim's
experience of the images of early sound films as 'incorporeal' resulted
not from any inherent flatness of the image, but rather from the historical fact that so many works of the period were devoid of this depth-
creating camera strategy.

But the creation of a sense of spatiality in APPLAUSE is not merely
a product of camera movement and visual mise-en-scene. Rather, it is,
to a great extent, generated by Mamoulian's use of sound. For as another theorist of the era, Bela Belazs, once noted in Theory of Film,
our very perception of optical space is intimately tied to our experience of sound:

"A completely soundless space . . . never
appears quite concrete, and quite real to our
perception; we feel it to be weightless and un-
substantial, for what we merely see is only a
vision. We accept seen space as real only when
it contains sounds as well, for these give it
the dimension of depth." [Italics mine] 8

It is this association of visual and auditory factors in the creation
of depth that Mamoulian intuitively grasped and articulated so adeptly
in the formal structure of APPLAUSE.

APPLAUSE was, of course, Mamoulian's first film. He was one of a
host of stage directors imported to the film industry during the first
panic of the coming of sound. Though Paramount was primarily interested
in him for the direction of dialogue,[9] Mamoulian's interest in cinema
was oriented toward more abstract modalities of sound. As he remarked
to Andrew Sarris in a 1966 interview:

> "I was convinced that sound on the screen
> should not be constantly shackled by naturalism.
> The magic of sound recording enabled one to
> achieve effects that would be impossible and un-
> natural on the stage or in real life, yet mean-
> ingful and eloquent on the screen." [10]

If one examines Mamoulian's previous theatrical experience, however,
one realizes that he was no newcomer to the notion of experimentation
with sound. As well as having directed stage plays, Mamoulian had directed many operas, and in his 1927 production of Porgy & Bess he had
used the following effect as an opening.[11] Mamoulian called it the
Symphony of Noises and described it as follows:

> "The curtain rose on Catfish Row in the early
> morning. All silent. Then you hear the Boum! of
> a street gang repairing the road. That is the
> first beat: then beat 2 is silent; beat 3 is a
> snore - zzzz! - from a Negro who's asleep; beat 4
> silent again. Then a woman starts sweeping the
> steps - whish - and she takes up beats 2 and 4,
> so you have: Boum! - whish! - zzzz! - whish! -
> and so on. A knife sharpener, a shoemaker, a
> woman beating rugs, and so on, all joining in.
> Then the rhythm changes: 4:4 to 2:4, then to 6:8
> and syncopated and Charleston rhythms. It all had
> to be conducted like an orchestra."

Many things are revealed by Mamoulian's description of his Symphony
of Noises. Clearly it shows that he was ripe for the new sound-film
medium, and that he viewed sound as a formal element to be manipulated
according to its unique aesthetic principles. It also demonstrates that

for Mamoulian sounds were an essential element in creating an environment, and that dialogue was by no means the sole conveyor of meaning.
Rather, concrete noise, as well, could be expressive.

But how exactly does Mamoulian handle sound in APPLAUSE, and how
is its articulation related to the creation of a sense of visual space?
First of all, when one compares the sound of the film APPLAUSE to that
of other products of the era, what most distinguishes it is the density
of its acoustic track. Many of the early talkies have an auditory as
well as visual flatness. If characters are talking that is all we hear
(except, perhaps, for some background 'musak'). The sound atmosphere
is thin and rarefied, lacking in perceptual truth.

Mamoulian's 'sound space', however, is always filled and it offers
an auditory counterpart for the visual 'clutter' we experience. Some
scenes that come to mind as exemplary of this technique are: the theatre
bar scene in which Joe King (Jack Cameron) shouts above the general din
in order to find a doctor to deliver Kitty's baby; the scene in which
April arrives at her mother's hotel and speaks to someone in the noisy
lobby; or the scene in which April and escort go to the raucous Harlem
theatre to see Kitty perform. All of these sequences are characterized
by what we might term several layers of sound: there is usually one lay-
er of dialogue as well as many additional layers of noise (talking,
music, street sounds, etc.). This sound density lends the frame an aura
of truth, for it seems to replicate our real-life perception of auditory
stimuli. In a text entitled Explorations in Communication, Marshall
McLuhan and Edmund Carpenter write of auditory experience:

> "The universe is the potential map of auditory
> space. We are not Argus-eyed but we are Argus-eared.
> We hear instantly anything from any direction and at
> any distance within very wide limits . . . Whereas
> the eyes are bounded, directed, and limited to con-
> siderably less than half the visible world at any
> given moment, the ears are all-encompassing, constantly
> alert to any sound originating in their boundless
> sphere." [12]

It is precisely this notion that Mamoulian seems to have grasped about
the nature of sound. He understands that in life we are continually

hit with a barrage of noise, a cacophony whose component parts are not
always discrete or distinguishable to our ear. As Siegfried Kracauer
explains in his Theory of Film:

> "In general one hears a row, that is -
> to use a mechanical analogy - a sort of result-
> ant of all the noisy forces within earshot." 13

In addition to conforming to our real-life perception of sound,
this density of the auditory track functions to emphasize our sense of
the spatial world depicted in the film. For as Carpenter and McLuhan
remark in the previously-quoted essay:

> "The essential feature of sound . . . is . . .
> that it fills space. We say 'the night shall be
> filled with music' just as air is filled with
> fragrance. . ." [Italics mine] 14

Another aspect of aural perception that Mamoulian seems to have
understood is that in life we can never turn off the melange of sound,
for there is no way to 'shut' our ears. Thus in APPLAUSE even though
characters change their position (leave rooms, go backstage, etc.),
sounds from other locations aggressively pursue them. When April and
escort approach the Harlem burlesque theatre, low-level noises from
within are heard before they enter. As Kitty sits in her hotel room,
having taken an overdose of drugs, a conversation between two lovers in
the hallway wafts into her chamber. When clapping begins as a character
is on the stage, it continues to be heard, in muted form, when he or she
goes backstage.

This modulation of sound, due to the location of the perceiver, has
obvious spatial implications. Since sounds are modified as we shift our
position (from onstage to backstage, etc.), they make us aware that they
pass through space. And since sounds continue to be heard when their
sources are no longer present, they remind us of locales beyond our view.

This comprehension of the omnipresent quality of sound was by no
means automatic in the early sound era. Even very skillful directors
like von Sternberg used sound with less auditory sensitivity. Thus in

THUNDERBOLT (1929) or THE BLUE ANGEL (1930) sounds virtually seemed to shut off when characters moved from one space to another.

Aside from replicating our real-life aural perception, Mamoulian's use of a densely layered soundtrack in APPLAUSE functions to create a sense of spatial ambience. The undecipherable background dialogue, the vaudeville music, the street noises, all construct for us a sense of the material world which the characters inhabit. They are 'character-istic' of the burlesque environment, and form a kind of 'tonal milieu'. Balazs writes most insightfully about this particular aspect of sound:

> "It is the business of the sound film to reveal
> to us our acoustic environment, the acoustic environ-
> ment in which we live . . . all that has speech beyond
> human speech, and speaks to us with the vast conversa-
> tional power of life and incessantly influences and
> directs our thoughts and emotions, from the mutter-
> ing of the sea, to the din of a great city." [15]

By creating a highly textured and layered acoustic atmosphere Mamoulian was again violating the contemporary rules of sound-film practice. For it was the aim of most dialogue engineers to eliminate all ambient noise in order to foreground the spoken text. Thus tech-nicians sought to counter the omnidirectional quality of early micro-phones, which tended to pick up all background sounds within their range. But for Mamoulian, ironically, these noises were crucial, and were to be accorded equal status to speech.

The density of the 'acoustic landscape' achieved in APPLAUSE seems all the more remarkable when one considers yet another prevalent prac-tice of the early sound era: that of extreme soundproofing of the set to assure a 'perfect' but sterile recording. As a Mr. Joe Coffman re-marked in a 1930 issue of the Journal of the Society of Motion Picture Engineers:

> "Unfortunately most 'deadening' materials
> do what the term signifies . . . on a dead stage,
> with absorbing materials used for set construction,
> the recording inevitably lacks life and brilliance." [16]

Yet on the soundstages of Paramount's Astoria studios (presumably the very same stages that were to produce in that year the comic, but acoustically lifeless, THE COCOANUTS) Mamoulian managed to create an aurally dynamic sound-film. Part of Mamoulian's success, however, was due to the fact that he stubbornly refused to stay within the confines of a studio situation. Thus one of the more interesting sequences in the film seems to have been shot in sync-sound, on location, in the New York city subways.

Another aspect of the new sound medium that Mamoulian intuitively appreciated was its capacity to reveal silence. As Balazs observes, the effect of silence can only be rendered when sounds are present, for there is never an absolute auditory void. What we mean by silence is that things are so quiet we can hear certain noises, distant or close, that we do not usually perceive:

> ". . . if we can hear the crack of a whip
> a mile away – then we are hearing the silence
> around us. We feel the silence when we can hear
> the most distant sound or the slightest rustle
> near us." 17

Thus Balazs's main point is that silence (revealed through the sounds of objects in the environment) is basically a spatial experience.

In Kitty's suicide scene, Mamoulian provides us with an example of this use of silence. In a prior sequence, Hitch has come home and told Kitty that she is no longer wanted for lead roles in burlesque; that she is an old, fat blonde who is past her theatrical and sexual prime. Kitty, panic-stricken, has called several agents in an attempt to prove herself a desirable property, but has been given the brush off in each case. Hitch tells her that her 'meal ticket' from now on is April, but Kitty knows that her daughter wants to leave show business to marry Tony. Hitch walks out on her and April goes off to meet her sailor. Kitty is left alone in the hotel room.

The scene, rendered in a virtuoso single shot, begins with Kitty standing in the center of the room. The camera pans away from her to a picture of Hitch on the mantel, and back again to her in the middle of the room. The camera pans in a similar manner two more times: first to a picture of Hitch on the wall, and then to a picture on a table of April in convent dress. Kitty, with a look of despair on her face, then turns her back to the camera, walks through the living room and bedroom, and enters the bathroom. The camera tracks behind.

Up until this point there has been an almost absolute silence - one that is quite unreal, as in a silent film. But as Kitty opens the medicine cabinet and begins rifling around for sleeping pills the noise of her breathing and the clinking of bottles becomes almost deafening. The scene ends on a sound dissolve - the jangling water glass in Kitty's room is transformed into the sound of a cymbal, played in the restaurant where Tony and April are eating.

This rendering of silence through sound is even more apparent in the following sequence in which we observe Kitty after she has taken the fatal overdose. She is sitting in a chair near the window, her face illuminated by an off-screen blinking neon sign. She says nothing. What we hear is a highly contrived collage of city noises: train whistles, bells, horns, and sirens. We are aware of a clock ticking in the room and a couple speaking the hallway. Through these 'acoustic close-ups' we are made profoundly aware of the physical silence that surrounds her: a void that permits the intrusion of sounds from the abrasive world outside.

What Mamoulian has, of course, done in this sequence is not to render absolute silence, but silence perceived. Though the scene is narratively situated in Kitty's point-of-view, we in the audience participate in her perceptual experience vicariously.

It is interesting to note that the creative use of silence was not new to Mamoulian, but rather issued from his background on the stage. A year before making APPLAUSE he had directed a play on Broadway entitled Wings Over Europe. In one particularly suspenseful scene Mamoulian had employed the following theatrical technique:

> "There was a clock on the mantel of the set. You never heard it of course. But during this silence I had the stage manager carry a

metronome from way backstage down to the
front. So the ticking of the clock becomes
louder, until the whole audience could hear
it." 18

The parallels to Kitty's suicide scene are clear.

It is also significant that the suicide sequence is characterized
by an asynchronous[19] use of sound: that is, the image of the object caus-
ing the sound is not present simultaneously on the screen. A contro-
versy concerning the proper use of sound had, of course, been going on
ever since its technological birth. Theorists had warned against a
simplistically synchronous use of sound and called for experimentation
in contrapuntal technique. Eisenstein, for example, had in 1928 bemoaned
what he feared would be an era in which sound recording would

> ". . . proceed on a naturalistic level,
> exactly corresponding with the movement on the
> screen and providing a certain 'illusion' of
> talking people, of audible objects." 20

His prophecy, as we know, proved correct and most early sound films
evidence a decidedly banal, causal relationship between sound and image
(e.g., the phone rings and we see it).

Mamoulian somehow avoids the trap and even makes asynchronous sound
one of his primary techniques. Examples abound. The city throughout
the film, although an important character, is revealed largely through
sound effects unaccompanied by images. (As April arrives in New York
it is mainly the sounds of the city that affect us; we never really see
their source.) One thinks as well of the scene in which we hear Kitty
and Hitch arguing off-screen, while the camera focuses upon a photograph
of Kitty as a young woman.

But Mamoulian experiments with sound in still other ways in APPLAUSE.
At one point he tries to create a kind of sound montage. After her first
night away from the convent, April dreams. On the screen we see a montage of grotesque close-ups of burlesque girls, musicians, and oogling
men, juxtaposed with serene images of convent life. The soundtrack
parallels this montage with an aural mix of burlesque tunes and the 'Ave
Marie'. In one of Mamoulian's later films, DR. JEKYLL AND MR. HYDE

(1931), he was to carry this innovative technique a step further. As
described by Arthur Knight, the transitions from the character of Jekyll
to Hyde were

> ". . . accompanied by a vivid, synthetically
> created sound track built from exaggerated heart
> beats mingled with the reverberations of gongs
> played backwards, bells heard through echo chambers,
> and completely artificial sounds created by photo-
> graphing light frequencies directly onto the sound
> track. The recordists referred to it as 'Mamoulian
> stew', but it was probably the screen's first exper-
> iment with purely synthetic sound." [21]

Still two other areas of Mamoulian's use of sound bear examination -
those of dialogue and music. As stated previously, one of the greatest
problems with early sound films was their concentration on dialogue.
Not only was there too much talking, but the nature of the language used
was often stagey and artificial. In theatre where the visual parameter
is generally less emphatic, words can carry a great deal more weight
than they can in film. When theatrical dialogue is transferred to the
cinema, it most often seems stifled and tends to impede the narrative
flow. [22]

To make matters worse, the filming of dialogue scenes in most early
sound films was highly unimaginative. The camera almost invariably
showed the person speaking, and while the conversation was going on most
background noise was eliminated (except, perhaps, for some conventional
theme music).

In APPLAUSE, however, Mamoulian avoids these pitfalls. The dialogue itself is conversational, colloquial, off-hand and seems to embody Balazs's notion of "weightless words". [23] One is also peculiarly
affected by the poignant quality of Helen Morgan's voice, and is re-
minded of Balazs's statement about the sound film's potential for reveal-
ing acoustic coloring:

> ". . . the spoken word is not merely the
> reflection of a concept - its intonation, its
> timbre, at the same time make it an irrational
> expression of emotion." [24]

For precisely this reason the <u>sound</u> of Ms. Morgan's voice stays with us
and haunts us, independent of the content of what she has said.

But what seems most noteworthy about Mamoulian's dialogue is the
manner in which it is embedded within the general aural texture of the
film. In many scenes (e.g., when Joe King and Kitty are speaking while
performing on stage) one can hardly hear the dialogue because of all the
other acoustic activity in the frame. In another scene (one which evi-
dences the first use of two-track sound mixing) Kitty sings while April
says her prayers. Almost never is a single thing happening acoustically
at any one time. Almost never (except, perhaps, in the scenes with
Tony and April) do we experience a flattening out of the acoustic environment in order to facilitate the foregrounding of characters' speech.

Mamoulian's use of music in APPLAUSE is also worthy of note. It
seems both surprising and logical that APPLAUSE is often classified as
a musical.[25] It is surprising because APPLAUSE lacks the artificial and
contrived use of production numbers so common in the movie musical; but
fitting in that music plays such an integral part in the creation of the
physical environment of the film.

But how exactly is music used? First of all, the film contains
only two brief instances of background or filler music – one being the
theme of 'Alexander's Ragtime Band' played over the opening titles, and
the other being a few seconds of band music played over a scene transition.[26] Secondly, the film contains only one instance of symbolic 'theme'
music: the use of organ music and the 'Ave Maria' for the convent scenes.
The rest of the film is suffused with music, but it all issues from a
causal source; it is all motivated by the events of the narrative (e.g.,
burlesque routines, marching band music, Kitty's singing).

Aside from having the music arise more naturally than in most musical films Mamoulian even downplays the musical numbers themselves. They
seem to embody the same off-hand, colloquial quality as his dialogue.
Mamoulian resists making his burlesque numbers glamorous productions and
keeps them as sleazy and down-to-earth as possible. He even restrains
from building musical numbers around his star, Helen Morgan, a woman who
was, of course, known for her voice. The times she sings ("What Wouldn't

I Do For That Man" and "Give Your Baby Lots Of Lovin'") she utters frag-
ments of tunes and sings them accappella. No disembodied orchestra, no
temporary halt in the narrative, no soft-focus close-up of the star.
Yet the beauty that arises from Mamoulian's sparse treatment is haunt-
ing and undeniable.

This use of causally-related music is important because it forms
one of the central aspects of the acoustic landscape rendered in the
film. The music is not so much important in itself, as it is in giving
us the sound and resonance of the burlesque world. For as Kracauer observes, ambient music

> ". . . resembles natural sounds in its
> strong affiliation with the environment . . .
> a hurdy-gurdy melody enlivens the street in
> which it lingers. It is the location of the
> melody, not its content which counts."
> [Italics mine] 27

Mamoulian does, of course, use music for certain dramaturgical purposes. When Tony and April are in the restaurant, at the moment that
Kitty is taking a drug overdose, the orchestra just happens to be playing the two songs that she has sung, thus reminding us of her back in
her room. But music never serves that function alone; it is always
integrally related to the environment from which it issues.

A final aspect of Mamoulian's use of sound in APPLAUSE remains to
be explicated, an aspect that is of crucial importance to the creation
of audio-visual spatiality in the film. Throughout APPLAUSE Mamoulian
seems acutely aware of the fact that sounds are modified according to
their distance from the perceiver. Although this seems an obvious perceptual point, the need for soundmen to follow the dictates of acoustic
perception was not at all an accepted tenet of the early sound era.
Rather than thinking sound theory through within a conceptual framework
most technicians simply did what they knew best how to do. Since most
sound engineers had been recruited from radio, they often followed broa
cast technique, a strategy that proved less successful in the sound-fil
medium. As Joe Coffman remarked,

> "In some ways it is unfortunate that the
> radio industry supplied most of the sound ex-
> perts of the film industry. In radio broad-
> casting it usually is desirable to present all
> sounds as coming from approximately the same
> plane – that of the microphone. And so levels
> are raised and lowered to bring all sounds out
> at approximately the same volume . . . But in
> talking picture presentations it is very desir-
> able to achieve space effects and dramatic var-
> iation of volume level." 28

APPLAUSE does achieve such 'space effects' through the subtle manipulation of acoustic perspective. When the distance between camera and subject shifts, the sound level changes accordingly. One thinks, for example, of the scene in which there is a change in voice level as the camera
shifts from a close-up of chorus girls singing on stage to a long-shot
of them from the audience's point of view; or of the scene in which a
change in sound level and quality accompanies the camera shift from an
on-stage view of a girl singing "Everybody's Doin' It" to a backstage
one.

What this reference to acoustic perspective makes clear is an issue
that has underlain our entire previous discussion: the question of auditory perception. For not only does Mamoulian create a palpable spatial
world in APPLAUSE; he creates a world that seems visually and auditor-
ially perceived. When coupled with the highly material sense of visual
space portrayed in the film, the effect upon the audience is not only
one of witnessing characters inhabiting a space, but rather of inhabiting that space themselves, of 'being there'.

It is this sense of a spatial world delineated and perceived that
explains the sensual power of APPLAUSE. For as Bela Belazs has so aptly
stated:

> "Just as our eye is identified with the
> camera lens, so our ear is identified with the
> microphone. . . In this way, in the sound film,
> the fixed, immutable permanent distance between
> spectator and actor is eliminated not only vi-
> sually . . . but acoustically as well. Not only
> as spectators, but as listeners, too, we are trans-
> ferred from our seats to the space in which the
> events depicted on the screen are taking place."29

Strangely, even the title, APPLAUSE, seems to 'bridge' the perceptual gap of which Belazs speaks. For it can be read as referring simultaneously to the burlesque audience within the cinematic diegesis, and to us, the audience, who experiences Mamoulian's monumental film.

Notes:

1. Rudolph Arnheim, Film (London: Faber and Faber, 1933), p. 235. Although this text was published in 1933, it is an English translation of essays written earlier in German. It was impossible to locate the original date of each essay.

2. Ibid.

3. An exception to this generalization is Bela Balazs whose writing on sound will be discussed later in this essay.

4. Arnheim, op. cit., p. 224.

5. James R. Silke, ed., Rouben Mamoulian: "Style Is The Man" (Washington, D. C.: The American Film Institute, 1971), p. 7.

6. I am thinking of such directors of the early sound era as Roland West, Josef von Sternberg, Howard Hawks, Harry Beaumont, etc., who made competent sound films, but did not demonstrate a particular sensitivity to the spatial aspects of the aural medium. Bryan Foy, of course, would be a prime example.

7. Silke, op. cit., p. 11.

8. Bela Balazs, Theory of Film (New York: Dover, 1970), pp. 206-207.

9. Silke, op. cit., p. 6. Mamoulian is quoted as saying "They wanted me to go in and direct dialogue for two years."

10. Andrew Sarris, Interviews with Film Directors (New York: Avon Books, 1967), pp. 346-347.

11. The Symphony of Noises was later used in LOVE ME TONIGHT (1932).

12. Edmund Carpenter and Marshall McLuhan, eds., Explorations in Communication (Boston: Beacon Press, 1960), p. 68.

13. Siegfried Kracauer, Theory of Film: The Redemption of Physical Reality (London: Oxford University Press, 1960), p. 67.

14. Carpenter and McLuhan, op. cit., p. 67.

15. Balazs, op. cit., p. 197. The term 'tonal milieu' used above is a
phrase Balazs uses on p. 211 of his text.

16. Joe Coffman, "Art and Science in Sound Film Production", Transactions of the Society of Motion Picture Engineers #14 (February, 1930),
p. 176.

17. Balazs, op. cit., p. 206.

18. Silke, op. cit., p. 19.

19. Although I object to the term 'asynchronous' as imprecise and con-
fusing, and would prefer the term 'acausal' sound, I am using it because
it is conventionally associated with the technique I am discussing.

20. Sergei Eisenstein, Film Form, trans. Jay Leyda (New York: Harcourt,
Brace, and World, 1949), p. 258.

21. Arthur Knight, The Liveliest Art (New York: New American Library,
1957), p. 158.

22. I mean to except from this generalization such films as Dreyer's
GERTRUD which purposefully use theatrical technique as part of the work's
overall formal and thematic structure.

23. Balazs, op. cit., p. 229.

24. Ibid, p. 230.

25. The Theatre 80 St. Marks, in New York city, has included it in its
repertoire of the movie musical.

26. The scene transition referred to is that which occurs between the
scene of Kitty and Joe King in her room, and April in the convent.

27. Kracauer, op. cit., p. 144.

28. Coffman, op. cit., pp. 173-174.

29. Balazs, op. cit., p. 215.

CITIZEN KANE:
The Influence of Radio Drama on Cinematic Design
by Evan William Cameron

". . . I spent a year cutting it [CITIZEN
KANE] and saw it 7000 times, but never since. I
can't bear to see myself up there; I keep noticing
things I want to change. When I made KANE, I had
a sort of innocent assurance. I hadn't learnt what
you aren't supposed to be able to do . . . In handling a camera I feel I have no peer. But what De
Sica can do, that I can't do. I ran his SHOESHINE
again recently and the camera disappeared, the screen
disappeared; it was just life . . ." [1]

Many arts have influenced the cinema over extended periods of time
One art - radio drama - is an exception. For we can date the onset of
its influence from the coming of synchronous sound to the cinema in 192
and the culmination of its influence with the creation of CITIZEN KANE
in 1941. Thereafter film and radio drama were to part company, each
having learned what it could from the other.

What had the cinema learned from radio drama? If we look closely
at CITIZEN KANE, we shall learn much about the virtues and limitations
of radio design, cinematic design, and the design of CITIZEN KANE itse
For CITIZEN KANE is a puzzling film to many, and ought to be puzzling
many more. By common consent it is a great film, yet its greatness ha
been misunderstood. For two questions have seldom been faced, much le
answered. First:

> Why, despite its reputation, has the design
> of CITIZEN KANE remained largely unemulated?
>
> (Truffaut may have been right, though one
> wishes he'd named names, in remarking that
> the film is "probably the one that has
> started the largest number of filmmakers
> on their careers";[2] but filmmakers, Welles
> and Truffaut included, have seldom <u>modeled</u>
> films after CITIZEN KANE.)

The answer to the first question is implicit in the second:

> Why, despite the accuracy and complexity of
> its characterizations, and the finesse of
> its effects, is CITIZEN KANE emotionally
> unengaging?
>
> (What sapped the <u>humanity</u> from CITIZEN
> KANE, and precipitated Welles's transition
> to the design of THE MAGNIFICENT AMBERSONS?)

A great film may influence films and filmmakers in one of three ways:

> Positively, by encompassing innovations of such
> fruitfulness that they enter forthwith the
> mainstream of film design (e.g., THE BIRTH OF
> A NATION, or UNDERWORLD);
>
> Negatively, by encompassing innovations of such
> unfruitfulness that they remain thereafter of
> only passing interest to film designers (e.g.,
> NIGHT MAIL, or THE LADY IN THE LAKE); or
>
> Both, by encompassing manifestly fruitful, and
> unfruitful, innovations.

Films are rarely great, for most are diffuse and hence unenlightening. CITIZEN KANE, however, is a film of the third kind - a film both positively and negatively influential - and we shall misunderstand its influence, and its lessons for us, if we pretend otherwise.

Let us, therefore, list the tactical innovations of CITIZEN KANE, distinguishing the visual from the aural, and the positive from the negative. By doing so, we shall delimit the effects of radio drama on cinematic design.

The Tactical Innovations of CITIZEN KANE

Positive - Visual

What visual innovations of CITIZEN KANE were productive, provoking
emulation? Principally two.

The first - the sustained use of deep focus (enabling us to see
sharply all objects from foreground to background) - had been attempted
earlier by Eisenstein, Renoir, and others. Success, however, awaited
the invention of short focal length lenses with wide apertures, the
development of fast panchromatic film stocks, the availability of source
of extraordinary amounts of artificial light, and the genius of Welles
(and Toland, his cameraman - the "greatest of us all" in Hal Mohr's
phrase) in forecasting its dramatic function.

Deep focus had ancillary effects. Since action was now unrestricte
to a single focused plane, events at varying distances from the camera
could be simultaneously recorded and contrasted. Longer takes became
possible from both stationary and moving cameras with less dramatic in-
elegance; and since follow-focus was unnecessary, longer takes permitted
flexible camera movements (e.g., roving tracking shots).

Deep focus, however, required visual content in breadth, depth, and
height, for the wide angle lenses not only saw more than usual, but registered it in focus. Sets, in particular, required ceilings, frustrat-
ing lighting directors constrained already to bring unaccustomed numbers
of lights to bear on a scene. With the ceilings in place, however, low
angle interior shots became possible for the first time, and Welles used
them to show detail and decor. (He was sensitive enough, on most occasions, to avoid using them symbolically, unlike Eisenstein.)

The second positive visual tactic of CITIZEN KANE - the sustained
use of low key lighting ('Rembrandt lighting', in Griffith's phrase -
a few highlights surrounded by shadow) - resulted in part from the requirements of deep focus in both a superficial and deep sense.

Deep focus required extraordinary amounts of light to register the

images. With more objects seen sharply within a shot, more objects had
to be lit. The fewer objects one needed to light, however, the more economical the production. Low key lighting, therefore, was the tactic of
choice if deep focus cinematography was to be economical.

But there was a deeper impulse toward low key lighting inherent in
the use of deep focus. For as Bazin soon noted, [3] if several characters
are simultaneously in focus within a shot, they may draw equal attention,
and hence become dramatically ubiquitous. (Or, put another way, the
event may lose its dramatic momentum and become ambiguous, for each
viewer is free to attend to whatever strikes his fancy.)

Bazin, I think, misunderstood Welles's response to this constraint,
for Welles faced the question head-on:

> Since, under deep focus, all events within
> a shot may draw attention, how is it pos-
> sible to restrict the attention of viewers
> to a single sequence of events as required
> for dramatic effect?

Welles's solution was to use low key lighting at all times (other
than in the footage mimicking newsreels), illuminating at any moment
only that part of the scene to which attention should be drawn. He
chose not to avoid shadows and accent highlights (the normal Hollywood
lighting technique of the 1930s), but rather to light for the highlights
and forget the unessentials. If (e.g.) the face of character ought to be
shadowed for dramatic effect, then shadowed it was.

The result was montage without cutting. Although the shots contained masses of detail, only significant details drew attention. Welles
then sequenced the film around these points of attention, maintaining
momentum and forestalling ambiguity (Bazin to the contrary notwithstand-
ing).

Positive - Aural

What aural innovations of CITIZEN KANE were productive, provoking
emulation. Again, principally two.

The first was an increase in the scope and accuracy of the sound effects contributing to the spatial sense of the scene (e.g., falling rain, echoes in large rooms, and the distancing effects of vanishing or approaching footsteps and voices).

The second was an increase in the effectiveness of the dialogue expressed by the characters, compared to the prevailing Hollywood (theatrical) norm. Distinct voices were keyed to distinct characters (Opposing characters? Opposing voices!), and the naturalness of the spoken lines was augmented by using ungrammatical constructions, overlapping conversations, and natural interruptions.

_____

Let us now list the tactical innovations of CITIZEN KANE which were negative and have remained unemulated. All are techniques for switching from one scene to another with a time transition in between.

Negative - Visual

What visual innovations of CITIZEN KANE were unproductive, remaining unemulated? Principally two.

Almost every technique used to indicate visually the passage of time between scenes was dramatically counterproductive (e.g., the swish pans between the scenes of Kane and Emily at breakfast; the changing circulation figures for the Inquirer; the costume changes at the opera; the jigsaw puzzle montage).

The problem was not that the transitions were unclear (every viewer could tell that time had passed, and how much), but rather that they were perceptually unnatural and hence emotionally empty; for a sustained emotional response can occur only when information is processed in perceptually natural ways. Emotions are felt responses occasioned by thwarted habits - physiological reactions to unconscious expectations gone awry (however pleasantly or unpleasantly). To evoke an emotional response, therefore, other than that of naked novelty, requires the presence and

prior assimilation of a context of natural stimuli naturally ordered -
for only to natural stimuli naturally ordered do we possess deeply conditioned, unconscious patterns of response.

The visual time transitions of CITIZEN KANE, being perceptually
unnatural, were symbols interrupting a context of events, and hence,
however clear their meaning, vitiated the possibility of sustained emotional response. Welles, sensing this, seldom again put them to use,
and observant filmmakers have followed his example. Straight cuts (or,
at worst, fade out - fade ins) now link scenes directly to one another
with no disengaging clutter in between.

The second visual technique which was unproductive is the lapse
dissolve (in which a new scene is gradually introduced and superposed
over the old, and the superposition is maintained momentarily before
the old scene is faded out). Welles used the lapse dissolve to relate
his character narrators to the scenes following which they were supposedly recalling - to place them visually 'on top' of the succeeding
scenes, as it were.

The lapse dissolve, like the devices of the first type, is a technique of time transition. It is equally unnatural in dramatic con-
texts, and hence emotionally stultifying, for we are unaccustomed to
perceiving visual mixes, and have no responses conditioned to them
from which deep emotional effects could be induced. (See also p. 215
below.) Welles, again sensing unfruitfulness, avoided the lapse dissolve in his future designs, and most filmmakers have followed suit.

Negative - Aural

What aural innovations of CITIZEN KANE were unproductive, remaining
unemulated? Principally two (each again a technique of time transition).

The first used spoken lines of character narrators as triggers to
flashbacks. The idea, again, was clear, but clarity came at the ex-
pense of naturalness and emotional continuity. For at one moment we
are watching a scene of a person reminiscing and responding naturally

to the events in that scene which we can see and hear, while at the
next moment we are shown a scene in the <u>mind</u> of the person which we
could not, in context, see and hear. The problem comes not from flash-
ing back to another scene, but rather from establishing the flashback
as a memory image - an image in the mind of a character - which destroys
the perceptual integrity of the establishing scene.

The problem lies embedded in the larger strategic hassle of using
perceived narrators in films (see p. 213 below). For the moment, however, we need only note that Welles was progressively to forsake the
technique, as have most other filmmakers.

The second unproductive effect occured whenever a transition was
made visually from one scene to another, while maintaining an uninterrupted synchronous sound continuity begun in the first scene (as in the
Thatcher montage, or the election speeches, when the transitions occur
in the middle of a sentence begun in one scene and completed in the
next; or when we cut in mid phrase from Susan at her singing lesson to
the opening of the opera; or when we cut between two scenes at different times of Kane doing tricks for Susan while maintaining a single
uninterrupted conversation.)

As with the swish pans at the breakfast table (see p. 206 above),
the transitions entail unnatural perceptions. The idea again is clear,
but the effect, at best, is clever - and perceived cleverness is an
undramatic intrusion, sapping emotional continuity. Never again was
Welles to use the technique, and most film designers, shunning inele-
gance, have avoided it as well.

We, thus, have four listings of the tactical innovations of CITIZEN
KANE (see Figure 1). The question becomes:

> What led Welles to the positive and negative
> innovations of CITIZEN KANE? (What were
> their distinguishing roots?)

The answer, as we shall see, was a susceptibility to the traditions of
radio drama.

Figure 1:   The Tactical Innovations of CITIZEN KANE

Positive - Visual

1. The use of deep focus,
and the concommitant use
of

    a. simultaneous actions
in diverse planes; longer
takes; and flexible camera
movements; and

    b. full sets with ceilings,
permitting low angle interior
shots; and

2. The sustained use of low
key ('Rembrandt') lighting -
montage without cutting.

Negative - Visual

1. The use of visual devices
to indicate time transitions;
and (included among them)

2. The use of lapse dissolves.

Positive - Aural

1. The use of many accurate
sound effects to contribute to
the spatial sense of the scene;
and

2. The use of unprecedentedly
effective dialogue, achieved
through

    a. distinct voices keyed to
distinct characters; and

    b. natural constructions of
speech (ungrammatical sentences,
overlapping and interrupted conversations).

Negative - Aural

1. The use of spoken lines of
character narrators as transitions to flashbacks; and

2. The use of uninterrupted
synchronous sound continuities
to bridge visual time transitions.

The Legacy of Radio Drama

Welles had been trained in the theatre, but his genius had found its focus in the new art of radio drama. He was brought to Hollywood to emulate the success of his War of the Worlds broadcast which had terrified the nation.

Radio drama, however, unlike the cinema, is a quintessential art of the ear, deriving its effects solely from the use of the voice, music, and natural (or unnatural) sounds. What, then, are the virtues and limitations of the way we hear, and hence of the design of radio drama?

Our ears, unlike our eyes, have no lenses. They register the presence of all sounding events in our environment simultaneously and indiscriminately. Unsurprisingly, therefore, our aural sense of the world at any moment is of a continuous spatial environment unbounded in any dimension.

Our aural sense of the world, however, is also uncacophonous, for at any moment we are attending (usually) to only one sounding event and not attending to the others. Since our ears have no lenses they are unable to focus on particular sounds to the exclusion of others simultaneously registered. Why, then, is the aural world uncacophonous? Or, more precisely,

> How is it possible for us to attend to a
> single sounding event in our environment,
> having no lenses with which to focus on it?

This perplexing problem, known affectionately as 'the cocktail party problem' in American acoustical science (How are we able to distinguish one drunken voice from another in a crowded room?), has only recently been solved. Our ears are frequency analyzers. When sound waves are received by one of our ears from a sounding object, they are (usually) out of phase with the waves received by the other ear, and both sets of waves are out of phase with the waves received from other sounding objects in different spatial locations. It is this difference in phase

of the waves received by each of our ears from spatially disparate objects which permits the brain to <u>attend</u> to one object rather than another, even though our ears have no lenses with which to <u>focus</u> on it.

The higher regions of our aural perceptual system, in short, encom-
pass a complex phase filter. For the phase filter to work, however,
the waves striking our ears from different objects must come from different spatial directions! Otherwise there would be no phase difference
between the waves to be filtered and analyzed.

But therein lies the source of the fundamental problem of radio
technique. For all sound waves emanating from a single radio speaker
arrive at our ears from a common spatial direction inphase! Were one,
therefore, to playback through a single speaker with absolute fidelity
a recording taken in the middle of a room at a cocktail party, one
would be unable to select from the mass of sounds a single sound to
which to attend – even though, had one been standing in the middle of
the room at the cocktail party, registering the same mass of sounds,
one could have done so with ease.

Designers of radio drama, therefore, faced a tricky problem. Listeners must attend to single events within a natural aural environment
to become emotionally engaged. But an accurate <u>phased</u> reproduction of
an aural event within its environment is impossible. Aural scenes,
therefore, must be constructed, not reproduced.

By 1941 designers of radio drama had learned to mimic our natural
aural experience of a scene through

> (1) sustaining a sense of a continuous sequence of <u>single</u>
> events to which attention could be drawn, by presenting at
> attentive levels only those events, and eliminating (or
> depressing) all others;
>
> (2) sustaining a sense of a continuous and unbounded
> spatial environment, by maintaining a constant, unobtru-
> sive background presence (room tone, relevant noises, etc.);
>
> (3) sustaining a sense of an accurate spatial distance
> between objects, by varying their relative loudnesses as
> they advanced or receded from the foreground; and

(4)   sustaining a sense of the immediate recognizability
and unquestioned credibility of characters, by using
distinct voices for different characters, and employing
natural (nontheatrical) patterns of speech and conversation.

The sources of Welles's positive innovations should now be apparent.
Welles came to Hollywood accustomed to conceiving of a scene as a sequence of single spatial events of unquestioned natural credibility,
existing within an unbounded spatial environment simultaneously present
but unattended. When he attempted in CITIZEN KANE to recreate the natural sense of the scene to which he was accustomed in radio, the results
were cinematically ingenious and fruitful:

By using deep focus and low key lighting (and
their concommitants), Welles achieved, through
natural visual techniques, the effect of unbounded spatiality with bounded attentiveness
to which he was accustomed; and

By transferring to the soundtrack the detailed
sound effects to which he was accustomed (the
effects of presence and distance, the distinc-
tive voices of characters, the natural patterns
of speech), Welles accentuated the natural spatial credibility of the events visually perceived.

What, then, were the sources of Welles's negative innovations in
CITIZEN KANE – those effects which he later recognized as unproductive,
and which have remained unemulated?

Our ears are marvelous tools for ascertaining the presence and distance of identified sounding objects. Unfortunately, lacking lenses,
they are astonishingly poor at ascertaining the spatial directions from
which sounds come. As Aristotle knew, therefore, and Leonardo da Vinci
reaffirmed, our eyes are our chief tools for ascertaining the spatial
and chronological identity of objects and events (i.e., the spatial and
chronological map of our environment).

Radio dramatists, therefore, faced a second tricky problem. Listeners must be oriented to the spatial and chronological map of their
environment to become emotionally engaged. Usually this must be done

by <u>describing</u> the dramatic environment to them with a human voice, for all other aural tools are insufficiently precise. But describing an environment is an unnatural use of the human voice in most situations, for we are accustomed to acquiring such information through our eyes, not our ears. (When walking with a friend, conversing, one is unaccustomed to saying (e.g.) 'There is a yellow automobile, and over there a brick building, and over here . . .' One may comment upon the environment, or express evaluations of it, but one seldom if ever <u>describes</u> it. Verbal descriptions customarily inform us of past or future events, not events present to us.)

Radio dramatists, therefore, were on the horns of a dilemma:

> A radio drama ceases to develop if its environ-
> ments remain undescribed, for listeners are
> then unable to identify the spatiotemporal
> setting of the action; yet if the <u>characters</u>
> describe their environment, they then lose
> credibility as characters, and (again) the
> drama ceases to develop.

To avoid the dilemma (to protect the credibility of the characters, while permitting listeners to identify the dramatic environment), radio dramatists developed a tool with precedents in the novel and theatre, but of genius in the new medium alone: the narrator.

By using a voice unlocated in the scene, a dramatist could identify for listeners the spatial and chronological environment of events with neither fragmentation nor loss of character credibility. Time transitions, in particular, could be made with simple elegance by shifting the tense or grammatical voice of a narrator's remarks: flashbacks and flashforwards could be effected with precision and consummate ease.

When Welles came to Hollywood, he was accustomed to achieving time transitions flexibly and accurately by means of narrators. Unsurprisingly, therefore, he (and Mankiewicz, his co-scriptwriter) designed CITIZEN KANE as a sequence of scenes encompassing major and frequent time transitions. (The story of Kane's life is presented chronologically (with minor overlaps) in four major flashbacks, each containing

multiple scenes having major flashforward time transitions between them.
The film ends where it begins, in Kane's mansion near the time of his
death.)

Given the strategy, the tactical problem was clear:

> What techniques could effect the time
> transitions, while maintaining dramatic
> continuity and momentum?

Accustomed to the sounds of radio, but not the sights of cinema,
Welles – with astonishing ingenuity – construed the sights as sounds
and subjected them to sound techniques! The results, however, were
unproductive in two ways.

Welles did not wish to forgo the flexibility and ease with which
narrators can effect time transitions. But he did wish to utilize the
immediate identification of characters which visuals provide. He decided, therefore, to use characters as quasi-narrators to introduce and
identify the flashbacks – not one character, but four!

Welles recognized that the only way credibly to introduce a flashback through a character narrator in a scene is to treat it as if it
were a memory image. Unfortunately, the introduction of a purported
memory image itself destroys the integrity of the scene, for memory
images are imperceivable by observers unlike the face and voice of the
character introducing them. (See p. 207f above)

(Perhaps disquieted by the effect of the multiple-character narration of CITIZEN KANE, Welles tried a voice-over non-character narrator
in THE MAGNIFICENT AMBERSONS, and then a voice-over single character
narrator in THE LADY FROM SHANGHAI. Finally, recognizing the root of
the problem to be his vestigial (literary) insistence on major and frequent time transitions, not the narration per se (Bresson's voice-over
narrations, and Welles's own in THE MAGNIFICENT AMBERSONS, after all,
are elegantly effective), Welles eschewed all three in TOUCH OF EVIL
with brilliant results.)

The second failure arose from a lack of understanding of the un-

equivalence of vision and hearing. Our ears, having no lenses, register complex mixes of sound - multiple sound events superposed on one
another. We, therefore, are accustomed to perceiving aural mixes (the
sounds of a cocktail party, for example), and sorting them out. Our
eyes, on the other hand, having lenses, focus on objects one at a time.
Visual mixes or superpositions are not part of our normal visual environment. We, therefore, are unaccustomed to perceiving them, and hence
have no rooted emotional responses to them.

Welles, in radio, was accustomed to using aural mixes and superpositions (e.g., cross fades, sound overs) to effect time transitions
with natural dramatic results, for aural mixes are part of our everyday
aural environment, and we have conditioned unconscious responses to
them. When, however, he attempted in CITIZEN KANE to use visual mixes
and superpositions to effect time transitions, or to unify disparate
events, the results were unnatural and hence emotionally vacuous. When
he attempted, similarly, to bridge disparate visual scenes with continuous synchronous sound, the results were again unnatural and dramatically unproductive, for we have no conditioned responses to such perceptual effects either. (See p. 206f above.)

The sources of Welles's negative innovations should now be apparent.
Welles came to Hollywood accustomed to the flexibilities of hearing.
When, however, he attempted in CITIZEN KANE to treat visuals as sounds
(and hence flashbacks as memory images), and subject them to sound
techniques, the results were uniformly clever but unproductive. For
the events became symbols, at best, and sapped the emotional development
of the drama.

The Legacy of CITIZEN KANE

CITIZEN KANE, despite its brilliance, is emotionally unengaging,
for its major and frequent time transitions, derived from radio drama,
compelled Welles to use tactics which were perceptually unnatural. Had
they been less unnatural, the film would be less brilliant. As it is,
however, CITIZEN KANE's many (de)vices cancel its virtues: its surface

engages the mind while disengaging the heart. Welles recognized this more quickly than anyone else, and when, one year later, THE MAGNIFICENT AMBERSONS appeared, the compulsions of radio drama were (largely) gone forever.

We can learn much from CITIZEN KANE about the virtues and limitations of radio and the cinema, but not by shutting our eyes and ears, closing our minds, and shouting 'masterpiece'. We must, instead, construe it as Welles did - as a "catalogue of effects" - most of them begotten by another art, radio drama, and half of them stillborn.

Only by following Welles's example shall we come to understand how great an achievement CITIZEN KANE really was.

Notes:

1. Orson Welles, quoted by Derick Grigs in his article "Orson Welles: Conversation at Oxford", Sight & Sound (Spring, 1960: Vol. 29, #2), p. 82.

2. Francois Truffaut, quoted by Pauline Kael in "Raising Kane", The Citizen Kane Book (Boston: Little, Brown & Company, 1971), p. 3.

3. See, in particular, "The Evolution of the Language of Cinema" in Andre Bazin, What is Cinema?, Vol. 1, trans. by Hugh Grey (Berkeley: The University of California Press, 1967), pp. 23-40. The surrounding essays "The Ontology of the Photographic Image", "The Myth of Total Cinema:, and "The Virtues and Limitations of Montage" are also pertinent.

Contributors

Evan William Cameron is Associate Professor of Communications (Cinema Sequence) at Washington State University, and President of Sparrow Productions. Former Coordinator of the Graduate Film Program at Boston University and President of the Board of the University Film Study Center, he has published widely in both film and philosophy and won major awards for his educational and commercial filmmaking.

Frank Capra is one of Hollywood's premier directors. He directed Harry Langdon's most successful silent film comedies; produced the remarkable "Why We Fight" series during World War II; and thereafter originated the Bell Telephone System's science series ("Our Mister Sun", etc.) for television. In between he won Academy Awards for IT HAPPENED ONE NIGHT, MR. DEEDS GOES TO TOWN, and YOU CAN'T TAKE IT WITH YOU, while directing such other successes as LOST HORIZON, MR. SMITH GOES TO WASHINGTON, MEET JOHN DOE, ARSENIC AND OLD LACE, and IT"S A WONDERFUL LIFE.

Julius Epstein has been writing and producing motion pictures for more than 40 years. Working as a team with his brother, Philip (until Philip's death in 1952), he won an Academy Award for CASABLANCA, has earned two Academy Award nominations for FOUR DAUGHTERS and PETE AND TILLIE, garnered five Writers Guild nominations for these and FANNY and THE TENDER TRAP, and was in 1973 awarded the Laurel Award by the Writers Guild and the Writer of the Year award by the National Association of Theatre Owners. Other credits include ARSENIC AND OLD LACE, MY FOOLISH HEART, THE LAST TIME I SAW PARIS, and THE LIGHT IN THE PIAZZA.

Raymond Fielding is Professor of Communication in the School of Communication of the University of Houston, Vice-President of the SMPTE, and Trustee of the American Film Institute and the University Film Foundation. He is past-President of the University Film Association, the Society for Cinema Studies, and the IFPA, author of numerous books and papers on the history of film and its technology, and a prize-winning documentary filmmaker.

Lucy Fischer is Curatorial Assistant in the Film Section of the Museum of Art of the Carnegie Institute, and teaches film at the University of Pittsburg. Her articles have appeared in Film Quarterly, Sight & Sound, Cinema Journal, and the Quarterly Review of Film Studies.

Douglas Gomery is Asssitant Professor in the Department of Mass Communication of the College of Letters and Science of the University of Wisconsin at Milwaukee. His work on the economic history of the film industry has been widely anthologized, and his writings on this topic and others have appeared in the Journal of the University Film Association, the Quarterly Review of Film Studies, Cinema Journal, Screen, the Purdue Film Studies Annual, and Wide Angle.

Bernard Herrmann was perhaps the most sought-after composer in film for over 35 years. He worked with many directors (including Welles, Dieterle, Stevenson, Wise, Mankiewicz, Hitchcock, Zinnemann, Walsh, and Truffaut), composing the scores for, among others, CITIZEN KANE, THE MAGNIFICENT AMBERSONS, JANE EYRE, ALL THAT MONEY CAN BUY (for which he won an Academy Award), THE DAY THE EARTH STOOD STILL, THE GHOST & MRS. MUIR, THE MAN WHO KNEW TOO MUCH, VERTIGO, NORTH BY NORTHWEST, PSYCHO, THE BIRDS, A HATFUL OF RAIN, THE NAKED AND THE DEAD, FAHRENHEIT 451, and THE BRIDE WORE BLACK.

Rouben Mamoulian came to film from the theatre in 1929, quickly expanded the horizons of the sound movie, and thereafter moved from film to the theatre and back again with unprecedented success in films such as APPLAUSE, CITY STREETS, DR. JEKYLL AND MR. HYDE, LOVE ME TONIGHT, SONG OF SONGS, QUEEN CHRISTINA, BECKY SHARP, HIGH WIDE AND HANDSOME, GOLDEN BOY, THE MARK OF ZORRO, RINGS ON HER FINGERS, SUMMER HOLIDAY, and SILK STOCKINGS, and in plays such as Porgy and Bess, Oklahoma, Sadie Thompson, Carousel, St. Louis Woman, and Lost in the Stars.

Hal Mohr, A.S.C., was one of Hollywood's foremost cinematographers for more than 60 years, photographing THE WEDDING MARCH, LITTLE ANNIE ROONEY, THE JAZZ SINGER, A MIDSUMMER NIGHT'S DREAM (for which he received an Academy Award), GREEN PASTURES, PHANTOM OF THE OPERA, THE CLIMAX, THE LOST MOMENT, and THE WILD ONE, among many others.

Gerald F. Noxon is Emeritus Professor of Film at Boston University, having founded the department in 1947. Prior to that he founded the Cambridge (University) Film Guild, worked for John Grierson in the G.P.O. Film Unit and later at the National Film Board of Canada, and wrote numerous radio dramas for the BBC, CBC, NBC, and CBS, including the first STUDIO ONE script. His writings on film have appeared in Sight & Sound, the Cambridge Review, the Journal of the Society of Cinematologists, and Cinema Studies.

Walter Reisch began writing and directing films in his home town of
Vienna, Austria, then worked for Ufa in Berlin, Gallone Productions
in Rome, and Alexander Korda in London before coming to Hollywood
in the 1930s to work 10 years at MGM and another 10 years at 20th
Century Fox. While in Europe he was awarded First Prize at the
1935 Biennale in Venice for the screenplay to the Paula Wessely
film EPISODE; wrote the story and screenplay for the first German
language 'Viennese musical' talkie, 2 HEARTS IN 3/4 TIME; and later,
in 1973, received the Great Gold Medal of Vienna for his artistic
achievements. In Hollywood he won an Academy Award for the screenplay of TITANIC, Academy Award nominations for the story of COMRADE
X and the screenplays of THE GREAT WALTZ, NINOTCHKA, GASLIGHT, and
JOURNEY TO THE CENTER OF THE EARTH, wrote and directed SONG OF
SCHEHEREZADE, and wrote the stories or screenplays to THE GIRL IN
THE RED VELVET SWING, STOPOVER TOKYO, THAT UNCERTAIN FEELING, and
other films.

James G. Stewart has been one of Hollywood's principal sound production
and post-production specialists for over 50 years. He designed the
original sound system for Radio City Music Hall, then moved to Hollywood and worked as post-production chief for RKO from 1933 to 1945.
From 1945 to 1950 he was technical supervisor to David O. Selznick;
from 1950 to 1963 he was at Glen Glenn Sound Studios in charge of all
post-production for Desilu Studios; now he works at the Burbank Studios. His credits include the sound work in post-production on CITI-
ZEN KANE and THE MAGNIFICENT AMBERSONS, and Academy Awards for THIS
LAND IS MINE and THE BELLS OF ST. MARY'S. His technical articles
have appeared in the Journal of the SMPTE and elsewhere.

Select Bibliography

Abbott, J. E., "Development of the Sound Film", Journal of the SMPE, June, 1942, p. 541.

Aiken, Joseph, "Technical Notes and Reminiscences on the Presentation of Tykociner's Sound Picture Contributions", Journal of the SMPTE, August, 1958, p. 521.

Arnheim, Rudolph, Film (London: Faber and Faber, 1933).

Balio, Tino (editor), The American Film Industry (Madison: The University of Wisconsin Press, 1976).

Belazs, Bela, Theory of Film (New York: Dover, 1970)

Bland, W. S., "The Development of the Sound Newsreel", British Kinematography, August, 1950, p. 50.

Cameron, Evan William, "On Mathematics, Music, and Film", Cinema Studies, #3 (Spring, 1970).

Cameron, James R., Motion Pictures with Sound (Manhattan Beach, N. Y.: Cameron Publishing Co., 1929).

Capra, Frank, The Name Above the Title (New York: MacMillan Company, 1971).

Chew, V. K., Talking Machines, 1877-1914 (London: Her Majesty's Stationery Office, 1967)

Coffman, Joe, "Art and Science in Sound Film Production", Transactions of the Society of Motion Picture Engineers, #14 (February, 1930), p. 176.

Conant, Michael, Antitrust in the Motion Picture Industry (Berkeley: University of California Press, 1960).

Crawford, Merrit, "Pioneering Experiments of Eugene Lauste in Recording Sound", Journal of the SMPE, October, 1931, p. 632.

Danielian, N. R., AT&T: The Story of Industrial Conquest (New York: The Vanguard Press, 1939).

De Forest, Lee., "Pioneering in Talking Pictures", Journal of the SMPE, January, 1941, p. 41.

Eisenstein, Sergei, Film Form and The Film Sense, edited and translated by Jay Leyda (New York: Meridian Books, 1963).

Fielding, Raymond, A Technological History of Motion Pictures and Television (Berkeley: University of California Press, 1967).

Franklin, Harold B., Sound Motion Pictures (Garden City, N. Y.: Doubleday, Doran & Co., 1930).

Gaumont, Leon, "Gaumont Chronochrome Process Described by the Inventor", Journal of the SMPTE, January, 1959, p. 29.

Gillings, Ted, "The Color of the Music: an Interview with Bernard Herrmann", Sight & Sound, Vol. 41, #1 (Winter, 1971/72), pp. 36-39.

Gomery, Douglas, "The Coming of the Talkies: Invention, Innovation, and Diffusion", in Balio, op. cit., pp. 193-211.

_____ , "Tri-Ergon, Tobis-Klangfilm, and the Coming of Sound", Cinema Journal, XVI, No. 1 (Fall, 1976), pp. 51-61.

_____ , "The Coming of Sound to the German Cinema", Purdue Film Studies Annual, #1 (August, 1976), pp. 136-143.

_____ , "Problems in Film History: How Fox Innovated Sound", The Quarterly Review of Film Studies, Vol. 1, #3 (August, 1976), pp. 315-330.

Green, Fitzhugh, The Film Finds Its Tongue (New York: G. P. Putnam's Sons, 1929).

Hampton, Benjamin B., History of the American Film Industry from its Beginnings to 1931 (New York: Dover, 1970).

Hays, Will H., See and Hear (New York: Motion Picture Producers and Distributors of America, 1929).

Hendricks, Gordon, The Kinetoscope (New York: The Beginnings of the American Film, 1966).

Heuttig, Mae, Economic Control of the Motion Picture Industry (Philadelphia: University of Pennsylvania Press, 1944).

Huntley, John and Roger Manvell, The Technique of Film Music (London: Focal Press, 1967).

Jones, G. F., Sound-Film Reproduction (London: Blackie and Son, Ltd., 1936).

Jones, L. A., "A Historical Summary of Standardization in the Society of Motion Picture Engineers", Journal of the SMPE, October, 1933, p. 280.

Kellogg, Edward W., "The Development of 16mm Sound Motion Pictures", Journal of the SMPE, January, 1935, p. 63.

_____, "History of Sound Motion Pictures", Journal of the SMPTE, June, 1955, p. 291; July, 1955, p. 356; August, 1955, p. 422.

Krows, Arthur, The Talkies (New York: Henry Holt & Company, 1930).

McCullough, John B., "Joseph T. Tykociner: Pioneer in Sound Recording", Journal of the SMPTE, August, 1958, p. 520.

Mueller, W. A., and M. Rettinger, "Anecdotal History of Sound Recording Technique", Journal of the SMPE, July, 1945, p. 48.

Narath, Albert, "Oskar Messter and His Work", Journal of the SMPTE, October, 1960, p. 726.

Pasquella, George Donald, "An Investigation in the Use of Sound in American Motion Picture Exhibition, 1908-1919" (unpublished Master's Thesis, University of Iowa, 1968).

Ramsaye, Terry, "Early History of Sound Pictures", Journal of the SMPE, September, 1928, p. 597.

Silke, James R. (editor), Rouben Mamoulian: "Style Is The Man" (Washington, D. C.: The American Film Institute, 1971).

Sinclair, Upton, Upton Sinclair Presents William Fox (Los Angeles: Upton Sinclair, 1933).

Sponable, Earl I., "Historical Development of Sound Films", Journal of the SMPE, April, 1947, p. 275; May, 1947, p. 407.

Stewart, James G., "The Rerecording Process", Audio Engineering Society Preprint #719 (New York: Audio Engineering Society, 1970).

Stanley, Robert, The Celluloid Empire (New York: Hastings House, 1978).

Swenson, Joel, "The Entrepreneur's Role in Introducing the Sound Motion Picture", Political Science Quarterly, September, 1948.

Theisen, W. E., "Pioneering in the Talking Picture", Journal of the SMPE, April, 1941, p. 415.

_____ , "Work of Lee De Forest", Journal of the SMPE, December, 1940, p. 542.

Wente, Frederick, MacKenzie, Stoller, Scriven, and Santee, "Synchronized Reproduction of Sound and Scene", a monograph reprinted from Bell Telephone Record, November, 1928.

Zuckerkandl, Victor, Sound and Symbol: Music and the External World, (Princeton: Princeton University Press, 1969.

Index of Titles & Names

Zecca, Ferdinand, 179
ZERO DE CONDUITE, 169
Zinneman, Fred, 167, 172, 173

Zola, Emile, 157, 163, 179, 180
Zukor, Adolph, 86, 88, 90